This book is due for return on or before the last date shown below

Property of the School of ECLS Resource Centre
Newcastle University
Ring 0191 222 7569 to renew

C000292844

From Village School to Global Brand

Changing the World Through Education

From Village School to Global Brand

Changing the World Through Education

James Tooley

P

PROFILE BOOKS

First published in Great Britain in 2012 by
Profile Books Ltd
3a Exmouth House
Pine Street
Exmouth Market
London EC1R 0JH
www.profilebooks.com

10 9 8 7 6 5 4 3 2 1

Copyright © SABIS® 2012

The moral right of the author has been asserted.

All rights reserved. Without limiting the rights under copyright reserved above, no part of this
publication may be reproduced, stored or introduced into a retrieval system, or transmitted,
in any form or by any means (electronic, mechanical, photocopying, recording or otherwise),
without the prior written permission of both the copyright owner and the publisher of this book.

A CIP catalogue record for this book is available from the British Library.

ISBN: 978 1 84668 545 3
eISBN: 978 1 84765 792 3

Text design by Sue Lamble
sue@lambledesign.demon.co.uk
Typeset in Photina by MacGuru Ltd
info@macguru.org.uk

Printed and bound in Great Britain by
Clays, Bungay, Suffolk

The paper this book is printed on is certified by the © 1996 Forest Stewardship Council A.C.
(FSC). It is ancient-forest friendly. The printer holds FSC chain of custody SGS-COC-2061

FSC
Mixed Sources
Product group from well-managed
forests and other controlled sources

Cert no. SGS-COC-2061
www.fsc.org
© 1996 Forest Stewardship Council

Contents

To Leila and Ralph

Foreword

THE GLOBAL COMMUNITY is rapidly approaching 2015, the year targeted for the achievement of the Millennium Development Goal of achieving universal primary education. But as we approach that important date, it is becoming apparent that too many children are not benefiting from education. Reaching the target requires innovative approaches, including the extension of access to high-quality education. Over the last decade in some of the poorest countries of the world, the growth in school places is coming from the private sector. Without this growth, the many benefits of schooling would not be experienced by the poorest. These benefits include the fact that on average another year of schooling raises an individual's potential earnings by more than 10 percent a year. More educated people have healthier lives. For the national economy, a more educated population tends to have a higher growth rate, a productive workforce, and lower levels of poverty.

Private sector involvement in education will continue to play a critical role in promoting access in under-served areas, leading innovation, responding to social demand, improving learning outcomes, and reducing costs while increasing efficiency.

SABIS® is an excellent example of a private education provider that is fulfilling this urgent need. Moreover, SABIS® has been engaged in the "global education industry" since long before the term was coined. SABIS® traces its origins back to 1886. The organization has educated children in its home country of Lebanon for over a century, even through civil war. The remarkable journey that has brought SABIS® to more than fifteen countries to date proves the company's commitment to education. The company went on to participate in one of the most important education innovations in the United States, charter schools, educating children in New Orleans, Louisiana, in the aftermath of Hurricane Katrina, among other states. The company has even opened schools in Kurdistan since the second Iraq war. SABIS® not only predates the global industry, but also many present-day emphases, such as, among others: schools for the disadvantaged, schools as a conduit for rehabilitation and reconciliation in fragile environments, and schools as market solutions for social issues.

In this engaging and inspirational book, Professor Tooley presents the story of one of the most enduring and committed players in the education field. It provides a rich background to the company and its approach. The book documents the contributions of the company and shows how a private company contributes to the public good.

Harry Anthony Patrinos
Lead Education Economist
The World Bank

Introduction

ACROSS THE WORLD, education is being radically transformed with the resurgence of a vibrant private sector. Sometimes this transformation is in collaboration with governments as "public–private partnerships" (PPPs) are created to improve educational outcomes in public[1] schools. In other places it's a result of students or their parents embracing private educational opportunities, irrespective of whether or not governments are offering something similar.

A seasoned observer of such developments is Chris Whittle. In his provocative and inspiring book *Crash Course: A Radical Plan for Improving Public Education*, Whittle surveys the history of his own roller-coaster ride in educational entrepreneurship. He dreams of "changing the education paradigm,"[2] challenging the shibboleths that hold back public education.

Whittle sees two important and related developments in education that are fundamental to this paradigm shift. First is the growth of *chains* of schools, which can afford to invest in R&D to create new and cost-effective educational designs. Second is the emergence of *"global education providers"*:[3]

These schooling companies seemed to intuit the same thing: education should be a global service. The languages people spoke were different, but the process through which children learned was universal, techniques of instruction traveled well, and significant portions of curriculum (the most notable examples being math and science) were effectively "global languages" already ... Though a McDonald's arch in Shanghai offended the aesthetic sensibilities of many, the trend toward a global village was irreversible.[4]

With big global education players emerging, the fundamentals of education will be transformed for the better.

This book is about one such global educational company, SABIS®.[5] Last year, SABIS was celebrating its 125th anniversary. I was asked to speak at the annual directors' conference. Over dinner, the president, Carl Bistany, suggested the idea of writing a narrative account of the company's history and philosophy. The idea appealed to me because SABIS seemed to embody several features that had the potential to reveal interesting dimensions about the private sector in education.

First, SABIS is proudly, even defiantly, "for profit" – even when it's clearly against its interests to say so. But secondly, I heard that it was active in countries like Iraq, and in environments like inner-city New Orleans, where it explicitly set out to serve children in difficult places, with huge needs. Indeed, their website announces that it grew out of a village school serving girls in a place – late nineteenth-century rural Lebanon – where girls were usually denied schooling. I've always been intrigued by the overlap between the profit motive in education and humanitarian outcomes. Could SABIS offer evidence of a profitable education business coinciding with a humanitarian vision, having beneficial outcomes for the poor?

Thirdly, the company's reputation is that it eschews much of what passes for "progressive" educational thinking. This contrarian approach interested me – particularly as the company also seemed to embrace advanced technology to enhance learning. Could these apparently contradictory approaches be squared? I was fascinated to find out.

Finally, SABIS was clearly involved in a range of business models – private schools, public–private partnerships and licensing models

– exploration of which would appear to have much to offer anyone concerned with the role of the private sector in education.

It must be said that SABIS's geographical range also attracted me. A reviewer of my earlier book *The Beautiful Tree* said that I clearly suffered from "a severe dose of wanderlust"; the fact that SABIS is operating on four continents, including in places like Iraq, Lebanon, the UAE, Egypt, and the USA, seemed too good an opportunity for travel to miss. So, with these five factors, it was easy to accept the invitation to write a book that would be a case study of SABIS, putting it in the context of the education industry in the early 21st century.

But what kind of book should I write? I was offered unprecedented access to the firm, including to Mrs Leila Saad and Mr Ralph Bistany, the elders of the company, both now in their 80s – and from whose surnames the name "SABIS" derives. The more time I spent with them, the more I heard of their story, the less I felt that a dry education or business book would be the appropriate vehicle to convey what I'd been given privileged access to hear and observe. I suppose it's a truism that the people within an industry matter – even more so, though, in terms of education, where the development of people is at the very core of the business. So I've tried to convey something about this education company through the people who are part of it, through their voices. For those who want an outline of the business or educational model, these can be found in the pages that follow (especially in Part 3); but I've tried to convey these not in isolation but as the living products of the people who have created them. But let's be absolutely clear, as Mrs Saad and Mr Bistany kept reminding me: the people are vehicles for the ideas and concepts. And in the end, for them, it is the ideas that count most.

One thing I hope to achieve with this book is to get more people excited about the education industry. Yes, private education is burgeoning, going through a renaissance. But because of this, it needs bright, enthusiastic, passionate people attracted into it, who realize that there is scope for their ideas and energy. In the education industry, they can really pursue something exciting and worthwhile. That's one reason to focus on the people who are making a difference. That's my hope in writing this case study; it turned out also to be Ralph Bistany's hope in allowing me this unprecedented access to the organization.

The book is divided into three parts. The first part ("War and peace") presents a journey through time – tracing the company from its humble origins in 1886 Mount Lebanon, through two world wars and the Lebanese civil war, to its initial phases of expansion to the Gulf, England and America. The history itself I found fascinating – how the school emerged in the ruins of one empire, founded as a school to serve girls, and how it expanded across continents almost by accident because of the exigencies of civil war. But as an educator, what was equally fascinating to me was how the educational model evolved over a considerable period of time, emerging out of mistakes or lucky breaks, being refined and honed during many years of trial and error, practice and experience. As we trace the history of the company, we can also trace the history of its educational ideas.

This is significant. Another important observer of the private educational scene, Steven F. Wilson, award-winning author of *Learning on the Job*, noted the striking difference between SABIS and all other educational providers seeking public–private partnership contracts in schools in America:

> Nearly every organization that proposed to manage public schools in the 1990s was a start-up ... Almost no organization could say it had run schools before, let alone point to academic results from a time-tested school design. Each would have to develop everything on the fly, from curriculum to infrastructure, policies to accounting systems.
>
> SABIS was the exception. An established, for-profit education company based in Beirut, Lebanon, SABIS operated private, tuitioned schools in many countries before it opened its first public charter school in the United States. While other EMOs [Education Management Organizations] assembled a school design only months before opening their first school's doors, SABIS had refined its college-preparatory curriculum over several decades and thousands of students.[6]

SABIS's education model emerged over generations and across continents. In the case of other education providers, like Chris Whittle's Edison Schools, for instance, this was entirely different. Whittle brought together a high-powered team to design the blueprint for his chain of schools. Even as they were in the process of designing the blueprint, they set out to scale the business.

Both are legitimate ways of creating a business, of course. But there is something rather appealing in the *organic* way in which SABIS's model *evolved*, out of many years of experience, hardship even; with SABIS the education model came first, the idea of scaling this as a global business came only once the founders – and, more importantly, others who invited them to open schools in their regions – were convinced they had a successful and worthy educational model worth scaling.

The second part is a journey through geographies, from Kurdistan to Katrina, although not in that order. Much of this part, as the title suggests, explores how and why the education company has set out to serve damaged communities. SABIS opened the first international (private) schools in war-torn northern Iraq, followed by innovative public–private partnerships there. It created charter schools in deprived American inner-cities, like Springfield, Massachusetts, and Flint, Michigan; it was also one of the first charter schools to reopen after Hurricane Katrina devastated inner-city New Orleans. It's a journey that shows SABIS going where other educational providers are reluctant or unwilling to tread, helping to rebuild lives shattered by war and natural disaster. But more than a journey through geographies, it's also a journey through the politics of education. Why is it so difficult for a company like SABIS to open charter schools in America, when it has a proven track record of helping the poorest to excel? And why – moving the story on to the Middle East – is it so difficult to get the public–private partnership model right in places like the United Arab Emirates, where a company like SABIS has decades of experience in educating its people? But the story doesn't end on this negative note; through its licensing business, SABIS has potentially created a model that can not only serve the disadvantaged – we show this in poor neighborhoods of Brooklyn,

New York – but could be the vehicle SABIS uses to expand dramatically worldwide, in both public and private schools.

In both Parts 1 and 2, aspects of the education model (through the eyes of a scholarship student, Hêro, for instance, in northern Iraq) and the business models (with the three models of private schools, public–private partnerships and licensing all highlighted) are revealed. Part 3, "The enterprise of education," then draws these themes together, to explore their interrelationships. Three of the chapters explore three themes – the logic of learning, the community of learners, and the evolution of the learning environment – that seem to encompass the coherent philosophy underlying the SABIS educational model. A further chapter explores important ideas arising out of SABIS as an educational business – such as, is for-profit education justified? And if so, what form can standardization in a global education business take? Finally, we bring together in one place further aspects of the SABIS business model. If the first two parts of the book describe journeys, then, to stretch the metaphor, this third part is a journey through the minds of committed educators, sharing with them as they grapple with the fundamental questions of how we educate young people in the virtues that have stood the test of time, while still enabling them to be prepared for the future of unknown possibilities.

***

My journey for the book began when Carl Bistany invited me to meet him in northern Iraq, to begin to see what SABIS was doing around the world. Possibly like others going to Iraq for the first time, I made sure my will was in order and didn't tell anyone from my family. Disappointingly, I wasn't to travel by "Flying Carpet," the airline on which the SABIS team had first traveled to Iraq. Instead, Middle East Airlines (MEA), the Lebanese national flag carrier, now had a direct flight from Beirut to Erbil, and this was unfortunately much more convenient for me. There was no connecting flight from England, so I flew into Beirut on Friday night and spent most of Saturday in Lebanon.

On a wonderfully warm and sunny November afternoon, I had a superb fish lunch with crisp Lebanese wine, with Amy Wesley, the blonde, American, right-hand woman of SABIS's president. We were in Byblos, the ancient Phoenician city on the Mediterranean just north of Beirut. It's known as the oldest continuously inhabited city in the world, a claim going back to 5,000 BC. It seemed especially fitting that my journey for the book should start in Byblos. For it is the birthplace of Cadmus, known as humanity's First Teacher: Cadmus was sent by his parents to rescue his abducted sister, Europa. He sailed to Greece, but couldn't find her. Not wanting to waste his time while there, he founded a city (now Thebes) and began to teach people the Phoenician alphabet, the world's first alphabet of 22 letters. His teaching brought the idea of the alphabet to the Greeks, which provided the foundation for the Roman alphabet, and the rest is not only history but all of European literature too. The story of Cadmus seemed a neat metaphor for the organization, SABIS, I was about to research. Originating from Lebanon too, they were also engaged in going to far-flung places as "first teachers." It seemed fitting that this first truly global school chain had its origins in the same place as the world's first teacher.

We flew into Kurdistan at night. As we flew over Iraq, we could see out of our windows the flares of the oil and gas fields of Kirkuk to our left and Mosul to our right. We landed at Erbil's brand-new airport, barely two months old. Amy and I were picked up by a special bus and whisked through to the VIP lounge, where our visas and passport stamps were painlessly arranged. I had never had such good treatment before on any of my travels: clearly SABIS was a much-respected organization in Kurdistan. We were met by Raed Mahmoud, SABIS's young and committed representative in Kurdistan, who drove us through the complex system of road barriers and army checkpoints that impeded access to and from the airport before we were out of the city on wide, modern roads, to arrive at a hotel adjacent to the International School of Choueifat, Erbil, the SABIS flagship.

Our hotel was comfortable, and everything certainly seemed safe and secure in Kurdistan. But just in case I was still feeling nervous about being in Iraq, one of the children I interviewed on my first day put me very much at my ease. Dina was a delightful, personable ten-year-old student in fourth grade at SABIS's first public–private partnership school in Iraq. She told me that although she was Kurdish she had been living in north London for the past few years and had only recently returned to Kurdistan. Why had she come back? "My mom said it was too dangerous in London," she told me earnestly. Her elder brother was getting caught up in "fights and stuff ... He was in a gang." So Mom had moved her to Iraq, to get away from the troubles in London.

I spent an exhilarating and packed five days in Kurdistan. I visited all three of the schools in Erbil – the private school (International School of Choueifat), and the two PPP schools (Fakhir Mergasori International School and Sarwaran International School). I observed classes, spoke to children, teachers and parents. I visited children in their homes too, to see how they were living and to learn their thoughts on the difference SABIS was making.

And then I journeyed into the mountains to Dohuk, the Kurdish city near the Turkish border, to visit SABIS's public–private partnership school there. Amy and I were guided by two terrific young people, Milad Daher and Mayan Gilly, both in their twenties and enticed to Kurdistan from comfortable lives overseas in order to help SABIS make a difference for disadvantaged peoples.

After leaving Erbil city, the road passed through rolling plains, dotted with trees and donkeys; there were sentry positions of the *Peshmerga* (Kurdish fighters) in the hills overlooking the road; periodically on the road itself there were also army checkpoints. At one of the checkpoints, we crossed what seemed a mighty river, although it turned out to be merely a tributary – albeit a broad one – of the River Tigris. It was inspiring to be where the cradle of civilization, Mesopotamia, arose on these fertile lands between the rivers Tigris and Euphrates. We crossed at the town of Kalak. In 2003, this town had been at the center of the Second Gulf War – the river was the border between Saddam Hussein's Iraq and the Kurdish autonomous region. The Iraqi forces had dug themselves in just across the river; most of the townspeople had fled into the mountains, afraid of what would transpire. But now, seven years on, it was peaceful and prosperous: boys were fishing on the steep banks of the river; lining the narrow road were vibrant market stalls, women and men selling their harvest; it was all full of color, of melons, oranges and pomegranates.

After Kalak, we climbed into rolling hills, and now we could see the flares of gas fields. And then, suddenly, there was a large city in the mountains, reached on a road whose hairpin bends were being widened and straightened. This was Dohuk, just two and a half hours from Erbil.

Memories of the recent wars seemed very much alive among the people I spoke to in Dohuk. Mr Uthman Rasheed Shivan, the unassuming, gentle director of the SABIS PPP School, had been sent to fight by the Iraqi government in the Iraq–Iran war in the mid-1980s, then again in the invasion of Kuwait in 1990. Escaping from the front line, he'd been part of the 1991 Kurdish uprising, fighting to rid his homeland of the Iraqi Revolutionary Guard. But when American and other allied support was not forthcoming, and the Iraqi army returned with a vengeance, he fled with the masses to the Turkish border. His grandmother had died on the way and had to be buried by the roadside. He stayed with his wife and two children in a tent in the refugee camp in no man's land between Turkey and Iraq for 26 days. On his return, he found his home completely destroyed.

But my two most abiding memories of the Kurdistan journey were these. First, I visited Hêro, the young student who had introduced me to all that was going on in the SABIS private school in Erbil and in her family home, having first met her in the school and been impressed by her intelligence and humility. We'd arrived in the early evening; there were no street lights on the road outside, so we couldn't see much of the neighborhood. "It's a good neighborhood," her father told me. I asked Hêro about her future ambitions. She wants to be an engineer. But most of all, she told me, she wants to serve her people and her country, Kurdistan. "It's my dream," she says.

As we parted, I asked her to write a note to me about her vision. I followed up through Skype at her school. When I contacted her again, Hêro told me that she was watching intently what was happening in Egypt on TV. She was particularly impressed by the revolution there and its conduct: "People there are very good, they actually did their own revolution and then they cleaned the streets. I liked that very much, you do a revolution, and afterwards you clean the streets yourselves." Here's how she finished her note to me:

> I continue to dare to dream. At first I saw myself becoming a teacher and teaching for free. Then I thought I'd become a doctor and treat sick people for free. I now hope to be an engineer and do my best to help as many disadvantaged children that I can in the best possible way. Even now as a student, I help my classmates in various subjects.
>
> My favorite pastime is spending time with my family. I love our simple life, I love my family and I am very proud to be part of it. It gives me great joy as my efforts and hard work have made my parents proud of me. I have been taught to be grateful for what we have and not to complain about something we do not have. We look at families that have less than we do, so we can be grateful for what we have. I thus belong to a happy and contented family, where we share and support one another and where we find joy in our simple life. Finally, I love the simplicity of my life and am happy with what I have.
>
> This freedom from complexity and wants gives me all the time in the world to dream ... dream of how I can do something for other people and especially my country.

The second abiding memory of the trip for me was when I happened to catch sight of Carl Bistany standing unobtrusively in a doorway, watching the dismissal of children from SABIS's school for orphaned children of martyrs (those whose fathers or grandfathers were killed by Saddam Hussein's regime). He looked deeply moved by it all. He looked so unlike any caricature of a business tycoon that critics of the education industry sometimes portray. I thought of how a man in his position doesn't need to be getting up at the crack of dawn, traveling thousands of miles, to help solve the problems of children like these. Clearly, and above all, he loved the challenge of seeing how he could serve disadvantaged children in distant and difficult places like northern Iraq.

On my last night in Kurdistan, over a wrap-up dinner, I told him about Hêro and her dream to serve. I also told him I'd seen him watching the children leave the school. He said, "Did you see their faces? They were smiling, orderly, waving. 'I can't wait to see you tomorrow morning.' Did you feel that's what they were saying too? Just, you know, this: If you told me, 'I want to buy that moment,' I can't put a price on it. I can't tell you it's worth a million dollars, or ten million dollars; it's priceless."

Where had these values that inspired him come from? And how had these values survived in a business environment, where surely the profit motive should edge them out? We left Kurdistan early the next morning, on my way to interview the two dynamic elders of the company, Mrs Saad and Ralph Bistany, back in Lebanon. It was to be an extraordinary few days, traveling back in time to trace the company from its origins in 1886 on the slopes of Mount Lebanon, seeing how the values that inspired the initial desire to open a village school for girls still inform all within the organization to the present day. It's the journey that takes up all of Part 1 of this book.

War and peace

CHAPTER 1

Climbing Mount Lebanon

The king's guest

In *The King's Speech*, the Oscar-winning actor Colin Firth plays King George VI, the man who didn't want to be king. His attempt to overcome a severe stutter, in a radio speech on the eve of World War II, wins over the hearts of his people. His father, King George V, and mother, Queen Mary, are portrayed less sympathetically – the king as impatient, irascible, his wife as distant, unapproachable. Some reviewers of the film think the portrayals unfair. Someone who might have agreed was the tall, handsome foreign guest at the vice-regal garden party in Dublin in 1897.

Published that year in the *Illustrated London News* is a facsimile of a photograph of the future king and queen with the handsome visitor, dressed, as the caption says, "in his native costume." Certainly the person with their royal highnesses cuts a dashing figure. He's taller than the future king, resplendent in his long flowing Arab robes, headscarf and headband. He sports a neat, trimmed beard and mustache.

The foreign visitor was the Reverend Tanios Saad, visiting from Mount Lebanon in what was then Syria. He had come to the United Kingdom because England was perceived as the beacon of growth and progress in learning; he was also there to raise funds for the village school he had co-founded eleven years previously with Miss Louisa Procter, an Anglo-Irish woman. The Reverend Saad was much helped in his fund-raising visit by "the kindness of the Archbishop of Canterbury," he wrote in his diary, who invited him to meet members of the royal family in London at Lambeth Palace, the seat of the archbishop:

> I wore my Eastern dress on that occasion, and their Royal Highnesses enquired who I was and both bowed to me very graciously. I here made the acquaintance of several who were able and willing to help me, among others the Archbishop of Dublin, who promised to preside at a meeting if I visited Ireland. Later on I went to Dublin and was invited to the Viceregal garden party and had the honour of being presented to their Royal Highnesses The Duke and Duchess of York [the future King George V and Queen Mary], who were most gracious to me. The Duchess told me that she remembered seeing me at the Lambeth garden party and was glad to see me again. The Duke told me that he had in 1882 visited Lebanon, and they both expressed much interest in our work.[1]

The Reverend Saad had a notebook with him. He was a bold man – traveling all that way from Mount Lebanon was in itself an audacious act in those days – and apparently not one given to abiding by protocol, or missing an opportunity. He offered his book to the future king emperor and queen, who were soon to take on the most powerful imperial roles in the world: "When I asked their Royal Highnesses to put their names in my book, they most graciously took me into the Viceregal Lodge and did so. I shall never forget this day and the graciousness of the Duke and Duchess of York," he wrote. Brandishing his book with his prized autographs within, the Reverend Saad became a hit with the other visitors:

> The guests were much astonished when they saw me go in with them, and when I came out many asked me why they had taken me in, and when I showed them my book with the signatures, they said I was much to be envied, as none of them had been so favoured, and several then signed my book also. The Duke and Duchess had used my pen

and I was asked if I would sell it, but I said no, but you may kiss it as I kissed their hands, and some actually did so.

I held this notebook myself. It's in the possession of Mrs Leila Saad, keeper of what remains of the SABIS archives, those not destroyed in the Lebanese civil war. She's an extremely elegant, refined woman, a sprightly 83 years old. She jumped up to fetch the notebook from a drawer in her chic apartment in Beirut when she told me this story. She showed me the pages. I cautiously held the notebook in my hand and ran my fingers over the rough ink of the royal signatures. In this way did I feel myself connected both to the history of the once mighty British Empire and to the 125-year chronicle of SABIS.

The Irish visitor

The Mount Lebanon that Miss Louisa Procter went to in 1880 was poor and breathtakingly beautiful. One visitor to the village she was eventually to make her home, Choueifat (then "Schwifat"), described it like this:

> Schwifat is beautifully situated on the lower slopes of Lebanon, about two hours from Beirut, with which it is connected by a carriage road (quite an innovation here), and with a splendid view of the sea, and overlooking a vast Olive garden, extending for miles along the coast, said to be one of the largest in the world.[2]

The name of the village, it was said, means "beautiful view" in Arabic, "and it deserves its name." The hill itself was cultivated with mulberry trees, the leaves of which were for feeding silkworms, for silk mills were an important industry in the villages of Mount Lebanon.

It may be that Miss Procter found herself in this village because of her acquaintance with a certain Lord Dufferin from what is now Northern Ireland. Lord Dufferin had been the British representative to the Commission in Syria investigating the causes of the civil war of 1860 that arose between two religious groups that are unique to

Mount Lebanon – the Christian Maronites – people of the Roman Catholic Church – and the Druze, connected to Islam. For reasons which are too complex to explore here (but which were in some way connected with the British desire to play off the French against the Russians, while supporting their Turkish allies, and vice versa), the British had a long association with the Druze population while the French supported the Christian Maronites. Lord Dufferin somehow upheld Ottoman rule in the area, preventing the French from establishing a client state in Lebanon. He also defended the Druze against the other great powers, who saw this as an opportunity to put them down.

Dufferin's familiarity with Choueifat may have been because it was one of the largest villages in the area, sufficiently close to the port of Beirut to be accessible. It may also have seemed like Mount Lebanon in microcosm, for its population of 7,000 was equally divided between Druze and Christian. Although nearly a quarter of a century had gone by, the sores of the past conflict and the potential for healing must have been some of the qualities that attracted a person like Miss Procter to the village.

In 1884, Miss Procter, who was 55, had recently lost her parents. For a Christian woman of her time, being "called" to work in the "Holy Land" would have felt an extraordinary privilege. A contemporary visitor observed: "Miss Procter had been visiting Lebanon and Palestine, the Land where our Lord lived and died, and had been much touched by the condition of the Druses (especially the Children)."[3] She took to her early work with vigor, responding to the needs of the women of the village: "She was a missionary and had dedicated herself to the service of humanity and proselytizing for the Christian faith. She began organizing the women into associations and symposiums and training them in healthy and scientific methods of childcare."[4]

After a while, however, she was called back to England; but she left her heart on the lower slopes of Mount Lebanon. When a letter arrived from the village, "begging her to return,"she rushed to seek advice from an old acquaintance whom she thought could help: Mr George Müller, a 79-year-old Prussian-born Christian evangelist, who had settled in

Bristol, England. He had created schools and orphanages in that city and had recently returned on a year-long missionary tour of the Middle East, including Syria – indeed, for seventeen years of his life, aged 70 to 87, he was to travel 200,000 miles on missionary work. The missionary society that he helped to create, the Scriptural Knowledge Institution for Home and Abroad, may have been the organization that helped Miss Procter go to Mount Lebanon. And her reasons for seeking Mr Müller's advice may well have been because he had played an important role in her decision to go to Mount Lebanon in the first place.

Mr Müller wanted to test her resolve: "He put before her the dangers and difficulties that a lady, single-handed, would encounter in such an undertaking." She waved aside these dangers and difficulties. Then Mr Müller said, "I will pray for you that the Lord will raise up some man from among the people suitable to be your colleague in the work."

In 1886, the Reverend Saad was a resolute young man of 28, Miss Procter nearly thirty years his senior. They met early on her return to Lebanon. It seems to have been the Reverend Saad's suggestion to her that "she open a boarding school for girls to make her work more effective and comprehensive." However, although the idea greatly appealed to her, she told him "she could not do it for economic reasons."[5] She received an income from her parents' estate of £100 per annum,[6] she told him. "Even now by the end of the year, this means I have to take my afternoon tea without biscuits." So how could she possibly afford to pay other teachers' salaries and boarding for the children, let alone fund rent for a building and so on and so forth? The Reverend Saad nodded upon hearing this and "left her to her work."[7]

A few days later, however, he came back with renewed determination: "We can open a girls' school, and I've persuaded the American mission to give us two of its teachers and pay their salaries. You and I can teach without salaries. We can live in the school, or easily build a house on the site, so we won't need any rent. The tuition fees will cover the students' room-and-board expenses, and ..." He paused for effect. "I promise you will have biscuits with your afternoon tea all year around."[8]

Nearly persuaded, Miss Procter saw how creating the school with this determined young man could be the answer to her – and Mr Müller's – prayers. But she could see an obvious practical obstacle: "Where will we site the school?" The Reverend Tanios Saad had the solution to hand, one of the reasons why he was so fired up with enthusiasm: "Just outside the village there are two silk factories. One of them burnt down, so the owner is discouraged and wants to sell the other. He's agreed to sell it to me!" Miss Procter may have rolled her eyes at this point. Patiently, she sighed: "And where, young man, are you going to get the funds?"

The Reverend Saad could barely contain his excitement: "The factory has got all of its equipment and machinery intact. Most of it is in perfect working order! The owner has agreed to give me two weeks to raise the money. By God's grace, I'll sell all the equipment and I'll have enough money to pay for the site!"

It didn't seem likely to Miss Procter, although she would pray for his success. But in fact that is precisely what Tanios did. He painstakingly dismantled all the silk-making machinery, and equally as painstakingly sold it piece by piece to other owners of silk factories in villages up and down Mount Lebanon. Remarkably, in the process he made more funds than were needed to purchase the factory. The school now had its building and a little funding to spare. And with that, Miss Procter readily agreed to come on board.

In October 1886, the school opened with 28 students, 15 boarders and 13 day scholars, all girls. Opening a school for girls fitted in perfectly with both Miss Procter's and the Reverend Saad's enlightened ideas. Girls in Choueifat and similar villages generally had no education outside of the home. They were usually married by the age of twelve. There's an African proverb, as Hillary Rodham Clinton reminds us, that says "if you educate a girl, you educate a community" – or even "a nation." The two school founders were equally convinced of the development potential of focusing their efforts on girls' education. While some in the village were suspicious of the motives of the school, many embraced its revolutionary idea. In two years, it had more than doubled in size, to 57 students. But the two founders were persuaded that the work they were doing could also positively impact on the village boys; in the third year, they admitted boys to the school – run as a mixed school until 1911, before being run as two separate entities, until being merged again in the 1940s. But for ten years, they were schooling more girls than boys.

The girls in particular were being trained as teachers. By 1897, a report on the school noted that some of these girl graduates were teaching as far away as Egypt, others "in different parts of the country." Overall, "the effect of educating the girls is ... beginning to be seen all over the country." Powerfully, the report noted, "The great difference made between boys and girls is dying out, girls are no longer looked down upon if they remain unmarried or are married at a very early age as formerly. One young Druse man is paying the school fee for his fiancée, she is about sixteen and a few years ago the Druses considered it a disgrace for a girl of twelve to come to school."[9]

For twenty years, Miss Procter worked tirelessly for the cause of the school she co-founded. Throughout that time she lived in a room adjoining the girls' dormitory on the top floor of the old silk factory, above the pale limestone vaulted hall used as classrooms. She used her connections in British society throughout this time to raise further funds for the school, including from Lady Hester Stanhope and other influential women whom she had acquainted with nineteenth-century Lebanon. It was through these connections that she arranged for the Reverend Tanios Saad's visit to the United Kingdom in 1897, and his invitations to the royal garden parties.

Two or three photographs of her have survived the school's bombardment during the civil war. One shows Miss Procter looking somewhat stern, surrounded by the children, both boys and girls, all looking equally grim. But that's the way people used to pose for photographs in those days – the grinning banality of today is a fairly recent phenomenon. Certainly a contemporary visitor, one Ellwood Brockbank, just before Christmas 1897 – a direct result of the Reverend Saad's fundraising visit that summer– was glowing in his praise for the warmth of the interactions between Miss Procter and the children: she, as well as the Saad family, "take their meals with the children, and the whole place is a model of simplicity and economy," he wrote. Indeed, Miss Procter appears as the matriarch of the school and family, for Brockbank observed that Miss Procter "feels more like a mother than anything" to the Reverend Saad. He warmly describes the school buildings too: "The buildings are very compact; formerly an oil mill and a silk mill they are improved beyond recognition, and the girls sleep in the large airy room where at one time the hum of the silk winders was heard. Nice, bright schoolrooms, decorated with pictures, open on the inner square, which forms a shady playground under the acacias. A new swing was evidently popular."[10]

Miss Lousia Procter died on 2 March 1907, aged 78. Reflecting her status in British society, present at her funeral on Sunday, 3 March was the British consul-general and a representative of His Excellency the Kaimakam, the governor of this province of the Ottoman Empire. In the English part of the funeral, the speech likened her to the woman of whom the gospels said: "She hath wrought a good work upon Me."[11] The Arabic part of the service spoke of her "unselfishness, her zeal and devotion to duty, her sympathy with child endeavour, her simple and heart-felt intercessory prayers, and last, but not least, her love to the Syrian." The "last act of her life was praying for teachers, pupils, &c."[12]

***

I saw her gravestone in the Saad family mausoleum on the site of the mother school (the original village school) in Choueifat. It's an odd place to have a mausoleum, on the grounds of the school, but I was told the children think having it there "is cool, very cool." Mrs Saad told me: "This is where we're all going to end up, on the campus of the mother school. I think that's the way we would like it to be."

The mausoleum is in a leafy white pine glade nestled just above the basketball court and the athletics track, reached by a narrow path up a rather steep hill. When I visited, it was an uncharacteristically hot, late November day, 35 degrees Centigrade, the bright sun relentless overhead. As we entered the glade and coolness of the mausoleum, poignantly we could still hear, as if in the distance, the cries and shouts of joy of young children playing games, although they were just a few yards away. But inside it was totally still. In the far wall were inset stones, with the names of the Reverend Tanios Saad, his wife, his son Charles, his two other sons, and two grandchildren who died as children. And there was the stone for Miss Louisa Procter. "Why would she have been buried with the family?" I asked of my guide. "Because she was part of the family, and this was her home," she replied simply.

In fact the gravestone for Miss Procter was damaged in the civil war and was now in five parts. Some laborers came and carefully fitted the parts together to show me. It was very moving reading this brief summary of the life of a remarkable woman, pieced together out of the destruction of the civil war: "In loving memory of Louisa Procter who entered into rest March 2nd 1907, in the 78th year of her age, after 27 years of service in Mount Lebanon, Syria."

In the cool and dark of the mausoleum I heard the school bell ring in the distance and the children leave the playing fields, soon to be replaced by others.

That's about all we know of Miss Procter. Mrs Saad – the living source of all there is to be known about the early history of SABIS – is disappointed that she knows so little about her. Over lunch one day in Le Paul restaurant in a fashionable suburb of Beirut, however, Mrs Saad did recall that Miss Procter had played the piano, and that the sessions where the whole family had gathered around the piano singing popular songs and hymns and carols may have been inspired by Miss Procter.

I have this image of Miss Procter from that one anecdote. I see her, a devoted Christian, bored with the social scene of late nineteenth-century England. Perhaps with a romantic disappointment in her life, she decides to devote herself aged 55 to the cause of deprived children.

Setting up the school for girls with the Reverend Tanios Saad was more than enough to fulfill her life's ambitions.

She worked empathetically and indefatigably for the cause of the school she co-founded. And in the evenings you could hear her playing inspirational hymns on the school piano with the children singing around her; and on Sunday afternoons, her adopted family stood around her as she played popular ditties of the day. I see her as a happy, fulfilled woman, a woman with many children who loved her as she was devoted to them.

The Saad connection

We know much more about the Reverend Tanios Saad, the other co-founder of the village school in Choueifat. One renowned Lebanese Druze commentator, Mahmoud Khalil Saab, described him as "the greatest educator ... one of the pillars of Lebanon's educational renaissance of the late nineteenth and early twentieth centuries."[13] The Reverend Saad was "a tall man of sturdy build," a man of "keen vision, dignified, solemn, resolute, bold in the name of justice, faithful and assured." All these characteristics are ones we saw in action as he persuaded Miss Procter of the virtues of opening the school and which kept him energetically running the school with her for those 21 years together. This intelligent and discerning man was also entertaining: "It was impossible to be bored in his company." In part this was because he was a man of letters, who had absorbed himself in "the stories of famous men," as well as "the holy book," and who loved to share these stories and their morals with others.

This was also because of his empathy with the people around him: "His interest in people's affairs and issues made him close to them and bound him to society." He was inquisitive about people, "interfering in what concerned him and what might not have concerned him."[14] This, however, was recognized as "an endearing quality," as he didn't do it "in order to discover people's issues and secrets, but rather to help with advice or action." One person on the receiving end of Reverend Tanios's enthusiastic advice, as we have seen, was Miss Louisa Procter.

Above all, Tanios Saad was seen as a good man, driven by "love and affection" for his people, a "beacon of morality" and "good counsel." In short, "The people of Choueifat loved and respected him and revered him generation after generation." This, remember, is written by a notable Druze scholar: the love for the Reverend Saad transcended boundaries of mere religion.

Tanios Khalil Saad was born in 1858 in Hadath, Beirut, into a family of Christian Eastern rites. The family home had been in Ras al-Matn, 29 kilometers from Beirut on the western slopes of Mount Lebanon, but his father had moved to Hadath to find work as a builder. The village Protestant church was very close to their new home. Even as a young boy, Tanios had been curious as to what this unfamiliar Christian denomination might be like (in Lebanon, the majority of Christians were Maronite, i.e. Roman Catholic). He liked what he found: "He was impressed with the religious service and its simplicity and order."[15] Perhaps aware of his affinity with this version of Christianity, his father sent him to the American Missionary School, later to become the Syrian Evangelical College and the American University of Beirut. Upon graduation in 1882 from the theological college affiliated to the American Missionary School, Beirut, he was appointed minister of Choueifat's Protestant church. The church ran two missionary schools in the village, for which the new Reverend Tanios Saad was ultimately responsible. Through his oversight of these schools, he began to develop his understanding of education and its importance to a village like his newly adopted one.

Four years later, he counseled Miss Louisa Procter and their own village school in Choueifat, in the converted silk mill, was born. As they expanded the school, bringing in boys in 1888, and greatly expanding the student numbers, the need for new buildings arose. The Reverend Saad negotiated further purchases of land around the school and constructed a new home for the boys' school, opened in 1896, which, as it expanded further, became the new family home.[16]

Their first graduation ceremony took place in 1890, for a graduating class of four girls. Two of these girls went on swiftly to open schools of their own and became headmistresses. One became a teacher in another school, and finally one, Eugenie Jureidini, became a teacher in Choueifat school itself. Five years later this "gentle Christian girl from the district"[17] was to marry the Reverend Tanios Saad, in 1895. As his young wife, she shared fully in the life of the school. Their home was adjacent to the school, and the couple took their meals with the school-children. Later still, she became the school's headmistress. In 1896 she gave birth to their first son, Fouad. In 1902 their fourth child, a son, Charles, was born.

An important milestone was passed for the school in 1911, when the future American University of Beirut, then still the Syrian Evangelical School, sent a delegation of two American and three Lebanese teachers to examine the graduation class of Choueifat. The graduating students passed their examination, and henceforth "graduates of the Choueifat school were accepted at the college without entrance examinations."[18]

In 1897, as we saw, the Reverend Saad made the first of two journeys to the United Kingdom, to raise awareness of what he and Miss Procter were doing in Lebanon and to raise funds. His second visit was in 1913.[19] "I have come to England," he wrote, "to endeavour to enlist the sympathy of friends, and with the hopes of raising money enough to clear off the debt ... and to raise £200 extra to be able to bring the water to the Schools from the neighbouring spring; a distance of about two-thirds of a mile." He was also hoping to "complete the endowment fund of £3,000" as a memorial to "my dear friend and colleague, the late Miss Procter." He writes that he himself is "willing to give £50 towards the endowment" and hopes that other friends will "raise up likewise, or half, or quarter of this sum, so that I shall be able to go back soon to the work which is awaiting me." This is a huge amount in today's terms – £50 in 1913 is worth around £18,800 at 2009 values, using average earnings, and shows a remarkable generosity on behalf of the Reverend Tanios Saad.

On this visit, he carried with him a letter of introduction from a Mr W. Glocker, writing from "American Press, Beyrout, Syria," in June

1913: "I have great pleasure in recommending to your notice the Reverend Tanios Saad, of the Shwifat [sic] Schools, Mount Lebanon, who has for many years superintended the above named schools without having received any salary for so doing." The letter continued, "He will be grateful for any assistance that you can render him by way of organising a meeting for him that he may address the friends and interest them by placing at their disposal Oriental curiosities and giving them an insight into Oriental manners and customs."

These visits to England were to lead to potentially big problems for the Reverend Saad. By 1912, the school had grown to one short of 200 students. World War I brought a halt to this healthy growth, with enrollment collapsing to 83 in 1914. As important, England now became the enemy to the Ottoman Empire that ruled Syria and Mount Lebanon at the time, and with this dried up any hope of funds and support from outside.

A few months into the war, early in 1915, some unwelcome visitors arrived at the Saad family home at the school. Soldiers arrived saying, "The Hakim, the ruler, wants to see you. Pack something. You may not be coming back." His wife began crying; thirteen-year-old Charles tried to comfort her. The Reverend Saad rode off with the soldiers to appear in the Turkish court of the Hakim the next morning. He was accused of being "a British spy." He stood erect and proud and asked quietly, "Why?" The court interrogator replied, "The proof is that you've considerable English connections. You've just returned from England. And," perhaps the most damning of evidence, "there is a picture of you with the Duke and Duchess of York in your home." There was indeed a large-scale painting he had commissioned of the photograph facsimile that had appeared in the *Illustrated London News* of 1897. He was incredibly proud of it and would show it off to anyone who came to the house.

The Reverend Saad was nonplussed: "Of course," he said, sternly, "and if you had had the opportunity to be photographed with the future King and Queen of England, then you too would have been honored and proud too." The interrogator was flabbergasted. "So what are you doing now?" he asked him. The Reverend Saad said, "I'm going to carry on with the school. And I know that His Royal Highness the Sultan would not approve of anyone who sought to close schools, in fact he is in favour of opening schools."

Comments like this and further refusal to budge convinced the interrogator in the end to dismiss the case against him. Indeed, he commented, "You must have needs at the moment, with the war hindering all that we do." The Reverend Tanios replied, "Yes, we don't have enough wheat and rice for the children." So they supplied him with wheat and rice, and sugar too, and he came back to the school loaded with supplies, instead of being convicted on a spying charge.

After World War I, the numbers in the school picked up again; from a low of 63 in 1918, enrollment was 159 the following year. But the school was never to regain its British connections – funding or teachers and volunteers – after the war. For Lebanon was now under a League of Nations French mandate and out of the British sphere of influence. The French government did propose some funding to make up the gap, but the Reverend Saad didn't want to take public funds, with what he felt would be inevitable curtailment of their freedoms, and so declined this.

By this time, the young Charles Saad had enrolled at the American University of Beirut, pursuing his studies in engineering. Upon graduation in 1923, he had been accepted at MIT in the USA and was keen on leaving Lebanon and going to America to finish his studies. His older brother Fouad had already gone overseas, to Manchester University in England. The Reverend Tanios Saad had other ideas, however, at least for the short term. He took Charles to one side and asked him to stay and help out with teaching in the school, but only for one year. Charles agreed, deferring his place at MIT until the following year. At the end of that year, his father said, "Well, you've achieved a lot, but you'll certainly want to consolidate what you've done." So Charles stayed for another year. By this time he had become hooked on all that the school could offer.

He worked outside of the school too during this period – mainly in a range of business endeavors – but he was very involved in thinking about the school. There was a long letter written by Charles in the late 1920s, unfortunately destroyed in the civil war, where he laid out his plan for the school, for overhauling the academic program and pointing to his concerns about the current inadequacies of the school buildings. He got deeply involved with both. To fund the school Charles worked in various engineering businesses, with considerable success, and poured money into the building program. Charles's older brother was also actively engaged in teaching and administration in the school. The Reverend Saad was sure that Charles's older brother was the one who would take over the running of the school when he was finally too old to carry on.

A double tragedy was to strike the Saad family in 1936, however. In February, the Reverend Saad's gentle wife, who had been ill for some years, died. In May, his eldest son died after a gall bladder operation, aged 40. One day, Charles returned from work to the family home on the school site. As usual, he walked in to greet his father in his study at the end of the day. The Reverend Saad, 78 years old, was sitting at his desk, with tears rolling down his face. In front of him were photographs of the two family members he had recently lost.

Charles tried to console him: "You are a man of faith, why are you crying for my mother and brother? You must have faith that you will be reunited with them!" The Reverend Saad looked up at his second son. "I'm not crying for your mother and your brother," he said softly. "I am crying for the school. Who is to keep it going, now that they are gone?" Charles touched him on the arm: "You don't need to cry," he said. "I will take it over. When you are ready."

In 1942, the still-energetic 84-year-old Reverend Saad was finally ready to hand over the running of the school to his son, who was now 40 years old and still a bachelor. In 1942, the school had 216 students. In the twelve years to 1954, under Charles's tutelage, it was to triple its numbers. Under Charles's leadership and passion for education, the school, reports the eminent Druze commentator Mr Saab, "continued on the road to progress until it became one of the country's leading high schools."[20] But, says the author, "the credit for the Choueifat school's phenomenal success does not go to Charles alone. Just as God had given his father a good wife and devoted educator who helped him manage and develop the school, He also blessed Charles with a good wife and headmistress for the school with a high degree of education and culture."[21]

In 1945, three years after taking over the school, Charles finally got married. His bride was Leila Baddoura, at eighteen years old some 25 years his junior. The new Mrs Leila Saad moved into the family home at Choueifat School.

***

I asked Mrs Saad how she had come to know Charles – or Charlie, as she lovingly calls him. We were sitting in her apartment on my first day of interviews in Lebanon. Sitting beside her on an easel, as if sharing in all of our discussions, was the almost life-size portrait of a handsome, urbane-looking middle-aged man. He is wearing a sharp suit and tie and appears at ease with himself and the world. "Charlie?" said Mrs Saad, in response to my query after his name was first mentioned. "He's the gentleman who is sitting here beside me."

"He was my mother's first cousin," Mrs Saad told me, "so my family used to come to Choueifat often." She shows me a photograph of a group of little children with their parents outside the school: "There were four of us, four girls, and my parents. Charlie was there, a young man." She doesn't really want to tell me more, but of course I am fascinated by this story. She gives me some snippets: As a family – a custom they continued while Charlie was still alive, and a custom that will resonate throughout this book – Sunday was a day when the whole family would descend on Choueifat for a communal meal. Sometimes there were as few as ten people, other times as many as 40. "We used to call him Grandpa – my future father-in-law – because he was the brother of my grandfather." As a child, Mrs Saad knew Charlie's mother, "who had been very active and very wonderful and a very bright woman, but she was bedridden for the last six years of her life. She was paralyzed completely. I remember her in bed. She became totally paralyzed in her late fifties. I was too young to remember. I knew them all. Charlie's brother who died – I knew the whole family." She reflects on her memories, but quickly moves the conversation on to other areas.

Eventually, on my second visit to Lebanon, when we were meeting at the mother school, after she had shown me around the house she had shared with Charles, two of his siblings, and her father-in-law, she tells me more: "I was always a little bit too old for my age when I was young, and I didn't enjoy very much the company of young people. So I always sought older company, even when I was young. And Charlie was there, and he was ..."

She gets distracted by other memories. But returns to say, "It's very funny. People, our closest relatives, would ask me, 'Who is older, you or Charlie?' Because I was always very serious, I'd dress in a way to look at least five years older than I was or ten years older even. And he was very young in spirit, and he loved life, and he loved to go out, and he loved to enjoy life, and he was very bubbly and full of life. Being older, he was much more interesting to talk to."

So they started seeing each other. "I knew him as a little child, and then I grew up, and I was no more a child, and he was more than a second cousin. It was a love affair, and people hardly believe it because of the difference in age between us, but it was all the same. We saw each other here and there. And then we used to go out. And ..." There is a long pause. "Anyway, I ended up here at Choueifat. I ended up getting married."

And so we come to one of the most extraordinary things about the history of SABIS. There is a living connection back to the school's roots in 1886, back literally all the way to its inception 125 years ago. The young eighteen-year-old Leila who married Charles Saad in 1945 is the 83-year-old Mrs Saad that I was meeting in Beirut. This immediately brought a distinct and huge richness to the SABIS experience. The more I got to know SABIS and its values, the more I came to realize how extraordinarily significant to all that SABIS is today is this living relationship to the past.

Those of us of a skeptical disposition may have read SABIS's claim on its website that it started as a girls' school in 1886, at a time when girls were not educated, as a lucky coincidence for the company. It certainly makes the company look virtuous, caring and forward looking. But could that really be anything much to do with the company today? The more one gets to know the company, the more one realizes how completely off base such skepticism would be. Because of the continuity in the person of Mrs Leila Saad, the values that drove the Reverend Tanios Saad and Miss Procter to open a girls' school in a remote village in Mount Lebanon are still the values that are driving the school and company today and have driven it through their long history. Throughout my interviews, I repeatedly probed Mrs Saad on her educational and intellectual influences. In the end I had to concede that she had only two – the Reverend Tanios Saad and his son, Charlie Saad. Their spirit, the spirit of the founders, informs all that the company has done and does. The values that drove the Reverend Saad and then his son are the same values embodied in the person of Mrs Saad today. The fact that in 1886 the company opened a girls' school now appears totally relevant to all that the company is, and is not just a convenient fact that the company is using for its own ends.

Clearly Mrs Saad is very proud of all that her father-in-law, the Reverend Tanios Saad, achieved. When we talk about his first visit to England in 1897, she says, "He had a lot of guts. And he was a very persuasive person. He could talk anybody into anything." "He was unstoppable," she says, with "the most fantastic motivation, drive and passion, to leave this country and go to England, all for the benefit of the school." The one time she crossed him, she recalls, was when she, the new bride in her new home, innocently suggested she might move the painting of the Reverend Saad meeting the future king and queen of England to another, less prominent location in the house: "At the mere suggestion, he almost removed me instead!"

And having known the reverend since she was a very young child, she saw how his amazing energy continued throughout old age: when she was first married, this man in his late 80s used to still ride on horseback, to and from the school. Mrs Saad was envious of this: "One day, he asked if he could teach me horse riding. I said I would love it, so he went to buy a horse to teach me. It was the year I got married. So with a lot of help, I got on that horse, in the football field. The minute I got on that horse I gave it a kick. What we didn't know was that this was an old horse from the races, the moment he saw open spaces ..." She laughs heartily and wistfully at the memory. "Need I tell you, that was the first and last experience I had on a horse. 'Thank you very much, Father, I've had enough. I don't think I want to learn riding.'"

"Anyway," she continued after time for reflection, "he was really unstoppable. And he went on giving meaning to his life in any way he could, until the very end." Others agree with this assessment: the Druze commentator Mr Saab concludes his study of his life with the observation that after he had handed over the school to Charles, "he did not retire from work and become idle until poor health forced him to do so. He died at the age of 95, and his mental faculties remained undiminished until his death."[22]

It's a great shame that none of the Reverend Saad's sermons or Charles's writings survives – they were destroyed in the upheavals described in the next chapter. All we have are some snippets of Charles's commencement addresses to the graduates of Choueifat. They point tantalizingly to a man of wisdom and elegant thought, illuminating some of the values that would have been part of his enduring legacy and influence.

First, education is tempered by morality, and there is a particular modesty and openness that comes with pursuing truth:

> If learning is the wind that blows into your sails and moves your ship, then your principles and moral values are the compass that charts your course through dark seas to the safe shores. (1980)

> Let your concern for the truth be greater than your concern for the triumph of your opinion. (1960)

> Be ready to live for what you believe in, but remember that changing

course when you realize that you are wrong is the true sign of the educated man. (1966)

Learning can liberate you from old shibboleths:

Equip yourselves with knowledge so that you may be leaders of thought in your times not copies of thought of our times. (1965)

A flame collects ashes with time. Learn how to blow away the ashes without extinguishing the flame. (1969)

He was an advocate of lifelong learning, as we call it now, and aware of the preciousness of time:

I want you to be aware that learning is a task that lasts a lifetime. Its limits are the throbbing heart and the conscious mind. (1956)

Organize your time so that you are its master not its slave. Wasted time is a treasure that is lost forever. (1979)

And, finally, the good society needs the protection of good people, perhaps particularly poignant in the light of what would soon be happening in Lebanon after he wrote these words:

Your personal success will not last if you turn a blind eye to corruption. Unchecked, corruption will eventually destroy all achievements. (1969)

Remember always that responsibility is the fence that protects the paradise of freedom. (1970)

The living bond that Mrs Saad has to the early history of the school can sometimes lead one into an embarrassing *faux pas*. Mrs Saad herself delights in telling the story of how she overheard some tiny children whispering at a function at the mother school as it began its 100-year anniversary: "How old is she?" asked one child. "Don't you know?" says the other. "She's one hundred." But it's an easy mistake to fall into: not because of her appearance, she's the most sprightly and energetic 83-year-old I've ever met, putting most 50-year-olds to shame. But once she starts talking about the history of the school, it's easy to become so absorbed in all the stories that you find yourself seeing her as the living embodiment of all that has gone before. Deep into one interview, juggling with so many facts and figures about the school's early history, I asked her, "So when did you first meet Miss Louisa Procter?" She shot me one of her firm, unforgiving looks and said simply: "James, she died in 1907. I was born twenty years later." I went deeply red.

***

Charles officially took over the reins of the school in 1942. Between 1942 and the year of his father's death, 1953, the Reverend Tanios Saad continued to play a role in the school. The determined and strongly opinionated father was often at odds with his kind and gentle son on how to run the school. Sometimes the disputes were about educational matters – about the introduction of a new subject or an increase in school hours – sometimes about the buildings and sometimes about the business.

World War II brought further insecurity to the region. Following World War I and the collapse of the Ottoman Empire, as we have noted, Lebanon became part of the French mandate of Syria – first as a Syrian enclave (the State of Greater Lebanon, 1 September 1920), then as the Lebanese Republic (1 September 1926), administered under the French mandate. After France had fallen to the Germans and the puppet "Vichy" government had been installed, in 1941 the Germans moved supplies and forces through Lebanon and Syria to use against the British in Iraq. The British responded by moving its forces from its mandate of Palestine into Syria, including Lebanon.

There was a short skirmish between the forces of the Vichy regime and the British, which ended in the British taking control of the region. The leader of the Free French, General Charles de Gaulle, then visited Lebanon and agreed that its independence would soon be granted. The new state of Lebanon was unilaterally declared on 8 November 1943, and finally accepted by the French, under international pressure, on 22 November 1943, now Lebanese Independence Day. As Charles witnessed these events, increasingly he became interested in the politics of nation-building (later, between 1960 and 1968, Charles was to enter the Lebanese parliament). His engineering skills were in any case in demand for the infrastructural work that the British were engaged in, including building railways. Any earnings were plowed back into the school – he had imbibed his father's sense of independence and didn't want to ask for funding from any government agency because he recognized that all funding came with strings attached, and he valued the school's freedom to teach as and what they wanted.

After World War II came to a close, Charles engaged in a thorough building program for the school, whose population was buoyed by the influx of students from Palestine. (This flow was interrupted for a couple of years after the creation of the state of Israel.) And Charles became the patriarch of the Saad family, every Sunday continuing the tradition of open house, eating in their very big dining room, relaxing on their terrace after lunch.

So the school grew and developed. In 1942, when Charles Saad took over, it had 216 students. In 1953, when his father died, there were 655 students. Clearly his work was successful. In the early 1950s, Charles wanted to have a much stronger focus on mathematics and the sciences, aware that these were important subjects that his students would need as they prepared for their futures. But then in 1954, the school academic director, and teacher of the key subjects of math and physics, left. He needed to be replaced, and urgently, but attracting good people into education was hard.

Perhaps Charles was also feeling that at last the school was his to run as he saw fit, after the recent death of his father. But with the exhilaration this engendered came the responsibility of leadership. In 1954, Charles wanted to bring fresh blood into the school to help him lift the school to new heights. He wanted a person who shared the same values that his father had imbued in him, but someone who could help him to develop and implement the vision of educational excellence to which he aspired.

He found this fresh blood in the unlikely guise of a callow 22-year-old youth.

CHAPTER 2

The good life

The other half

Twenty-two-year-old Ralph Bistany was at the American University of Beirut studying, on his father's recommendation, physics with mathematics. He was a young, extremely bright, opinionated rich kid. He was also very short. His businessman father had bought him a bright green Oldsmobile 88, with a V8 engine, which he, a tad insensitively, drove to the university – General Motors' bestselling automobile cost maybe four times the annual salary of one of Ralph's lecturers.

At twenty, he had married a petite seventeen-year-old French woman. He had met her at a party – he was asked to go to parties mainly on account of his Oldsmobile, not because people especially liked being with him. In his turn, he loathed parties, preferring his own company. At this event, however, a pretty, blonde, blue-eyed French girl caught his eye, and she didn't seem to mind his attentions either, however clumsy they may have been. He met her again at a second party, and they seemed to get along even better. They then went out in a group of young friends, and he contrived to spend as much time as he could close to her. And still she didn't seem to mind. At the end of the evening, he offered to drive her home. She said, "Yes." In the car he asked whether she would marry him. He heard her say "No," so he said, "Okay," was quiet for a bit, then gamely tried to talk about something else. After a while, she said, "You are a strange person." He shrugged, absorbed in his own thoughts. "Why's that?" "You asked me if I will marry you. I say 'yes' and then you stop talking about it; you even change the subject." Ralph was cross. "You said 'no.'" "No," she replied, "I said yes." So, on their first time alone, went their first argument.

The young Ralph was passionate about learning but not so keen on turning up to lectures and the like; as for lab work, he found this tedious in the extreme. The head of the Physics Department at AUB was Dr Salwa Nassar, who had studied in Chicago with Enrico Fermi, the Nobel laureate who worked with J. Robert Oppenheimer on the Manhattan Project and is often known, with him, as the "father of the atomic bomb." As one of her top students, Dr Nassar was fond of the young Ralph and protected him where necessary (for instance, by convincing others in the department to overlook the fact that he didn't often attend lab classes). The two became very attached, and after graduation he continued to his master's under her tutelage.

Perhaps the news of her mentor's severe illness made her reflective about life's deeper meanings (Enrico Fermi was diagnosed with stomach cancer and was to die before the year was out). One late summer's day Dr Nassar took the young Ralph aside. "You know, you've really got to do something for your country." She wanted to see whether he had the potential for another side to him, to push him in a better direction. She wanted him to prove to her that he wasn't just a spoiled, rich kid. He said, okay, what should he do to please her? "I'd like you to help in a local school." One local school had come to the attention of her university department – Mr Charles Saad had an innovative deal with the university whereby the freshman class would do their first year of study at his school in Choueifat and then be allowed to take an exam to join the sophomore class at the university. She was also aware that Mr Saad had told her of his great need for a mathematics and physics teacher at that time, subjects he was rightly prioritizing. So, on her recommendation, Ralph went to meet Mr Charles Saad.

The first meeting was not a success. Charles was 52, now firmly in charge of the school after his father's death, feeling the heavy duty of responsibility for the children in his care. Dr Nassar had forewarned him about this bright but bumptious young man, and so he carefully thought of the right words to convey the importance of the school's work in a way that the rich young man might understand: "Education is a mission ..." he began. Ralph stopped him. "I don't believe in missions. I'm exactly like the guy who sells cheese in his shop. He is selling cheese. I will sell mathematics and I have no more merit than he has, provided neither of us is cheating on the product."

The meeting broke up pretty soon after that. Dr Nassar was very annoyed: "I didn't send you to discuss deeper issues," she said. "I sent you for a job interview." She called Mr Charles Saad again, smoothed things over – Charles as always was affable and willing to give the young man the benefit of the doubt – and sent Ralph back.

On the second visit, Ralph and Mrs Saad encountered each other. They each tell the story of their first meeting in slightly different ways; but it was clear that neither had much respect for the other on first meeting. They were both young – Mrs Leila Saad at 27 was only five years older than Ralph. Neither thought the other's youth much of an advantage.

Mrs Saad's version is that she didn't even notice Ralph at first. She had been sitting in the car without proper air-conditioning, in the most terrible August heat, the young wife impatient for her husband, who had promised to be only a few minutes, but who was keeping her waiting. Eventually, at 2:30 p.m., he came rushing out with his briefcase. Charlie, the great charmer, said, "I'm sorry, darling, I'm sorry. Did I keep you waiting?" Mrs Saad let him have it: "What do you mean, did you keep me waiting? Of course you kept me waiting ...!" Charlie tried to calm her down: "But you know, I was interviewing this math and physics teacher. We really need him for the school." Mrs Saad said, "But I didn't see anyone come out of the gate." Charlie said, "No, no, he just came out a minute ago." Mrs Saad exploded: "You mean to tell me, that short, dark fellow with the open shirt is a mathematics teacher? And what a mathematics teacher he is going to be!" Dismissing in her mind the unimposing, hot and miserable youth whom she had hardly noticed walking past the car a few minutes earlier.

Ralph had certainly noticed Mrs Saad. His version is that he had been sitting with Mr Charles Saad, on the beautiful balcony of the family home, with the tremendous sweeping views over the olive groves and down to the sea. "I heard shouting, and there was this young lady shouting at somebody doing some work on the walls and very displeased at what was going on." Ralph was rather surprised. "Here was the boss, this young lady is shouting, there was obviously a big age difference between them." Telling me this story, in his apartment with Mrs Saad sitting near by, he leaned over to me, *sotto voce*, but loud enough so that she could hear: "Then I found out she was the real boss." Mrs Saad confided in me: "I'm not often wrong in judging characters, but I made the mistake of my life that day. I'm so glad Charlie didn't listen to me because we would have missed someone who was truly irreplaceable."

Mr Ralph Bistany joined Choueifat as mathematics and physics teacher. He taught the freshman class from the university for twelve hours per week, while simultaneously studying for his master's at the university too. He initially joined the school for one year. At the end of the year, Charles Saad invited him to review his year and convinced the young man, just as his father had in his turn convinced him, "Why don't you give us another year and consolidate your achievements?" And so in this way Ralph eventually got hooked on the pleasures and potential of education. He had had no prior wish to go into teaching. Perhaps he would follow in his father's footsteps into business. Failing that, he wouldn't have minded going into academic research, in mathematical physics. But education? Never had he given that a thought. But slowly, working with the children and young people, he saw that this was very much an area that could combine his interests in academic development with his business sense.

Miss Louisa Procter had introduced the Saad family to the English tradition of afternoon tea and biscuits. This tradition had been maintained by the Reverend Tanios Saad, and by the time his son Charles took over the household, afternoon tea was firmly ingrained in the culture. At 5 p.m. sharp, no matter what else was happening, Charles

Saad would call Ralph and Leila to take tea with him. "What new ideas did you have today?" he would ask Ralph.

Sometimes there were fires to put out – just as there had been disagreements aired over tea between the Reverend Tanios and his son, so now sometimes disagreements arose between Charles Saad and this new young man in whom he had invested so much. (Charles and Leila didn't have children of their own – the one source of regret that Mrs Saad tells me about in her own otherwise entirely fulfilled life: "We never had any children, and I think in a way Charlie looked at Ralph as a child of his, who was continuing to promote the message that he believed in.") Putting out the fires fell on Leila's shoulders.

One area of disagreement was relationships with government. Charles had been deeply engaged with the process of Lebanese independence back in 1943 and was impressed by the potential for change that politics could bring. Charles thought they should engage with politics as a way of improving education for the masses in Lebanon – and in the end was to convince Ralph that this could be a useful way forward. Politics was one thing but Ralph drew the line at mixing with politicians. The very well-connected Charles often invited senior politicians to the school, and Ralph was not very cooperative. Charles, the sociable person who loved being with people and talking ideas at dinner parties, would organize important dinner events, and Ralph would usually refuse to attend.

Sometimes the area of disagreement concerned teaching and learning methods. Ralph might be trying to implement a certain approach. Mr Saad would tell him he was misguided. But he knew the young man was sincere and brilliant and wanting to make a difference in the educational experience of his school. So he would ask: "Why do you hold this view?" Charles would listen and more often than not be persuaded that Ralph's approach might be the better way. And once he'd supported Ralph, Charles had the vision to let him take the school to where he wanted it, backing him all the way, sometimes against everyone else, including his young wife.

One teatime, however, a more substantial disagreement erupted. Charles had mentioned in passing that the school was again in some financial difficulty, but that they needn't worry, he would again sell property to provide the needed investment in the school. He was only really updating his wife and Ralph. Finance was not something with which they needed to be concerned.

But Ralph wouldn't let it be mentioned only in passing. He was genuinely puzzled: "How come?" he asked. "You should be making money in the school." It was in the late 1950s, and the school had reached around eight hundred students, most of whom were paying good money for their tuition. But instead of making money, the school relied on Charles making money in his other businesses and spending this in the school. "This is not sustainable," said Ralph. "It's also not possible." He firmly believed that education could be run as a business, a normal business able to make a profit. Charles tried to brush him off, telling him not to worry about the financial side of the business. Ralph persisted, "According to me you should be making money, if you're not making any money something is wrong." Charles said, "Ralph, leave the accounts aside and concentrate on the academics." Ralph said, "No, I want to take over the accounts."

The school already had an accountant, an older person who had been with Charles for many years. Ralph said, "I want the accountant to report to me." Mr Saad was calm, but this young man sometimes took it all too far. "Well," he said, "first thing, you are not an accountant." Ralph asked him what he meant by that. Charles said: "You don't know accounting." "Fine," said Ralph, "when I know accounting, will you agree to let me take care of this issue?" A little irritated, but not thinking that anything would come of it, Mr Saad agreed.

A day or two later, Ralph went into Beirut and bought the latest accounting books. Every spare moment he got, he devoted himself to their study. After a month of this, he brought the subject up again at afternoon tea. Ralph said, "I'm an accountant now." Charles dismissed him: "You can't be, not so quickly." Charles had friends who were auditors. Ralph said, "Call your auditors, let them come and interview me. If they tell you I'm not a good accountant then I'll forget it." This was done. "Yes," they said, "he knows accounting."

When Charles made a promise he stuck to it. After that Ralph took over the financial side of the business. And some problems that had been hidden away beneath the surface were now revealed and rectified; finally the school began to make money.

Genesis of ideas

During this period, the educational philosophy of SABIS was also evolving. The first of the key elements to evolve were the "SABIS Point System®,"[1] the "teach-practice-check" cycle and the "pacing charts." These evolved, Ralph Bistany said, from a "very bad experience" – and the detailed and emotional way in which he told me the story 50 years later showed how deeply the impact of the experience is still ingrained in him. He was teaching fifteen students a "very tough program" in mathematics: "It included calculus, add to it the conic sections; it treated geometry in three different ways, one of them through radical axes; transformations in geometry, including inversion, a transformation that would change a sphere into a plane; it included a short course in astronomy; descriptive geometry; a heavy course in trigonometry; a heavy course in number theory ... Maybe I forgot something."

He had the class for twelve periods a week, with additional time at noon and over weekends. "I thought I had solved every possible problem that could be asked, every trick anybody could think of," he said. "And as I taught each area I asked: 'Do you understand?' And they would all say, 'Yes.' And in June they all failed."

In the Choueifat school, Ralph used to start his days at six in the morning and carry on until 11 p.m. "I was happy until that June. They failed, all of them, so I cried." He really did cry: "I went to my room. I had an apartment at the school although I was married and had a home, for when I worked late. After crying for a moment, I washed my face, prepared my resignation letter, and went to Mr Saad."

It was late afternoon. As was usual at that time of the day, Charles was in his study taking tea. Someone brought Ralph tea and biscuits, but he couldn't partake. Instead of the usual sharing of ideas, pushing forward the boundaries of their educational understanding, Ralph sat morosely. Eventually, Charles said: "What's the matter?" Ralph told him that he had failed the students, failed his mentor, failed the school, and that he should go. Mr Saad listened patiently. Then he said, "You are not going anywhere. Review in your own mind what went wrong and work out a way of making it come right next time."

What Ralph realized is that, first, he shouldn't ever be satisfied again simply asking students whether they understood or not. They had to be able to confirm, in writing, that they had – hence the need for the "teach-practice-check" cycle.

Why would the children say they had understood, when clearly they had not? It took him some time to realize that they weren't simply lying. "They were sincere; they *did* think they understood." If a student is reading or listening, then it's easy to carry on reading or listening. "I *can* sort of fool myself that I'm understanding if I'm listening to something or if I'm reading it." But you can't fool yourself if you have to write. That was the trick he soon realized. He told his students: "When you study something and you think you've understood it, close that book and write it so that someone who reads it will also understand it. In trying to do so, anything you haven't really understood will cause you to stumble and eventually you'll have to go back to the point at which you have not understood and will be able to build your knowledge from that point onwards." The key was to write, not listen or read.

Moreover, the teacher had to be sure what he was trying to confirm that the students knew. Ralph realized that the curriculum needed to be painstakingly dissected into "points," the specific areas that were required for students to learn.

A common criticism that often comes SABIS's way today is that they "don't trust the teachers," and that this is a big problem with their education model. (We shall explore aspects of this contemporary criticism in Chapter 11.) Ralph Bistany doesn't like the use of the word "trust" here. In the mid-1950s, for instance, Ralph says: "We were extremely close to our teachers. We knew everybody inside out; we ate with them; we went out with them; we were with them all the time." No one should question whether or not they trusted each other. Rather than talk about trust, the issue was more about the integrity of what it means to be an educator.

In February 1957, Mr Charles Saad made Ralph assistant director general, and Mrs Saad director general, giving Ralph increasingly more say in the running of the school. The next September, Ralph was teaching math to students who were now in their exam year. "They had so many gaps. When I checked, I couldn't find out whether they had done this material and forgotten it or whether they had not done it at all. They had no idea." To his shame, as assistant director general, neither did he.

Ralph realized that education – like any other profession or business – would have to be more methodical than that. Thus was born the first "pacing chart." Ralph took the requirements of the external exam the students were to sit in June and wrote a chart of all the material that had to be covered, in minute detail, in order to get the students to cover all the material by June. Having done it for this class, he then asked himself, "Why wait years to determine if there is a problem?" Thus began the construction of the pacing charts in all subjects and for all levels, starting with the goal of the final exams and retracing all the concepts back to the earliest grades.

So far so good. But then there arose the issue of how to check that teachers were following these. "I had no way to check. How did I know if anyone was a bad teacher or a good teacher? It troubled me. It meant that we didn't know." So Ralph and Mrs Saad talked this through. "We don't know anything about our teachers. And if we don't know, are we going to leave things to chance?"

The solution was that no assessments should be written or administered by the teachers who had taught the particular classes. "Nobody can do without outside checking. It's so easy to fool oneself," said Ralph, who, as we've already seen, was aware of how he had been open to fooling himself about the progress of his own classes. But he was fooling himself again if he thought his teachers would respond so readily to their own shortcomings. The Choueifat faculty "went raving mad" when he raised the prospect of others writing and administering their class tests. "You don't trust us," they said. Some teachers left because of this.

But it was not about trust. Then as now, it was about giving students and parents what they deserve to know, an objective idea of how well they're doing. "Early on, we just did not accept that the teacher should design his own lesson, his own course, his own tests. To us this would have been the equivalent of having a building where every floor is designed by a different architect and built by a different contractor. Amazingly this is what many people still promote. It makes no sense to me," says Ralph.

But the "points" and the "pacing charts" were not enough. A further idea, that of "essential knowledge," emerged from another foundational experience in the late 1950s.

Charles and Leila Saad had a close friend who was an emir of the Druze community. By coincidence, he was also a friend of Ralph's grandparents; Ralph used to call him "Uncle." He came to the school with a young Iranian student. "This boy has problems," said the emir. "His brother is one year younger than he is, yet one year ahead in school."

Ralph shrugged, and gamely said, "Okay, let me test him." As the boy was supposed to be going into tenth grade, they gave him the appropriate test. He got zero. They tested him on ninth-grade material; again zero. All the way down to fourth-grade material, still zero. Ralph went back to the emir: "I'm sorry, we cannot teach him," he said. The emir was not so quickly swayed: "You are not going to let me down, are you? You have to do it."

Ralph mentally kicked himself. He'd been thinking only of academics. But now he was responsible for financial matters too. And he remembered that the child's father was immensely rich. He said to the emir: "I will take him, but he will be in a class of his own. I'm going to charge his father what a whole class costs." The emir said, "Why not?" Ralph worked out the costs: "I want so much. So much it is, said the emir. And the deal was made, without any argument."

Now the educational challenge arose. What concepts does this boy absolutely need to know in order to be able to tackle tenth-grade mate-rial? And what are the prerequisites that he needs to know in order to tackle *those* concepts? Ralph knew he would have to go all the way back to the beginning, finding out what the boy did and didn't know of these areas, filling in the gaps as he went along. Ralph assigned the boy to a number of teachers. "I don't want a grade for him," he told them. Instead, he wanted a detailed checklist of all he had learned, pointing to the areas he still needed to master. For two years, the teachers took part in this process of finding out what the boy knew, teaching the new essential concepts and checking for their understanding. At the end of that time, the boy was ahead of his brother again. They had found that by taking a student back to the basics, the things he did know, they could build up mastery of the essential knowledge that he needed in order to get on.

Clearly the method used – one child with a personal, dedicated teacher – was not replicable, except perhaps for the very rich. After this experience, the school began to get a reputation in Lebanon and beyond that if you had a child who was unteachable, "then bring him or her to Choueifat, and they will perform miracles." But clearly it was not just for special-needs students that the school had uncovered an important idea. Ralph Bistany and Charles and Leila Saad realized that the method that had got the special-needs boy through was actu-ally applicable to *all* of the children in their school. So the ideas of "essential knowledge" and the logical sequencing of the curriculum were born.

These ideas evolved further, as more needy cases were brought to Choueifat.

On a sweltering hot, mid-August afternoon in 1959, Ralph Bistany was alone in the school office, having difficulty getting anything done in the heat. He decided to close the office at 3 p.m. As he closed the door behind him, an elderly gentleman arrived. In an American accent he asked whether he could talk to the director. Ralph really didn't want to stay; he was tired. The gentleman had made this long journey all the way out from Beirut, however; Ralph saw his sweat and his weariness, and thought, "Okay, I'm not going to tell you to come back tomorrow." So Ralph reopened the office and asked what the problem was.

The man was a Mr George Fleischman from the American embassy, working for USAID, the American government aid agency. Initially, he said that two young people from Yemen were causing him grief. They knew practically nothing, but the Americans wanted them to have a crash course so that they could qualify for the American University in four years' time. Mr Fleischman talked about Yemen: until recently, there was only one car in the country, they had no schools and it was all very backward. Now the country was opening up, and the Americans were very keen to educate a cadre of people to help serve the new Yemen, as engineers, doctors and other professionals.

Ralph's mind was racing. The experience with the Iranian boy was recent: he knew that the school could rise to an educational challenge like this. But then doubts: that boy at least knew some English; these Yemenis, on the American's own admission, "know very little." Would it really be possible to take two children of fifteen, who knew no English, little Arabic, whose mathematical skills were pretty non-existent too, and get them ready for the American University in four years? Ralph went back and forth in his mind and wondered, however much he wanted to help, whether he could do it. After two hours Mr Fleischman apologetically said he hadn't been completely truthful earlier. "It's not two kids; it's eighty-five." At that point, Ralph asked the American whether he could come back in a couple of days.

For Mr Fleischman, two kids seemed a good way to ease into the problem without putting the listener off. For Ralph, it was the opposite: the fact that there were 85 made possible what would have been impossible with only two. For 85 students meant big money. They sat down again and discussed the sums involved. Ralph calculated that the 85 students would bring in funds that would effectively double the existing income from the school's 700 children.

Mr Fleischman and Mr Bistany reached a deal. The Yemenis would board at the school for twelve months a year. Mr Bistany called a meeting with the heads of department; Mrs Saad was present at the meeting. He explained the immensity of the Yemeni problem and asked for the staff's views. One by one, Mrs Saad included, they all said it couldn't be done, that they shouldn't touch it. When they were finished, Ralph said, "Fine, I'm happy I've heard your views; now we are going to do it, I've already committed to it." But Ralph had cleared it first with Mr Charles Saad, and that's why he felt able to override the staff misgivings at this stage.

The school followed the same approach that they had trialed with the Iranian boy: they realized for these Yemeni students, giving grades as one would normally do was of no use at all. They needed something far more granular, detailed and informative. First they needed to break down all the requirements of the American University curriculum and build checklists of all the concepts that needed to be known, the prerequisites for knowing those concepts, and the order in which they had to be known. "I don't want a grade," Ralph said, "I want to know what each kid has learned. I want to know things like, Mohammed has learned how to factorize X squared minus A squared, but Yosef has not." This soon led to being swamped with paper, however – you really needed thousands of these concepts to check, and it very quickly became unmanageable. Ralph was frustrated, but had to relimit their objectives. Instead of the level of detail he required, he had to settle for rougher measures – but these "units" were still manifestly better than simply giving grades, as would be the custom in any other school at the time.

So the process for the 85 students was to develop the essential building blocks of the curriculum and divide it all into "units." A unit might be: "A student can derive the roots of the second-degree trinomial." This of course has many sub-components – and here was Ralph's frustration, that ideally he'd like to know the detail of where the student stumbled on any of these sub-components. But nevertheless, the data gained were immensely useful in getting the students up and running.

What particularly inspired Ralph and the Saads again was that the ideas they were trying out for the 85 Yemeni students were clearly appropriate for the existing 700 students. What was possible with pen and paper for 85 students, however, was simply not possible for the larger number of students. The frustration this engendered led to Ralph's desire for a way of coping with the level of data he wanted from each child. He wanted data, the more the better, for he could begin to see now how using this data could help create the flourishing educational environment he was seeking. Soon he realized that he needed a computer. It was this experience, then, which led the school to be one of the first to experiment with the potential of information technology, to eventually create what are called the "history files" for each child in each subject.

There was a further twist in this story, which showed how the SABIS village school was way ahead of anything else at the time. It transpired that American aid distributed through USAID should be given only to American companies; consequently, before approaching the Choueifat school, Mr Fleischman had first explored all the American schools in Lebanon and elsewhere in the Middle East, but nobody else would touch the Yemeni program. Hence he felt able to offer it to the non-American school.

At the end of Choueifat's first year with the Yemeni students, however, Mr Fleischman came back to the school. He was deeply embarrassed. He told Ralph Bistany the that proprietors of the other American schools had complained to their ambassador. They pointed out that Choueifat was not an American institution, and so, therefore, USAID was breaking its own rules by offering the program to them. Embarrassed and somewhat drained by the whole affair, Mr Fleischman had gone to see the ambassador: "But I offered it to all the American schools and they turned me down," he protested. The ambassador was nonplussed: "Well, they turned it down, but now they've changed their mind. They want the children." Mr Fleischman told Ralph how he had put up a fight, and at the end persuaded the ambassador to keep one third of the student body in Choueifat and allocate the remaining two thirds split equally between two of the American schools in Beirut. The new cohort of students starting that year was to be divided in the same way.

The term started in October. The students were split between schools in the way required by the American ambassador. A month later, Mr Fleischman called Ralph again. Could staff from the other schools come to see the Choueifat program? Ralph Bistany was blasé about this: "Fine, they are welcome."

Ralph Bistany called his heads of department together again. He said, "We're going to get a visit from two schools. Whatever they tell you, you agree, don't argue about anything. Let them see anything they want to see, answer their questions, but don't argue." The visitors arrived. They went around the school, spoke to the members of staff assigned to them, and said, "But this can't be done. The kids won't learn like that." As promised, none of the teachers argued with them. The visitors left, firm in their disbelief that Choueifat could actually have achieved what it was saying it had achieved.

Just before Christmas, Mr Fleischman called again. By now Ralph was used to his apologetic tone. "I'm embarrassed, but, how shall I put this? Could you please accept the Yemeni children back again?" Ralph chuckled. "What happened?" he asked innocently. Mr Fleischman said: "The other schools say they are not teachable."

So all the Yemenis returned to Choueifat, and nobody complained to the ambassador any more. The program was immensely successful, the vast majority of the students going on to an American university, to become doctors and engineers and the like. In the end, politics intervened, as so often was to happen with SABIS: in 1967, the program was terminated because Yemen and the United States severed relations. But the effect of the program on SABIS was immense and enduring.

One of the ways it had an enduring influence on SABIS was in the need it created for technology, and hence to SABIS acquiring one of the first computers on sale in Lebanon in the late 1960s – inspired by the need to analyze the large amount of data it was amassing because of the Yemeni students and the detail they required about the granularity of student understanding.

In those early days, Mr Charles Saad and Ralph Bistany had gone to visit the computer company Olivetti, which had just brought out its first computer in Lebanon, the Audiotronic. Charles and Ralph were shown the machine and asked the price. "It was almost the price of a building at the time," Ralph recalls. But it didn't matter. The man from Olivetti wouldn't sell it. It didn't have any software, and the software engineers had only just started their eight-month training. Once they'd finished and had prepared suitable software, only then could they start selling the machines. A bit disheartened, they left. "Two days later the machine was at the school." Mr Charles Saad had bought it. He had also bought the ten books that the software engineers were being trained on. "I'm sure you can read them," he said to Ralph. So Ralph wrote the first software for their first computer. He's been influencing much of their technological innovation ever since.

In the late 1950s, another experience became the basis from which important ideas on the community of learning evolved. One weekend at Choueifat, Ralph was watching the kids play soccer. He saw that the referee was a boy who limped heavily. He had suffered from polio when he was young, so he couldn't play. He observed that there were no adults involved, "they had organized it all themselves." Ralph was impressed. He noticed that the boy was refereeing perfectly and that the other children obeyed him instantly, nobody argued with him.

The boy was a young Kuwaiti who later went on to become governor of the Bank of Kuwait. Ralph started thinking: "If this boy who is actually physically handicapped can control all these other kids, then this has implications for the way we run our school!" Clearly, they could be free to hand over some responsibilities to students within the school. But how many? And which? "We were much too slow in our reaction," he muses now. But what emerged was, over time, whenever they had problems within the school, or things to be done, "Let's see if there is any student who can take on the responsibility." He reflects on his reaction: "It all came very slowly and I blame myself for not reacting faster. Here I was sitting on something that could have helped our school and I just didn't know. I'm not as smart as I think I am."

The "something" that could have helped their school which emerged from this early experience was the Student Life Organization®.[2] This has become an absolutely crucial part of the SABIS educational model, and we'll devote much of a chapter to it later in the book.

***

Mrs Saad, reflecting on these examples when I visited her in the mother school, mused: "In retrospect, I admire my husband more and more, the more I think about all this. Because I see the conflict of age and what it does to people. I've seen people just wave away an idea because it is being proposed by a younger person. And when you are the head of an organization, and a young man comes and tells you what you are doing is wrong, or that you should do things differently, there aren't many people who would let that conversation carry on. But Charlie's reaction used to be, 'Why do you think it is wrong? Explain it to me.' And if he was not convinced, he would ask him to spend more time, because Charlie's basic driving force was, what is the best for the school? He was willing to listen to anything that was in the best interests of the school."

***

In June 1960, Charles, at the age of 58, got elected to parliament. This was the first government installed after the Lebanese crisis of 1958. For the eight years he was MP, he was also chairman of the education commission in parliament. He handed over the running of the school to Ralph Bistany, now 28. Mrs Saad became vice-principal, and in charge of two departments, English and Social Studies. She was also heavily engaged in her own studies, pursuing a degree in English literature and pedagogy at the American University of Beirut, graduating in 1963.

Charles had in the end persuaded Ralph of the potential of political change to improve the educational opportunities for ordinary people in Lebanon, and Ralph strongly supported him in his attempt to get elected and helped him with his work on the education commission. The longer they tried, however, the more frustrated they became with the impossibly slow pace of change – and the way in which extraneous factors impinged upon the political process, so that in the end, you were not really working on educational change, but on other factional issues. Toward the end of Charles's time in parliament, they had a visitor for afternoon tea at the family home in Choueifat. He was a senior official from the Ministry of Education. As much to make conversation as anything, he put to the assembled group, including Ralph Bistany, "So, how can the Ministry of Education help?" Ralph said, "They can get out of the way." Charles politely moved the conversation on to something else. But by this time it probably summed up the Saad–Bistany combined worldview on education and government.

The 1960s and early 1970s were a time of growth and consolidation in the school – which doubled its numbers from 770 in 1960 to 1,480 by the end of the decade; they had increased again to 1,806 by 1974. Just as Charles had created a committed young team around him in the late 1950s, Ralph now did the same. Some of these people are still with the company today. These include Ramzi Germanos, who joined in February 1960 – and who now in his early 70s is executive regional director for all the SABIS schools in the Gulf.

Ramzi, twenty years old, was roped into teaching physics early on, although his major subject was chemistry. For most of the course, he recalls, he was just two or three weeks ahead of his students. When his first class finally took the external exams, however, Ralph called him to his office: "I want to congratulate you on your results." Ramzi thought he couldn't be serious. The class average was 60 percent, and a large number of students had failed outright. But Ralph reassured him: "I consider it to be a very good result. The person who taught this course before you is a first-class honors physics graduate from Oxford. On this same test his students scored forty percent."

Ramzi resided in the school, which had six rooms for teachers, with two teachers per room. "All of us shared one bathroom," Ramzi muses. It was an immensely exciting time for them all. Ralph and the other young teachers were "eating, drinking, breathing together." After school, someone might say, "Okay, let's go and have dinner at Faisal's";

they'd go swimming first, and then eat fish. "And then," remembers Ralph, "we would have vivid discussions; someone would be preparing a course in philosophy, and we'd explore with her all that she was thinking. Or the same in English or in physics. And then we'd stop and play backgammon and then go back. They were heady, exciting days." It was all a great bonding experience for Ramzi: "I think what kept me there was that when I would come across interesting ideas, different from what is normally expected, I would present them to Mr B, as Ralph came to be called, and instead of hearing, 'No we don't want this,' he would look deeply into them, be challenged to see if it was something they wanted."

One of the ideas that Ramzi presented to the school which Ralph Bistany thought was of immense value fitted in neatly with their other methods for efficient learning. This was the idea of "classic" or "basic" questions. Ralph had first seen it in action when Ramzi was teaching the equivalent of A-level dynamics. He had given the students a list of nineteen questions which he'd painstakingly worked out. He told them to try to find any problem in any of the course books that was not a combination of those nineteen questions. And no one could. Hence, by carefully going through the curriculum and finding these "classic" questions, he was able to reassure any student that, provided they too mastered these nineteen questions, they would not falter in the exam.

Ralph was so excited by this idea that he asked all the teachers to do the same. Ramzi himself was the one who extended it across each of the sciences when he was head of sciences at the school. After the classic questions, a related idea was to think about the minimum vocabulary they would require of children in a SABIS school, at particular grades. And then they explored what mistakes children were making in language, and how these could be eradicated for every child.

Ramzi also wrote much of the science curriculum for SABIS. Ralph says now, "He wrote beautiful books." These are the very same books that SABIS is now revising and adapting.

Early on, under Ramzi's guidance, the school changed how they taught science. Rather than introducing all the physical laws and getting children to simply memorize these, or taking them to the lab and getting them to replicate an experiment, saying "this is the proof," Ramzi wanted the school to introduce the *scientific method*, to introduce children to the idea of what it is to think like a scientist. Ramzi remembers how he would explain this to his classes:

> Consider a boy who doesn't know anything about physical laws, who gets lost in the forest. He needs to keep warm at night. He knows that some objects burn, but he doesn't know which objects. So on his first day he collects a whole range of objects, branches, sticks, keys, stones, a broomstick. Then he experiments, finds that the broomstick and the branches burn, but the keys and the stones don't. So he starts thinking, why? Why would these burn and not the others? And so his first thought – his first hypothesis – is, maybe it's related to their shape? Perhaps it's cylinders that burn? So the next day, his search is refined to look for cylindrical objects. He brings back old pipes and ignores an old door. And he spends a cold night because the pipes don't burn. So he has to go back to the drawing board. The point is, his initial hypothesis that cylindrical objects burn is *not* nonsense; it was justified within the bounds of the experiment that led to this rule, considering the objects he had experimented with. This is how scientists should think. We come up with a hypothesis and then we try to prove it wrong. We can never prove it right, but it only takes one instance of failure to prove it wrong.

At the same time, rules like Newton's laws, although proved not to hold under speeds approaching the speed of light, are still very useful at much slower speeds, which are what apply most of the time. The difference between the predictions of Einstein's laws of relativity and predictions based on Newton's laws of classical mechanics are far too small to be detected in most cases. Therefore, under normal conditions, it makes sense to use the simpler rules of classical mechanics rather than using the "more accurate" relativity rules.

So the SABIS science curricula that Ramzi designed started with children doing series of experiments to get a feel for nature. Then quantitative measurements are introduced around the age of twelve, to show them that measurements are possible and that hypotheses can be drawn from the data and made into mathematical models – for a mathematical model "is nothing more than the summary of many experiments, all of which can be summarized into that small formula." It's important, says Ramzi, that students realize that these formulas are not laws of nature. "Newton did not discover laws of nature; he invented rules, or mathematical models, that were reliable within the bounds of his experiences. When scientists went beyond Newton's experiences and found measurements that didn't make sense under Newton's rules, Einstein had to come up with more general rules that we call laws," which again are likely to be superseded one day. "If students get into this spirit, then they can start to understand what science is. Our approach gives them initially all the foundations: the skill to measure, the skill to collect data, the skill to put the data on a graph, the skill to find a mathematical model. Once they have these skills, then we can tell them, 'Now you know how laws are built. They were put together by human beings, just like you did.'" Then you can introduce them to the laws that others have formulated.

The results obtained under his teaching in physics seemed to bear out his insistence that young people learning about the scientific method was beneficial. In the Lebanese baccalaureate, physics is considered the toughest subject. When one of Ramzi's earliest classes of exactly 40 students took the scientific baccalaureate exam, the class average in physics was 85 percent, a high distinction. Performance in biology and chemistry was also dramatic under Ramzi's guidance. The result, by any measure, was outstanding, said Ralph.

One instance when Mr Germanos was not convinced that Mr Bistany was right, however, was when Ralph wanted to introduce yet more testing in the school. Math, for example, was taught for six periods a week, and Ralph wanted one of those periods to be handed over to testing. Ramzi, aware of the likely teacher revolt over this, challenged Ralph: "But how can we finish the syllabus? If you take one period out of six, that's over fifteen percent of time lost!" Ralph demurred: "Yes, but if you use this period for testing, the benefits to you will be so great that they will more than compensate for your loss of time."

Ramzi met with the teachers – he was the one in the firing line, not Ralph – and they were as shocked as he had anticipated. Eventually they accepted a plan which Ralph proposed. They would cut three chapters – around 15 percent of the curriculum – from the syllabus, revise the pacing chart, and then they could fit in these new-fangled weekly assessments.

But the curious thing – curious at least to the teachers and Ramzi, although Ralph clearly had foreseen this – was that, after the system had bedded down, now that the teachers knew who had learned what, they were able to go through the curriculum more quickly. "The knowledge made them go faster." In the end, Ralph was able to reinstate the cut three chapters and restore the full curriculum.

Ramzi too was involved very early on in the new Student Life Organization. His own view is that his contribution grew out of his informal "advising" classes that he used to hold – when he would take time off from physics and talk to students about putting in the extra effort for study, exploring questions about motivation and where they were going in life. One day, one of the students asked, "Sir, why don't you give us advising lessons?" Ramzi said that it wasn't up to him to structure the syllabus. So the students went to Mr Bistany and persuaded him to create this as part of their curriculum. And it became a formal part, with books written for the sessions and a structure drawn up. Out of this, in Ramzi's view, grew the idea of students creating a positive atmosphere, positive peer pressure, and positive support for their colleagues. And out of this many of the ideas for Student Life became real.

"It was really about challenging the group of students in any school who are irresponsible and selfish, who don't care what happens, by helping the group of highly responsible people take risks to improve their school and society. It was helping those children to develop the guts to challenge their classmates who were being destructive, being negative. They could tell them, 'You're harming yourself; you're harming us; everybody has to work harder after school because of your actions.'" And so the school began to change through positive peer pressure. And the more students got involved, the more they wanted further involvement.

The school introduced yet other innovations, being one of the first to see the potential of the new information technology to transform and improve their educational model. The school improved its physical facilities, to cater for the increasing demand, building new boys' and girls' dormitories, laboratories, libraries and a cafeteria, among other facilities. The team was also responding to the business imperative of making sure at all times that they were financially viable, by cutting out things that were unnecessary and increasing the efficiency of their work. In many ways it was pleasing for Ralph to note how many of these changes, which led to the improved viability of the business, also made perfect sense educationally, something we follow up in Chapter 12.

It was an incredibly rewarding and fulfilling life for them all. They were engaged in running a school for nearly two thousand children, from across the Middle East, which was now known as one of the finest schools in the whole region. Many visitors came to admire what they were doing. They were seeing how their teaching and learning methods, evolved over many years through a multiplicity of different experiences and pressures, were raising standards, aspirations and educational engagement among their students. They were witnessing their alumni taking positions of responsibility and importance across the region and shared in their joy and success. And they were enjoying the benefits of the refined business model, now making a reasonable income from the school, feeling self-sufficient and comfortable.

And to cap it all, they were living in Lebanon. Given the bad press this little country gets today, it is hard to imagine this, but the Lebanon of the 1960s and early 1970s for them was paradise: "The quality of life was unique," Mrs Saad told me. "None of our European or American friends who came here wanted to go back; they wanted to settle."

Lebanon's prosperity was driven in part by its banking sector – it was dubbed the "Switzerland of the Levant," given its prominence in the Arab banking world. Another key industry was tourism, with the capital Beirut dubbed the "Paris of the Middle East" because of its French architecture and cuisine. In the middle of winter, you could bask in the sun on the Mediterranean shoreline in the morning and go skiing in the dramatic mountains in the afternoon. Its food and wine were second to none – it's one of the oldest wine-growing areas in the world. It was their beloved country, paradise on earth.

And that could possibly have been the culmination of the Saad–Bistany story – after all, there are many extremely successful schools in the region and elsewhere (think of the great elite private schools in England such as Eton, Harrow, Winchester, and Rugby, or in the USA, such as Emerson Prep, Milton Academy, Choate Rosemary Hall, Phillips Exeter Academy, and Groton) that consolidated their enrollment at 2,000 or fewer students, content to rest on their laurels ever since. And nobody would have thought there was anything wrong with that. We'd still be celebrating the 125th anniversary of a great school. And perhaps I'd still be writing a book to commemorate this. But the International School of Choueifat had one huge disadvantage compared to those other schools in their leafy suburbs. It was situated, literally, on a demographic fault line. And this fault line erupted on 13 April 1975.

On that fateful day in Beirut, local Phalangist militias (belonging to the Christian Maronites) were diverting traffic away from a church where a baptism was taking place. A lorry carrying members of the Palestine Liberation Organization (PLO), which was allowed to operate from Lebanon at the time, refused to be diverted. In the ensuing scuffles, four people were killed, including the father of the child being baptized. Sporadic fighting between the groups degenerated into street fighting; in its turn, this became the civil war that was to last until 1990, resulting in an estimated 100,000 to 200,000 civilian casualties.

The civil war was to change the lives of the Saad–Bistany families forever.

CHAPTER 3

Out of Lebanon

Living through the war

When I climbed up to the top of the hill on whose slopes the International School of Choueifat sits, past the family mausoleum containing the graves of the Reverend Saad, Charles Saad and Miss Procter, I could see why the school geography could bring it such problems as the civil war developed. It was clearly a prime site to capture. From the hilltop there is a 360-degree panorama, with a commanding view down to the airport and the port of Beirut. But it is exposed too, which is why the militia needed to find suitable hideouts to conceal their positions. Even today, in a disused corridor of one of the school's buildings, there are obscene graffiti scrawled by militiamen, whose presence would lead to the bombardment that destroyed the school.

The Lebanese civil war made the Saad–Bistany families more determined than ever to serve children anywhere. It stiffened their resolve and made them willing to risk danger for the sake of their ideals. The civil war's major impact was to expose the Saad–Bistany family education business to the wider world outside of Lebanon. "In effect, we were kicked out," says Ralph Bistany, and in being forced to survive, they discovered that their school model could be successful elsewhere.

But what of the impact of the civil war on their lives in Lebanon, on the country they cherished and the people they loved? For the younger members of the family, the civil war was like "a typhoon that came in from nowhere." Carl Bistany, now SABIS president, was a young man of nineteen when the civil war started in 1975. He stayed for a year before fleeing like so many of his contemporaries to the USA – and then didn't return for some years because of the ever-present danger and insecurity of his home country. During his year in Lebanon he lived "day by day, appreciating what each day brought to you." He said, "We had to carry arms and be there and stand guard at night, long, cold nights; sometimes we got shelled."

But for the older members of the Saad–Bistany families it was truly devastating. No more so than for Mrs Saad. The school at Choueifat – her home for all the years since she had been married, the home that she had visited as a small child, that connected her to the rich history of her husband's and father-in-law's school, which she had made her own life's mission – was on the civil war's fault line and was badly shelled. Many of the buildings were completely destroyed.

Mrs Saad showed me photographs taken when she had returned to the school when the civil war had finished. The buildings were a mess of shell holes; some had been destroyed completely. Debris was all around; one particularly poignant photo showed Charles Saad's study and desk, with shell holes shattering the walls beneath the windows. Half-burnt books and papers were all around. It was chaos. "We left in a hurry," she told me, "and most of our old papers were destroyed." This included so many of the writings of Charles Saad and his father that are lost forever. "The war was madness in this country. I was heartbroken."

The day she returned to Choueifat after the war had finished, Mrs Saad recalls, "I didn't want anybody to see what I looked like. I insisted on going through it alone. I didn't want anybody to see the emotion I felt; it was awful. I didn't want those who had destroyed the school to feel that they had achieved their objective." There is a photograph of the architect who had built the school, scratching his head, apparently saying to Mrs Saad, "Do you really want to do this?" "Yes," she insisted. "They are not going to get to me or to anybody. The school is going to be rebuilt and it is going to be better than it ever was." She continued: "I'm not going to let a silly conflict like this kill a school that so many people have struggled to build. With those who are not here, and those who are still alive, giving their youth and their lives to it, I'm not going to let it go." Ralph Bistany, however, was not keen at all on rebuilding: "We can rebuild it elsewhere, why Choueifat? They have not been nice to the school." Mrs Saad dug her heels in. "They want to be known for destruction; I want us to be known for creating. We are going to rebuild this school." Ralph said, "You are very stubborn," but knew this was a struggle he should not try to win.

The civil war in 1975 made life a challenge for everyone; but particular challenges were opened up for educators wishing to persevere with their chosen work. From 1,806 students in the school year 1974/75, the school had slumped to 694 students by January 1976. This was one problem; a larger problem was how to cope with students' erratic attendance. One week, things would quieten down, children would come back to school. But then the violence would flare up again, and children's attendance would be sporadic if not non-existent. Some of the educational ideas that the Saad–Bistany families had been working on prior to the war helped them through this period. Mrs Saad decided to focus her students' attention mainly on the "basic" subjects, languages and mathematics, and sacrificed the peripheral subjects. And within the basic subjects, they focused only on the "essential" concepts. So when a new group came, "we would take time from the peripheral subjects, social studies and the science in the primary school, to allow them time to catch up with the others." They planned it carefully. Mrs Saad takes some pride in recalling this: "I can tell you, not one student fell through that net, not one. It meant a lot of monitoring, personal follow-up, frustration, work after school. There were times when we stayed up all night to figure out how we could structure the rest, so that no child would lose out. We did not sail through; we struggled through that period. But in the end, successfully I think."

Ralph Bistany meanwhile was setting up a school in Sharjah, in the United Arab Emirates, something we'll turn to in the next section. He had taken with him the head of math and head of science: "I knew enough to guide people but when it came to tough questions I put out a cry for help," said Mrs Saad. It was difficult for Ralph himself to come back – indeed, Mrs Saad wouldn't allow it – because Ralph's background was as a Maronite Christian, the perceived enemies in the school region. As a Protestant Christian, the daughter-in-law of the founder, Mrs Saad felt at the beginning of the conflict that she could continue to work in Choueifat.

Mrs Saad was kidnapped once. "Not for long," she says, shrugging it off. "For about a day." She doesn't want to talk about it, "These things are not important," but when I press her on a later visit, reluctantly she tells me a horrifying story of being kidnapped with her sister-in-law and driver, in her car. They were taken to a remote spot, surrounded by militia. One of the kidnappers' associates recognized her as the principal of the school. She was told she and her sister-in-law could go, but that she had to leave her driver behind. She refused and persuaded them that she didn't know how to drive, and that she and her sister-in-law were too old to walk. Eventually, her persistence paid off and all three were let go. During those years, however, there were other kidnappings that had sadder endings.

In the middle of the civil war, to add to all the difficulties, Mrs Saad lost her lifelong companion and mentor. Toward the end of 1980, Charles Saad had begun feeling unwell. It was a mild heart problem, the doctor said. Mr and Mrs Saad had Christmas together in Lebanon, but Mrs Saad had to pester her doctor: "I don't care what you say, he doesn't look well." In early March 1981, Charles was diagnosed with cancer of the colon. "He didn't know it; I knew it." He went to hospital for an operation in March. His condition deteriorated greatly in late May 1981; he was again hospitalized and "he was no more communicating with us," recalls Mrs Saad. At this time, Ralph was away from Lebanon, exploring possibilities elsewhere. In early June, Mrs Saad was at Charlie's bedside in the hospital when Ralph returned and came to visit. "On seeing Ralph," Mrs Saad remembers, "he opened his eyes wide, motioned for help to sit up in bed, and asked Ralph for all the details of what he'd been finding. The doctor could not believe what he was seeing." The truth was that Charles's interest in his beloved school – above all, his interest in its continuity in spite of the vagaries of war – "left him only when his heart finally stopped beating."

Charles passed away on 14 June 1981, at the age of 79. In his will, Charlie entrusted his wife with Choueifat school: "Charlie wanted the school to continue and he knew if anything could be done, I would do it. I felt that if I didn't, I would be betraying the trust of the people who spent their lives ... my father-in-law, Miss Procter, Charlie, and all the others. So I couldn't abandon them just because I was afraid for my personal safety. There is that tie that at times of difficulty supersedes everything else."

Mrs Saad became principal of the school and Ralph director general. Somehow Mrs Saad kept going, comforted by the memories of Charles, as she struggled to run the school while her beloved country fell apart. "I tried to; it was difficult to pretend it was business as usual for me," says Mrs Saad. "I think that without Ralph's support it would have been impossible."

On 6 June 1982, on the day of the school's "open house," they were hoping as usual for many new parents and students to come and see what they were doing. But the expected guests did not appear. There was the sound of explosions, just as usual. But then they heard that the Israelis had invaded Lebanon.

That was the beginning of a very tough period. "That June, soldiers came all the way to Beirut, then all the way up to Choueifat and terrified the kids," Mrs Saad tells me. There were still boarding students at the school at the time. The soldiers wanted to search the house and told her to leave. Mrs Saad said, "Over my dead body. If you want to come in you can, but I'm not leaving the house." They went through the buildings, terrifying everyone around.

But then things calmed down again, and the academic year 1982/83 started "acceptably well" in September. On the first day of the Christmas holidays, the whole thing erupted again. The school still had boarders at this time, around two hundred and fifty, and most of these were still at the school on the first day of the holidays. Choueifat by this time was a predominantly Druze village, the neighbouring villages predominantly Maronite Christian. The Israeli soldiers were there in the midst of it all too. "So there would be fighting, back and forth; sometimes you didn't know who was shelling whom, or why," Mrs Saad mused sadly. That first day of the Christmas holidays, Mrs Saad was having her morning coffee when a huge explosion came very close to where she was sitting. She urgently summoned the boarders and supervisors to get down to the shelters. Some group was shelling the school. The first shell had fallen immediately in front of the dining-room door. Had it been a school day, the students would have been lined up there, and there would have been terrible loss of life. As it was the first day of the holidays, breakfast was served later. Reflecting on that memory, some of Mrs Saad's braveness dissolves: "I don't like to think ... it was a horrible day; I was so scared."

Almost every night for the next few months they would be shelled, and every time they would have to go down to the shelters. They were in the heart of a conflict that had nothing to do with their school and the values they were endeavoring to promote. By the end of that school year, they were all completely drained. The village still wanted Mrs Saad to continue running the school in Choueifat. Increasingly, she doubted how much longer she could continue. Eventually, some of the village militias suggested that they should accompany her up into the Druze heartland, to meet with their leader. This was a pretty dangerous mission to undertake; as ever, Mrs Saad put on a brave face and said, "Yes, why not?" In an open-top jeep, surrounded by heavily armed militia, she allowed herself to be escorted into the Chouf mountains. When they were granted an audience with the Druze leader, the militias asked, "Can Mrs Saad go on running the school in Choueifat this year?" He was dismissive. "Are you crazy?" he snorted. "Of course she cannot." That settled it. They would have to move the school.

By then it was mid-August 1983. They had to scramble to find an alternative place in Beirut. They found a building, not one of which they were proud, but it was the only one available. They signed a lease for three months, hoping that their sojourn in town would be brief. In the end they stayed there for nine years: "Nine long, horrible years," reflects Mrs Saad. School numbers dropped from 1,466 to 698 that first year. But there was no way they were going to deprive any of their children of their schooling, those who wanted to stay with them. And from then on, the school was to stay open throughout all of the civil war years.

The years 1984–89 were "pure hell," Mrs Saad reflects now. "There was a big flare-up. The airport was opening and closing and opening; you didn't know where you were. Those were years when even I couldn't go to Choueifat, even I; it was impossible. There are ugly details that I don't want to share with you ..."

Living through the war strengthened her resolve and made her think deeply about the nature of human society and the place of religion within it. The school's tolerant approach to religion can perhaps best be seen in the context of these experiences. It also made her aware even more acutely of the value of education to people in conflict-affected areas: "We want to teach the students to achieve the best they can, so that if they ever should have to leave their country, they will have the baggage that no one can take away from them, because education is one thing that no one can take away from you. They can take away your possessions, your wealth, but they can't take away what's in your mind. Probably this is why we are so keen on giving our kids the very best we can." Clearly it makes them well equipped to serve children in some of the world's difficult places.

Exodus

Ralph Bistany is disarmingly candid when he talks about the expansion of the company out of Lebanon. "I would have liked to tell you that I saw potential development in future. In fact, I never saw anything like that. We had an invitation to expand outside Lebanon in 1970, from a group in Abu Dhabi, and stupidly I turned it down ... Now I see there were opportunities all over the world that I was either too stupid to understand or too lazy to look at or didn't want to see. You become too lazy; you're enjoying life; comfort makes you soft ... Lebanon, after all," he repeats, "was paradise."

But as the civil war erupted and showed no signs of abating by the end of 1975, they realized that they were likely to be bankrupt and bereft of their beloved school. Like many of their compatriots, they realized they had to leave and take their business elsewhere. Ralph used to tell others who would listen: "World War II lasted hardly six years. We're a small country, Lebanon, so our war can't go on for very long." But crucially, even if it went on for two years, "that was enough to bankrupt us for good; that was why we had to move." He adds ruefully, "Not for a second did I think it would last fifteen years ..."

Teatime in Choueifat in mid-December 1975. As Ralph Bistany and Charles and Mrs Saad were taking tea, Samir Koukaz, a cousin of Mrs Saad's, arrived. He was about to leave Lebanon for Sharjah, one of the smaller emirates in the United Arab Emirates. They were all worried about the civil war. What had seemed likely to be confined to a few small street skirmishes was now impinging on all they were doing. Samir said that the American advisor to the Sheikh of Sharjah had asked him whether he knew of a school that would be interested in coming to Sharjah. Ralph was immediately interested; this could provide the opening he was seeking to continue the school on a more solid footing away from Lebanon. "Would you like me to introduce you to him?" asked Samir. Ralph said, "Yes, of course. When are you leaving?" Four days later, Samir and Ralph left for Sharjah.

The conflict flared up a few days later, and the telephone was cut off to the school at Choueifat. In the middle of a very cold night, the Saads were asleep in their home at the school. They were awoken by knocking at the door. It was a man from the village gendarmerie. "What's the problem?" Charles asked. "Monsieur Bistany called from Sharjah, to the gendarmerie, and he wants to urgently talk to you." Charles and Mrs Saad got dressed. It was pouring with rain. They donned raincoats and lifted umbrellas and marched off to the gendarmerie, worried about what they would hear. But their concerns were unjustified. "We could hardly hear each other on the phone," Mrs Saad tells me, her voice full of affection for the memories. "But Ralph was saying, 'The prospects are wonderful ... I think we should—'" Ever the pragmatist, Mrs Saad interrupted him. "Ralph, come home and we will discuss it here." He said, "The sheikh is in a hurry. I've promised we are going to start in January." Mrs Saad was furious: "How can you start in a country that you don't know, that you haven't seen, where you have nothing, in one month's time?" But Charlie was excited too. "I told him, 'You two are fools! You two are crazy!'" she said.

**

With Mrs Saad and Mr Bistany together, in her apartment, we take tea, and reminisce over that fateful decision:

> Mrs Saad: "There was a lot of groundwork that had to be done. You see, that's not his problem. He's full of great ideas, but there is a fantastic team to support these ideas. It's easy to throw up an idea, but then implementing it ..."
> Ralph Bistany: "That's not my problem." (laughter)
> Mrs Saad: "It's never his problem." (also laughing)
> Ralph Bistany: "It was a question of remaining alive. Actually it should have been impossible. But Mrs Saad, once she's committed, doesn't let impossible things get in the way."

**

The day after Christmas, Charles and Mrs Saad flew out to Sharjah, to see the site that Ralph had been promised, an old, dilapidated British air force camp, "with one mess hall that would serve as a dining room cum classroom cum games room cum whatever you want." They drew up a list of all the things they needed – beds, equipment and the like. Ralph asked Mrs Saad to buy these goods. "You don't know what Sharjah was like in 1976," she comments. "It was not yet developed and even the basics were not readily available. Anyway, we bought what we could, but most things were unavailable. We spent New Year's Eve there. I was very miserable; it was my first New Year's Eve away from home. I was very unhappy."

Back in Lebanon, things were deteriorating rapidly. Many of the teachers in Lebanon volunteered to go to Sharjah to help start the school there. It was an unknown place for them, but they were fleeing what was unknown in Lebanon too. Ramzi Germanos, the dynamic science teacher, by now head of science, recalls memories of his last weeks in Choueifat, of "armed groups rushing into school with their machine guns, accusing us of harboring people who were firing at them. They would come in and check, and eventually they would station themselves in our school, so they could use it as a base to fire." Days before he was due to leave for Sharjah, a school supervisor was killed. "When the shooting started, everybody gathered in this corridor because it seemed the safest place to be. A rocket bomb came in and exploded and shrapnel ricocheted around, killing the supervisor." For Ramzi and the other teachers, "it became obvious we had to leave."

But the financial situation for Ralph and the Saads was desperate. Ralph had to tell the teachers that they could not immediately pay any salaries. The teachers would get only "pocket money" until the financial situation picked up. In the end, for a whole year, they lived without salaries, before Ralph was able to honor his commitment to them with substantial back pay.

During early January, Ralph was in Sharjah, getting the school ready for opening. In the end, he needed most things sent from Lebanon: textbooks, copybooks, kitchen utensils, pens and pencils, sheets, towels. Mrs Saad started getting organized. The first tranche of what was required was neatly packed in marked cases, ready to send. Then Beirut airport was closed. Ralph started pestering her with telexes: "When are the teachers coming? When are the goods arriving?" Then the telex stopped functioning and communication ceased between the two.

Nothing happened for a while. Suddenly, at the end of January 1976, there was a window of opportunity: the airport was reopened. Ralph was in his hotel room in Sharjah when he heard the news on his radio that Beirut airport would open that night, and its first flight would be to Dubai. Ralph immediately perked up. He went straight to the hotel manager, a friend whose children had studied at the mother school in Lebanon: "I want a bus for tonight," Ralph said. The manager asked, "Why?" "It's for my team. The airport in Beirut has just opened, so my team will be arriving tonight." The manager pointed out that, if Ralph couldn't contact Lebanon, how did he know Mrs Saad would be sending stuff that night? "I know Mrs Saad well and if there is a plane getting out of there tonight, she is going to send me the team tonight."

The manager helped Ralph muster two buses. He sent these buses to the airport. The plane arrived. The *only* people on board were the SABIS team.

A key player in the Sharjah experience was Elie Sawaya, a Lebanese, who has been with the Saad–Bistany families since 1970 and is still working with them to this day. When Elie first joined them, he was a tall 25-year-old man. He was a star player on the national volleyball team and was invited to join Choueifat to coach the children in volleyball. "He was quite successful," recalls Ralph, but in the end Ralph wanted to let him go. Mrs Saad told him that he would be making a big mistake: "This guy is in the wrong place; he should be involved in the business." Ralph said, "Okay, I'll wait." When an opening came up on the business side, involved with purchasing, Ralph invited him to accept that position. "And he suddenly bloomed. He was so effective from day one." Ralph is contrite: "I was glad Mrs Saad alerted me that this guy had something in him. Definitely she can read people better than I can."

Elie's contribution in Sharjah was "absolutely enormous and absolutely indispensable," says Ralph. Elie, Ramzi and Ralph were the core management team; but that didn't mean they were exempt from all other duties as well. All three had to take on multiple roles. The former British base they'd been given was the lowest point in a large plain, so when rains came, the buildings flooded. "There was mud and water everywhere," recalls Ramzi. He and Elie took up brooms and got working on clearing the flood water away. Ramzi had a car, but it wouldn't start because it was completely flooded out. Ramzi took a photograph of Ralph's shoes floating in the water.

One of the first pupils remembers it well. Ahmad Tabari, now a highly successful US businessman and qualified lawyer, was around eight years old when he first joined the Sharjah school as it opened. "When there was quite a lot of rain, and there were one or two rainstorms a year, it would absolutely overflow with blackish water, sewage if I may say so, and we would have to walk on planks to get from place to place. And a couple of times if I remember we actually sat in soggy classrooms! There was water at our feet. We actually sat in the classrooms listening to science or whatever, with our feet in the water."

The school did start to attract displaced Lebanese and others. Sometimes this meant that Lebanese politics flowed into the classrooms, with "children repeating what they might have heard in the salons of their parents," said Ahmad. "It was weird because we didn't understand what we were talking about but you heard things like, 'Oh, you [group], you ruined our country,' or 'We hold you personally accountable!'" But then these skirmishes petered out as the school became more cosmopolitan, with Chileans, Indians, Pakistanis, other Arabs, British, Italians, and Americans all adding to the population of this growing school.

Elie's role as company purchaser was tested to the limits, for they had to be very careful with money. His ability to learn quickly about new environments soon came in very useful. Having watched and observed the daily routine of the market traders, he would venture down to the wholesale food markets in the overwhelming heat of the early afternoon, as the traders were reloading their trucks. Elie would point out that their remaining perishable goods – fruit and vegetables, fish and meat – would spoil now. Why didn't they give them to him for a very reasonable price? And so Ralph and his team were able to eat reasonably well. Ralph said, "We had occasional luxuries; we had cherries for next to nothing for many days; we ate the best fish for twenty cents a kilo. Elie would always take the trouble to wait until the best bargains could be had."

Elie was also put in charge of the construction of the new school.

Again, Elie quickly got to know everyone in the business. At the time, there was a crisis in the Emirates and many contractors were going bankrupt. He would hone in on the bankers who were having problems of this kind. "So," he would say, "your contractor has equipment for forty bathrooms unsold, but he owes you the money." And he would negotiate to pay one third of what was owed to the banker to take the unsold stock off his hands. "Essentially," said Ralph, "we ended up building our first school at maybe forty percent of normal price. That was his talent."

Elie's skills as purchaser were supplemented by the discovery of Ramzi's skills in the kitchen. "We wrote a menu for each day based on the purchases of the previous day. So today as dessert for lunch we'll have oranges." So Elie would have made sure they had found oranges. "But what about dinner? We used to collect the orange peel after the teachers peeled the oranges – they didn't know that. Then we'd wash them, roll them, put them on a string, boil them with some sugar and cloves and they would have that as dessert and they would love it! We had to be inventive like that."

Early on in Sharjah, it became obvious that Ralph Bistany had inadvertently offended the minister of education. Ralph had been dealing directly with the sheikh's office and had understood that the school could be opened before a license had been obtained. The minister disagreed and was "absolutely furious." Ralph protested his innocence and eventually the office of the sheikh intervened to say that the minister should give Ralph the license. So Ralph went to the ministry. "I went at the appointed time. I sat there for about four hours. I was told, 'But the minister has left.'" Ralph asked what he should do. "Come back in two days." So he came back two days later, and again sat for three or four hours. Again, the same story, "Oh, the minister has left now, come back in two days." "By the third time," Ralph remembers, "I realized it was going to be a long process. I had math books that were of interest to me, so for the next meeting I'd go and I'd sit there in the waiting room, I had my math books and I studied. And then usually three or four hours later they would come and say, 'He has left. Come back in two days.' This comedy lasted between three and four months. And you can't believe how much math I studied during that period. We finally got the license."

Three days after the team arrived from Lebanon, after the unexpected opening of the airport, the new school was operating. At the end of January, the school had 25 teachers, six administrators and just seventeen students, scattered between first grade and twelfth grade. By the end of February, student numbers had increased to 37; by June there were 141 students. By the beginning of the next school year they had 400, doubling to 800 the year after. The school was set to become a huge success.

Ah yes, I remember it well

The 1958 film *Gigi* – "the last great MGM musical" – features Maurice Chevalier and Hermione Gingold in their touching duet "I remember it well": "We met at nine," he sings; "We met at eight," she corrects. "I was on time," he recalls; "No, you were late," she chides. "Ah yes, I remember it well," he muses.

Being with Mrs Saad and Ralph Bistany as they reminisced over past times often reminded me of that song. No more so than when I was with them in Dubai and we ventured out on an excursion to visit the site of the original Sharjah school, SABIS's first adventure outside of Lebanon. Elie Sawaya had just conveyed the news to them that the site was now a Lebanese supermarket, and offered to show us around if we met him outside.

We drove along the freeways of Dubai, past the World Trade Center, a rather modest-looking building now, but which apparently was the only high-rise building in the vicinity when Mrs Saad and Mr Bistany first moved here. "Driving from Abu Dhabi, when you saw that building rising in the desert, then you knew you were in Dubai," Mrs Saad said. As we passed the massive expanse of Dubai International Airport, a new Emirates Airbus A380 – the revolutionary new double-decker airline – approached to land. They reminisced about when they had first traveled on a Boeing 747, an earlier revolutionary airplane: "It was 1969, I think," said Ralph. "1971," said Mrs Saad. "We took it from Rome to London, and it was very fine; it felt like a whole building was flying."

And then we reached Sharjah. Mrs Saad said, "This is not the Sharjah we knew." Sharjah certainly feels less affluent than Dubai – only six-lane highways instead of twelve; and as we came nearer to the district where they opened their first school, the buildings were only six or seven stories high; there was even washing hanging outside on apartment balconies.

After a few false turns ("This is it"; "No, not it at all"), we came to a roundabout, where some ugly prefabricated low-rise buildings were incorporated into a larger supermarket. A new mosque was on the other side of the street. The low-rise, dirty and dilapidated buildings had once been a British air force base before becoming the first SABIS school outside of Lebanon.

Elie Sawaya joins us – it's the first time I've met him, and I'm touched by this gentle giant of a man, who stands very tall against me and dwarfs Ralph completely. On his business card Elie carries the title "Personal Representative to Mr Bistany." After spending time with him, I could see exactly why Ralph Bistany wanted Elie to be the person who accompanied him to difficult places – on his first journey to Iraq, for instance, as we'll discuss in a later chapter. At the time, Elie would have been around 60, while Ralph was 75. "He's a tough guy with a heart of gold," Ralph reflected later. "He could still fight ten people and beat them." A useful companion to have, then, as you ventured into unknown and potentially fraught places.

Now it's Mrs Saad's and Elie's turn for a duet:

Mrs Saad: "I don't think this was the actual building."
Elie: "It is the actual building."
Mrs Saad: "I don't remember it so big."
Elie: "It was so big."

The big hall, which was used for many purposes, is now a vegetable market. I take their photographs by one of the food counters. Ralph says, "I am just trying to get things back and now I regret that we didn't document all of this. But at the time it was the last thing on our minds. I was worried all the time; we had no money; we couldn't stay in Lebanon; we only had to survive."

Where an ice-cream counter is now, Mrs Saad said, "I think it was in this corner where we had our seating area, where we sat in the evening and watched television. There were tables that were used by children as classroom tables during the day, and in the evening we had them in here."

"We've come a long way," says Ralph Bistany. Mrs Saad says, "We sure have!" But then she becomes subdued as we wander down the aisles of the market, past the meat counter and the pharmacy. "Too many memories," she says, with a sigh.

Elie then suggests he drive me to where the Sharjah school moved – and where the highly successful school still stands on its 400,000-square-meter site. "I want to show you something," he says.

When he had first found the piece of land where they were to move the school, he told me, it was in the middle of the desert, there was no road and they used to have to come by four-wheel drive. The only way he could locate the land was by a tree. "There was only one tree in that part of the desert," he said. And it was near the corner of their land. "And over the years, however inconvenient it was to builders and developers, I made sure no one harmed the tree." And sure enough, intruding into part of the car park now, on the edge of the basketball court, stands the tree. Now there is so much vegetation around – so many palm trees and bougainvillea – it's not a tree that you'd particularly notice.

Mrs Saad and Ralph Bistany arrive in their car, having followed us there. Mrs Saad is delighted: "Ralph, you remember what the landmark was? Do you remember? It was a tree! And here it is!" Ralph said, "Yes, yes, I remember it well." Mrs Saad continued, "A lonely tree that stood in the desert, and when we saw it we knew we were at our land."

I asked what sort of tree it is. "I don't know its name," she said, "you see them occasionally in the desert. One of the very rare trees that do not need much water."

Seeing the beautiful tree was a fine way to end our excursion.

Expansion to England and America

Looking back on the impact of the civil war on SABIS, Ralph Bistany is philosophical: "In life, you never know what will happen. I would have been delighted had the problems of Lebanon stopped very quickly. And had it been possible for us to continue what we were doing in the first school, I would have considered myself lucky and I would have said, 'Well, we had a close call, thank God. The war did not flare and we were so lucky it didn't.' Instead, the country was very unlucky with the way it happened. But it turned out to be a huge advantage to SABIS."

For now, having successfully opened their first school outside of Lebanon, they realized that this didn't have to be a one-off. Ralph put it like this: "Having realized how close we had come to being bankrupt, I felt personally we had to have as many schools as we could in as many different places as we could, and this would represent security for us." Mrs Saad thought this was true, but reminded Ralph that another reason was much more important when they started their further expansion: "It was all a response to demand. After Sharjah, others came asking for further schools, when they saw our school. We were being approached all the time."

First had come demand from Abu Dhabi. In 1978, the Saad–Bistany team opened a school there in a camp that had until recently been used by a construction contractor firm. It opened with 422 students. Just a year later, in November 1979, it moved into its purpose-built campus in the heart of the city, where it remains to this day. In October 1980, the team opened a school in Al Ain, the oasis town and resort, home of the former president of the UAE. This again started in a temporary location with 90 students, before moving in the fall of 1983 to a purpose-built complex similar in design to that in Abu Dhabi.

The year 1983 was a momentous one for the now developing SABIS. Not only because of the new school in Al Ain, and the forced move of the mother school from Choueifat to rented accommodation in Beirut; SABIS also now started its first private school outside of the Middle East.

In 1982, Mrs Saad and Ralph Bistany, together in the Emirates, met with George, a Lebanese friend working in the Gulf who had an English wife. He was interested in partnering with SABIS to buy a school in England. In June 1982, Ralph and Mrs Saad went to England to find the site for their new school. Many sites in the south and Midlands of England had been selected for them to look at. The first was Ashwicke Hall, a fine Victorian manor house some seven miles outside of the ancient Roman city of Bath.

"The minute we went through the gate," recalls Mrs Saad, "I told Ralph, 'This is it.'" Ralph protested that there were many other places to go and see. "I said you can go and see them," said Mrs Saad, "but this is the place I want to open our school."

Ralph gamely went to see the next place on the list, but then gave up. He told George, "I know her and she's not going to change her mind, why waste our time?" In September they were ready to sign. Ralph was in England having completed negotiations, but Mrs Saad was meanwhile back in Choueifat pursuing important work there. But Beirut airport was closed again. "I had to go overland to Damascus, to take a plane from Damascus to London." Leaving Choueifat was the most hazardous part of the journey to Damascus.

Stunningly beautiful though its location is, the Bath school wasn't a particularly successful venture for SABIS. The schools that SABIS were opening across the Gulf were international schools – with nationalities drawn from across the world, not just from the host countries. Bath, on the other hand, possibly because of the timing of its opening, became, according to Mrs Saad, "a sort of Choueifat transplanted in England." Very quickly it filled up, but with a majority of Lebanese escaping the civil war. Unfortunately, this had an undesired impact on the way the school was perceived. It became known as an Arab school. And because of this, few Europeans wanted to go there. "It wasn't anything to do with racism," Mrs Saad stresses, "but the British have always been very proud of their educational system and the Arabs were not known for being great educationalists, so I can't blame them for not wanting to give us a try." Indeed, she points out, many Arab students from other countries were also put off attending their school: many wanted to go to England to mix with the British to improve their knowledge of the English language and culture. They too didn't want to go to a transplanted Lebanese school.

When the civil war ended in Lebanon, most of the children returned to their home country. SABIS decided to close the school, and it eventually shut its gates in September 2001, the intention being to sell the property. The vagaries of the English planning laws, however, meant that the buyers who came forward – who wanted to convert it from a school to other uses – were stymied and couldn't get planning permission. If SABIS couldn't sell it, then they would reopen it. In 2008 it reopened as a summer school. In September 2012 it will reopen as a fully fledged school again, the SABIS International School-UK, Bath, England.

In 1985, SABIS began its expansion into America. As with much of their development until then, their first private school there began as a word-of-mouth invitation: "There was a lady of Egyptian origin who had a relative at our school in Bath. She visited and was very impressed by all she saw. She went back to Minnesota, where she lived, and got a group of people interested."

Breaking into America was to be a huge challenge for SABIS. "Boy, was it a struggle," said Mrs Saad. But why was it so important for them? "We wanted to go to America because America is the center of gravity of our world and of our cultures," Ralph explained. They wanted to be in America because that would mean they had arrived in the cultural epicenter of the modern world. "And besides," he continued, "as a business, we have to think, 'Where is the largest market?' Any person in our business would see America as a major market."

Although they also had offers to set up a school in Washington, DC, they decided to open first in Minnesota: "In *Fortune* magazine at the time," recalls Ralph, "it was considered the state with the best public secondary education. Minnesota was number one." So if they could show they could do well in Minnesota, "we would have made the grade."

Their new school was opened in September 1985, in a temporary building, while their purpose-built campus was constructed.

There were teething problems, though. Their intention initially was to start with all SABIS-experienced teachers from the UK. They even rented houses and furnished apartments for their use. But then, "all their visas were turned down ... all of them!" For some reason which they've never fully understood, the British teachers were not allowed to enter the USA: "It was a huge shock!" Ralph recalls. So they had to start again. They hired American teachers and opened the new school. That first year Ralph spent a lot of time tutoring them, on the job, in the SABIS methods.

Another issue concerned sport. Ralph Bistany and Mrs Saad are quite candid here: "We simply did not understand the American mentality." Ralph was clear that he didn't want the school to have American football on its sports curriculum. It wasn't so much the danger to the students, although that was an issue, it was that he felt that the sport would become all-consuming of young people's energies and loyalties. He didn't want this kind of distraction from children's academic work in SABIS schools. What he hadn't realized, however, was that "if you refuse to offer American football, many parents are not interested." Their enrollment suffered, he is sure, as a result of this simple factor.

If Ralph and Mrs Saad thought these problems were big, however, they hadn't seen anything yet. Once in America, they began to explore other business models for schools. For a few years after their Minnesota private school opened, the possibility of creating "charter" schools came up. Legislation there arose as a response to the crisis of low standards and low expectations in American public schools, particularly among ethnic minorities and disadvantaged groups. Individual states were free to set up charter school laws, with two common characteristics: first, schools had new freedoms – from local school districts and unions – to liberate the energy and talent of educational providers. Secondly, no public funds could be transferred without concomitant accountability, so charter school boards would be set up to hold schools accountable, academically and financially. Charter schools, then, would be publicly funded schools, free at the point of delivery, but which nonetheless would have some of the freedoms and advantages of private schools.

The possibilities here were immensely exciting to Ralph Bistany and Mrs Saad, who saw the huge potential for making a difference through the education of some of the most deprived youngsters in America.

The story of SABIS's trying to make a difference in American public education is a roller coaster, however. In its complexity, the story has made me in equal measures energized and deflated, in equal parts inspired and downhearted. Inspired by a company that continually seeks to prove that it can reach the most deprived youngsters and equip them for college and for life. Downhearted because it seems such an uphill struggle; there always seems to be a battle for the right to serve the poor. In the next two chapters, we explore this story of SABIS trying to make a difference in America's public schools. Hold on tight.

PART 2

Making a difference in difficult places

CHAPTER 4

An American roller coaster

Trying to make a difference in America

It's not the easiest thing in the world to make a difference in public education. Sometimes those with power and influence really baffle me. Not least in the case of charter schools in America.

Does this story also leave you puzzled? Here are the bare facts as I see them. Some fifteen years or so ago, a school district gave one of its worst-performing schools to an education company to manage, to improve what was on offer. The company proceeded to make a big difference in the lives of the children and families. It invested $20 million of its own raised capital in building a school which is probably one of the finest public school buildings you'll see anywhere. It invested too in adapting its educational model, used only in elite private schools before, so that children from deprived families end up with the same education as their privileged counterparts elsewhere. The company incidentally takes less funding per child from the state than other public schools.

The school they created is extraordinary. Talk about closing the achievement gap: from a school that was once an educational basketcase, for ten years now every single child who has ever graduated has been offered a place in college. Remarkably, the African-American population at the school outperforms the white population in the state. But it's not all about academic achievement: visit the school and you'll find a wonderfully engaged student population, taking part in a range of music, drama, sports, and outreach. One girl, herself a child of poor refugees from Laos, calls the school the "give-back" school, giving back to the local and global communities. One African-American student, who had been in huge trouble in all his previous schools, says that it's like "a family," a "caring" school that has helped him on the road to success. He's now deputy head prefect of the school's Discipline Department, sorting out troublesome boys like he himself had been, helping them on to the road to accomplishment.

The school is a resounding success. It has a waiting list of three thousand students – a genuine waiting list, revised every year to make sure that every person on the list is still actively seeking a place.

Now suppose this same company then applies to have a second school in the same district, to extend its tried and tested model to help more deprived children. Can you guess what happened?

I couldn't. I was dumbfounded when I found out that SABIS's second application for a charter school in Springfield, Massachusetts, was turned down. SABIS's first charter school in Springfield was a resounding success – in all the pertinent details I've described above. It was ready and able to replicate what it had already successfully done. But the state of Massachusetts turned down its application.

This and the next chapter catalog SABIS's roller-coaster ride through American public education. It's in equal measure both inspiring and perplexing. The story begins in Massachusetts, with the events leading up to the opening in the fall of 1995 of SABIS's first charter school.

Six characters in search of a school

The history of SABIS's involvement in charter schools in America goes back to the early 1990s and has a list of sparkling *dramatis personae*. These include Dr Peter Negroni, the radical school superintendent who wanted to shake things up; Udo Schulz, the businessman of German origin finding a new opportunity; Beth Conway, the skeptical committee member wooed to change her mind; Michael Glickman, the giant principal who couldn't resist a new challenge; and Maretta Thomsen, the skilled educator, who laid the groundwork for change. Steven F. Wilson, the author and entrepreneur, whom we meet properly in Chapter 8, also makes a cameo appearance.

Udo Schulz was born in 1939 in Silesia, now Poland but then part of Germany. Toward the end of World War II, his mother fled the Russian assault with five-year-old Udo to shelter near the city of Hanover, only to suffer through the Allied bombing of that key transport hub, which destroyed 90 percent of the city and killed 6,000 people. Could these early experiences have made him sympathetic to SABIS, an organization used to surviving the exigencies of war?

Having moved to Minneapolis to head the US operations of a German-Swiss Company, Udo, aged 53, was looking for new challenges. His three sons had got him interested in education. SABIS's first American private school had opened in 1985 in Minnesota, and Udo had heard good things about it. The school had systems; this is what he liked – for these seemed to have the potential to mitigate the luck of peer group or bad teachers obstructing your future.

Udo's third son was flourishing in the SABIS school. At a school open evening, Udo collared Ralph Bistany. He told him that he thought SABIS was not taking advantage of opportunities for expansion in America. He badgered him several more times. Eventually Mr Bistany said, "Maybe you want to join us and we'll do it together?"

So in 1992 Udo joined SABIS, initially as a consultant, later as vice-president for business development. Initially looking for opportunities in private education, Udo heard talk of a "new type of school"; the first charter school in Minnesota had opened in 1991. Could this be an opportunity for SABIS to get involved in *public* education? Udo attended a conference in October 1993 in Boston; Massachusetts was just about to pass its charter school law. Here Udo met with Jose Afonso, a senior official in the charter school authorizers' offices. Together, they started thinking how SABIS might get involved. Mr Bistany and Mrs Saad almost immediately saw the potential. Udo recalls that they "were excited pretty quickly because they saw it as a way to help disadvantaged minority and deprived kids by using their successful system."

Dr Peter J. Negroni styles himself a "career educator." He started as a public school teacher in New York City and then served as school principal and district superintendent. In September 1989 he took up the position of superintendent of Springfield, Massachusetts, where he served until he retired in June 2000. The Commonwealth of Massachusetts made him Superintendent of the Year in 1998. He accumulated many other awards, including the Association of Latino Administration and Superintendent Lifetime Achievement award (2006) and the National Puerto Rican Coalition Lifetime Achievement award (1996). As well as his personal doctorate, he has an honorary doctorate from Springfield College.

By the time he moved to Springfield, he'd got a reputation as someone who could shake things up. And Springfield needed shaking up. The school system was not functioning well. Perhaps as a consequence, the city was stained by violent crime: Springfield ranked eighteenth highest out of 354 American cities for violent crime when he arrived. The more Dr Negroni met with community leaders, the more he realized the school system needed change from the bottom up. His desire to create a system of school choice gelled with the growing movement in Massachusetts, where Governor William Floyd Weld, elected in 1991, had recently introduced charter school legislation, drafted by Stephen F. Wilson, then a policy wonk working for the governor.

Dr Negroni set out to introduce charter schools to his district, Springfield. He was looking for that "lightning bolt" that could shake up public schools, bring in competition, and raise their standards. But he had to convince the school committee first.

Beth Conway, a feisty and energetic woman who does not suffer fools gladly, then with three young children, was an elected member of the Springfield School Committee. She, in common with the other members, didn't think much of Peter Negroni's predilection for charter schools. They had their minds pretty much made up. When it came to any vote, they wouldn't be lining up behind their superintendent.

Dr Negroni organized first a meeting with Edison Schools – the

education management company set up by Chris Whittle, serial entrepreneur. Edison was offering a computer for every child to take home,
but Beth was suspicious of what looked like a gimmick. "Their delivery of education seemed no different; bringing a computer home really
wasn't a fix for anything," she thought.

Aware that Edison hadn't inspired his committee, Dr Negroni went
looking for other alternatives. William Edgerly, the Boston business
leader who had been a catalyst in getting the charter school legislation
through in Massachusetts, had met Mr Ralph Bistany on one of his
early visits to the USA, and had been impressed by what he had heard
from him. Edgerly encouraged Dr Negroni to visit SABIS's first private
school in Minnesota, where he had met Mr Bistany.

In some ways Peter Negroni and Ralph Bistany are similar: both are
driven, sharing a vision for education and excellence. But they're also
very different: Peter Negroni is a people person, a smooth operator who
can make anyone feel at ease. Mr Bistany is not known for his social
skills – indeed, he *is* known for his *lack of* social skills. And yet at that
first meeting he persuaded Dr Negroni that SABIS could be the right
team to win over the Springfield committee. How? "I sensed that he was
a caring person, really committed to what he was doing," reflects Dr
Negroni now. He was "intrigued" by the fact that he was "very smart,
probably an intellectual genius." And he liked the fact that, with Mr
Bistany, "what you see is what you get: there is no bullshit about him,
no pretense. You knew you could trust him from the outset."

It impressed him greatly that SABIS had spent long years perfecting
its model before it sought to expand: "I think that Mr Bistany believes
that he was put on this earth to educate kids," said Dr Negroni. And Mr
Bistany introduced him in their private school to children on scholarships – poor children who didn't have supportive parents. Dr Negroni
saw that the SABIS system – designed for typical private school children – was nonetheless working well for the scholarship kids too.

Peter came back and told his committee about what he'd seen: "All you
need do is walk into the school and you'll see that the model would work
here. It is so well defined." The committee members were nonplussed.

"Will you meet with them?" he asked Beth. "Sure," she replied, "but you know most of us are dead set against charter schools, period."

Against that background, the committee – seven people including Beth – was assembled to listen to the SABIS presentation. The team included Mr Bistany, some parents and teachers, and Udo Schulz. Arriving in the conference room a few minutes earlier, Udo set up a flip chart and overhead projector – cutting-edge technologies at the time. The school committee arrived. Beth Conway pointed to where he had set up and said, "That's where we're sitting." As Udo Schulz moved everything across to the opposite side, he was not alone in thinking things were not getting off to a good start.

The team delivered their presentations, but, Beth recalls, for some reason Ralph Bistany didn't say a word. Perhaps he was trying to gauge which way the committee would go. Beth knew that she was not alone in not being persuaded.

The presentation apparently at an end, Beth threw down the gauntlet. "What makes you think you can do better than what we already do?" With that question, Beth recalls, "Mr Bistany motioned for everybody to stay still. And he got up and he started to talk."

He talked about SABIS's educational experiences over many years, in countries different from theirs, but where children's needs and aspirations were the same. He described in his quiet, measured way, in his soft, lilting accent, how you could construct systems so that even average teachers could draw out tremendous things from their children – any and all children. He believed, he told them, that all children in the community they sought to serve were capable of going to college. But they were let down by the public education system. In particular, they were let down by the way so much was left to luck, to chance, not to good systems.

What you needed to do – what SABIS has already done – was to break down into a logical sequence all that was required for college entrance. SABIS had already created hundreds of books for children from kindergarten upwards built on that logical sequence, and they would adapt these for America, and for Massachusetts.

Some of the concepts he described were the "essential" concepts mentioned earlier in this book, concepts which it is essential to master before moving on to others. "*It's no good,*" he said, emphasizing every word, "*assuming children have mastered these concepts. You have to check that they have.* And that means checking quickly and often ... In SABIS," he told them, "we check every week. Every week we make sure that the essential concepts have been learned, and if they haven't, we go back and teach them again. *But wisely.* We use children who have understood the concepts to help their peers who have difficulty. Children love the responsibility of this. And their understanding is deepened as they help their peers."

As he talked, Beth became "mesmerized": "I bought in hook, line and sinker. He was like a gentle giant, so passionate about educating all kids." Many in the committee were clearly of a like mind. Another whole hour went by. They were so wrapped up in what Mr Bistany was saying that they didn't notice. The description of him as "a gentle giant" is apposite; Mr Bistany is very short. But he came across as someone with a giant heart for education, and that's what held the committee in thrall.

He also disarmed them with his candor. He knew that in America everyone was clamoring for smaller class sizes. He guessed, he said, that the committee felt the same. He could probably make himself popular by promising them this, as he was sure his competitors were doing. He wasn't going to do that. In SABIS schools, class sizes are larger than the average. That was because the notion of "individualized instruction" was a complete myth. "Simple arithmetic will show why," he said. "Even with a small class of only twenty students, and a forty-minute period, that would mean that the teacher has only two minutes per child. That's hardly individualized instruction! If you want to teach individuals twenty is too big, ten is far too many, maybe you can do reasonable work with four, but not more. It amazes me that people don't think this one through." Ralph can be passionate and intense, but he can also be disarming. His candor was like that. With a twinkle in his eye, he said, playfully, "Forty in a class is *better* than ten."

Beth and the other members liked the fact that he wasn't trying to impress them by telling them simply what they wanted to hear. Someone *less of a giant*, she felt, would have hidden behind what they'd wanted to hear. Someone less of an educational giant, in any case, would not have had the experience to know what the truth of the matter was.

Instead of discussion about class size, he continued, more profitable discussions could be had considering how a "class" needs to be defined: "In education a class is defined necessarily by the course, and if you have a course that's well defined, that starts at a point and ends at another point, and that has a set of concepts that are prerequisites, then any individual can be in this class taking this course if and only if he or she has the prerequisite knowledge." And with SABIS's diagnostic tests, they aim to construct classes where all individuals are prepared with the prerequisites in order to learn.

He discussed discipline problems in schools – something he knew would be near the top of their concerns: "Our experience," he said, "is that very often poor behavior is triggered by learning difficulties that are not properly addressed. If you make sure that children have the correct background knowledge vis-à-vis their course, then you will have fewer disciplinary problems." Furthermore, he told them, you can also build on the principle of peer learning that he'd already mentioned: "If you get children to be responsible for discipline in your schools, as we do in SABIS through the Student Life Organization, then you can harness their youthful energies for your academic gains." You don't need costly administrators to control students: students can do it better themselves, and SABIS had the systems and experience to show how this is possible. "The school is a community. The Student Life Organization brings students into the school discipline process. Students help instill discipline, prevent bullying and intimidation, ensuring the environment is conducive to learning. In this way, we also encourage cooperation not competition between students."

He wasn't afraid of addressing other educational "myths" too, as he dismissively called them. "Every educationalist today," he said, "is against memorization, thinking it is the same as 'rote learning.' It's not

– rote learning is memorization without understanding. But there is no learning without memorizing. It's very difficult to memorize something you don't understand. The role of the teacher must be to help children understand and to provide them with the tools to help them memorize too."

What about American football? He knew enough about America now to know that this would be on their minds. "We won't have football in our schools. If it's not done on a high professional level, it can be dangerous. It's not something you can do sloppily. But that's not the main reason – because I know that our school *could* do it well, if it really pulled together. No, the main issue is the time and commitment it demands. If we take over a school, we'll be working with children with very low academic standards, who will need a lot of time to catch up. The last thing they need now, or will need in the future, is this distraction for their time, energy and loyalties."

Ralph could see that even his own team was jittery about this – they had wanted him to compromise on what they felt could be a deal-breaker. But in the end it was Ralph who read his audience right. Although they loved their football, mused Beth Conway, what Ralph said gelled with them. Academic teaching was more important, especially for the kind of children that they wanted to serve.

Dr Negroni came in as the meeting ended – pleasantly surprised at the transformation in the committee members. Beth came straight up to him. She said, "I like this company. I think they can do good things for our kids." Other school committee members joined in: "Well, this isn't what we thought it was going to be. It seems good." Dr Negroni seized the opportunity: "I want a charter school. You can see Mr Bistany is telling the truth, right?" One by one, the committee members nodded. "So let's do it," said Peter. The committee agreed to award one charter, to a school partnering with SABIS.

Once the decision was made, Mr Bistany and Mrs Saad came and stayed in a Springfield hotel for two whole months. The duo balanced each other. Peter Negroni said of Mrs Saad: "She is a delightful person, a good business woman, great fun to be with, very personable." Beth said:

"I found her to be very soft spoken but somebody that you definitely paid attention to. I mean, she's just a lady in every sense of the word."

Beth and Peter brought people to them, so that they could talk personally to the visitors: "Because they're the ones that really sold you on the whole program. Because it wasn't a sales job of giving you a computer or something that didn't mean anything, it was a whole philosophy of how their teaching methods had worked and the struggles they had gone through in their other schools to make this happen." But more than their philosophy, Beth and her fellow committee members remarked on something else: "Their compassion was just palpable. Everybody that we met with just bought into how sincere they were." Part of their sincerity was conveyed in the fact that "they were willing to take all the financial risks."

Beth conveys some of the excitement of it all. "My husband didn't see me for a month," she said. The more she heard Mrs Saad and Mr Bistany speak, the more energized Beth came to be about what SABIS had to offer. What she realized – and what she still tells parents to this day – is that the new charter school "would be giving a private education for public school dollars. And you won't find that anywhere else." There was one downside, however: "Mr Bistany didn't believe in doing anything unless food was involved, so everything was usually done at breakfast, lunch, dinner, or a snack at night. I think I gained forty pounds that month."

A charter board of trustees was put together, including the mayor, a city councillor, the head of the urban league, the head of the Puerto Rican cultural center, a couple of businessmen, and a few parents. Beth went after parents who would represent different parts of the city. She told them all she knew about SABIS – and some of them met with Mr Bistany and Mrs Saad. The answer to the question "Would you be interested in sitting on a board?" was often "Sure, but only if our kids can get in." Beth had to tell them, "No guarantee on that!" (Indeed, the mayor of Springfield's daughter is on the waiting list today.)

Next, they had to find a school – and convince the parents that they were the right people to take over. Ralph Bistany was clear: they were ready and willing to take over the worst-performing school in the district. This turned out to be De Berry Elementary School. It was in a bleak area of the city, with boarded-up and burned-out houses on the same street. It was in a dangerous area too – SABIS people were told that they shouldn't drive through it at night. Even during the day you could see drug dealers and drunks on the streets. "It was a pretty desperate area," says Udo, reflecting back. "We drove around the district and we visited the school and Mr Bistany said, 'I'll take it; we'll do it; we'll turn it around!'" Mrs Saad and Ralph went to visit parents in their homes, to talk about what SABIS could offer to them. "It was pretty rough, pretty rough," says Mrs Saad. "I really had my eyes opened to the desperate ways in which some people lived in America."

A major obstacle stood in their way: the teacher unions. They were fighting against the charter movement because teachers did not have to be unionized to work in a charter school. Now that a specific school had been highlighted, the unions orchestrated a scare campaign aimed at parents and teachers: "SABIS," they said, "is going to take your school away from you, the community. They'll cream off the best and take more money. They're a for-profit company; all they care about is profit, not your kids."

It all came to a head in a meeting in a school auditorium.

Returning to our *dramatis personae*, Michael Glickman was at that meeting. He truly is a *physical* giant of a man, with a huge personality and a warm smile and hearty laugh to match. He had been working for some 27 years in the public education system, as teacher, assistant principal and principal. He'd heard the furor about the De Berry School and decided to go to the meeting where its future would be decided. His union – he was vice-president of the Administrators' Association – was against charter schools; that may have added piquancy to the interest of an independent-minded thinker like Michael Glickman. But he certainly had no desire for anything else: he was very comfortable in a rather pleasant and small elementary school. He'd been principal for ten years, it was simply a great school, "great kids, great parents, great faculty."

Michael remembers how unruly the crowd was at the meeting: "They weren't listening; they were a little bit challenging." Michael called for respect: "Hey, guys. Give them a chance to make their presentations," he said. But the meeting didn't go SABIS's way. The parents, swayed by the unions, rejected SABIS's overtures.

Peter Negroni remembers the meeting as if it were yesterday: "I was so furious. I looked at the parents and the teachers and I said, 'You are giving up a wonderful opportunity for your children. I'm going to put your feet to the fire and make sure that you live up to the promise to your students.'" They had promised that they didn't need a company like SABIS in order to turn themselves around. The next day this was all over the Springfield newspapers. The union was furious with him. But the school never turned around.

After the meeting, Michael Glickman introduced himself to Mr Bistany. "Bad luck," he said. "I liked what I heard from you. But I don't think you'll be able to get round the difficulties in any school here. You'll leave empty handed." Ralph looked at him and said, "No, I'm going to stay and we're going to win."

If the worst-failing school in the district couldn't be taken over, then it would have to be the second-worst-performing. By coincidence, this school was the Alfred Glickman School (it had nothing to do with Michael Glickman). SABIS met with the parents here, and this time got them on board. But there was a further problem: it turned out much to Dr Negroni's surprise that his department didn't own the schools, the city council did, so although he could decide that the charter should go to the Glickman school, and even though the parents agreed that they wanted this, still the city council could get in the way.

The final showdown was at the city council. Outside a group of 200 parents were protesting – but this time *in favor* of SABIS opening. The city hall was jam packed, standing room only. Mr Ralph Bistany and Mrs Saad were at the front. Dr Negroni spoke, addressing his remarks in particular to the nine voting members of the city council. SABIS needed five in order to get a majority. Beth spoke, some parents spoke. But getting towards the end of the evening, SABIS was short of one vote. "The atmosphere," says Mrs Saad, "was electric." Their last remaining chance – the only person who had not made his position clear – stood up to speak. He went on for a long time, saying how he was against charter schools, period. Mrs Saad looked at Ralph Bistany, sensing his dejection. At the end of about twenty minutes, the speaker stopped. And he concluded, "But I have nothing against SABIS, so I vote for them." Mrs Saad said: "You could have heard a pin drop! And then the uproar on our side was unbelievable! This happened ... seventeen years ago! I can still live it now, the atmosphere there and the excitement."

With the vote won, they could have the building for the Glickman School.

"We were just ecstatic," says Beth. "I wouldn't have ever missed that excitement for anything."

"It was exhilarating," says Mrs Saad. "And then the feast with the city mayor, who was very much for us. And then the work started."

They had their school; now they needed their principal. Peter Negroni and Ralph Bistany discussed the principal Ralph had met at the abortive De Berry meeting. The more he heard about him, the more Mr Bistany thought he would be the right man for the job. A meeting was arranged. "Mr Glickman, do you want to come on board?" Ralph said. With a handshake, Michael Glickman became the new principal of the Glickman charter school. Michael Glickman had never been able to turn down a challenge.

Peter Negroni had to accommodate all the current teachers of the Glickman School within the system. They were all invited to apply for jobs at the new charter school. None did; their union told them not to. This suited Michael Glickman. It meant that he could start with a completely new staff. He had no distractions now either: as soon as word got out that he was to join SABIS, phone calls from other principals seeking his advice in his role as union vice-president suddenly ceased. This stiffened his resolve to make it all work. He didn't like political games when the well-being and life-chances of children were at stake.

"It was a great luxury to be able to hire your own staff," says

Michael, something that he'd never experienced in all his years in the public system. It carried the "luxury" of being able to make your own mistakes, too. But with a charter school, you could correct your mistakes, unlike in the public schools, where, once appointed, it was very difficult to get rid of a teacher, however badly he or she performed. And mistakes were made in the first year, with at least one teacher being let go, for the sake of the children.

One key person who was definitely not a mistake was Maretta Thomsen, who had been working with Michael at his earlier school. He saw that she would fit in well in the SABIS school and appointed her as academic coordinator: "We were an effective team. She would take care of the academics, and I would do all the other stuff for the school."

The staff were all new to the school; they were also all new to SABIS. Michael himself had been inducted into the system with a long visit to the Minnesota private school. He was really impressed with the people, the program and the facility. Could he make the same system work in an inner-city public charter school? People from the Minnesota school came and trained the Springfield staff in the methods.

At the beginning of July 1995, SABIS took over the school, opening it in Grades K–7. Every child who had been at the school previously was allowed to stay, and most did, apart from one severe special-needs class, which Springfield district itself had decided to move to a brand-new school, with a swimming pool complete with a ramp for disabled access, and other purpose-built facilities. "Boy, did the union come down on us about that," says Michael ruefully. "But it wasn't our doing at all." Indeed, school enrollment for the first five years of the school was entirely controlled through the district, as the city of Springfield was under a racial-balance bussing program, ordered by the federal government back in 1975 to overcome the disadvantages of neighborhood patterns. So for five years, Springfield balanced the intake at roughly one third white, one third Hispanic, and one third black.

SABIS wanted the whole program brought across lock, stock and barrel. It was surprisingly straightforward adapting the SABIS model from the international private school setting to the inner-city public charter school setting. There were minor details – such as having to "translate" all the SABIS books and materials from British English to American English. There were other technical issues, such as making sure that the curriculum fit the state standards when they came in – sometimes this involved redistributing the pace of how and when subjects were learned, so that children would be ready for the exams when they were due. A lot of the "translation" and adaptation work was down to Maretta's effective hand.

The academic aspects worked well. But they couldn't get away from the fact that the children they were dealing with came "with more baggage than kids who are privileged," says Michael Glickman. It was much harder to create a conducive and disciplined education environment than anyone had expected. It took two full years, Michael says, to sort out discipline. For a year there were problems of fights between students. Eventually he had to draw the line and say, "If you solve the problem in a physical way, you are going to be held accountable." Accountable meant being suspended. Not expelled – Michael and his team were adamant that they weren't going to expel children; that would be abandoning their duty of care. But suspensions of a day or two would be enough to make the student have time to reflect on what they were doing and usually see sense.

Apart from fights, there was the general high level of disruption. The teachers in public school were used to low standards. They took it for granted that there would be one or two disruptive kids in a class who would make life miserable for everyone else. Michael was adamant: "I don't want a child interrupting the class and taking that time away from other kids!" A lot of Michael's and Maretta's time was, therefore, spent on improving their teachers' classroom management skills. SABIS was realizing that this had to be an even larger element of its program as it moved into managing its first charter school in Springfield. So they created more replicable systems – involving students in the Student Life Organization and members of staff – to deal with the additional burdens.

Mrs Saad and Mr Bistany would be in Springfield at least three or four times a year; they'd meet with new staff, exploring techniques of learning and classroom management together. They organized an annual meeting of staff, hiring a room in the Marriott; Mr Bistany always made sure there was sumptuous food laid on. "People really got a sense, you know, that these are the people who started this, and they're right here with us," says Beth. "It was part of what made people loyal to the school and the system."

They couldn't get away from the fact that there were children with issues that they weren't used to dealing with in the upmarket schools. When their first graduation class came, one of those graduating was an eighteen-year-old girl, who gave a speech from the dais. She'd been happy at SABIS, she said, but she wanted to tell them now that she'd been married to an older man for the last few years while she'd been in school. He had two children, and she'd been doing her own homework in between raising his two children. SABIS had given her an opportunity which she would never forget. Michael says, "There were tears streaming down *my* face as I listened to her story."

As the school's success became clear to the community, pressure on enrollment increased, and because charter school legislation permits only lotteries for over-enrolled schools, the cozy situation of the district allocating students couldn't continue. So the school had to create a lottery for admission, a situation which continues to this day.

The school expanded and outgrew the original Glickman facilities, leasing land from various sources and putting up portable classrooms until at one point they were on three separate sites at the same time. They found a piece of land attached to a cemetery: more and more people were going for cremation, the owners said, so the additional land they had acquired wasn't required. Over two years, they built a new state-of-the-art school, in a brick and mortar and steel construction, with extensive sports facilities and fields. SABIS invested over $20 million of its own finances in this new building. At the same time as SABIS was building this facility, the city of Springfield was building a similar-sized school, but for twice the cost, around $40 million. The city had to go through the public procurement process, through unionized labor at all times, which pushed up the cost. But no one would say that the public school building built by the city was any better than that built by SABIS. SABIS moved into their new school, now called SABIS International Charter School, in 1998.

Michael Glickman served as principal of the school until 2000, when he became regional director for SABIS in the USA. Maretta Thomsen took over as principal. In 2010, she in turn handed over the school to Karen Reuter. It's been a hugely successful school. It remains SABIS's flagship charter school to this day, now in its seventeenth year, having had only three directors during that whole period. The systems that they've built there have been replicated in other charter schools in America: at the time of writing, SABIS has eight charter schools, with four in addition under license.

Successfully closing achievement gaps

When SABIS took over, the Alfred Glickman School was the second-worst-performing school in the District of Springfield. Only around 35 percent of the children were on grade level. Now the SABIS International Charter School, as the school is known, is one of the highest-performing schools in the district. One of the simple, easy-to-remember facts is that, in the ten years since the school has been graduating high-school students (Grade 12), 100 percent of these students have been offered college placement.

SABIS is a huge success story for Springfield. When the city was suffering a high level of crime, the mayor of the city told Michael Glickman, "We have families that have stayed in the city because of SABIS." The crime led to a lot of middle-class flight out of the city. Some people stayed because at least there was a great school they could send their children to.

SABIS opened other charter schools across different parts of America after the success of Springfield. The second-oldest SABIS charter school is the International Academy of Flint, in Michigan (which we'll say more about in the next chapter). It's worth looking at the success of these two oldest SABIS charter schools together – they're the only two SABIS charter schools that currently go all the way from

K to 12, so we can get a sense of how they fare on college admissions. And they're the ones where the system has had time to bed down, so we can see how SABIS works at its best. For ease of reference, we'll dub them "SABIS Springfield" and "SABIS Flint" in what follows.

The former superintendent of New York public schools, Joel Klein, who recently left to join News Corporation as an education advisor to Rupert Murdoch, frequently referred to education as "the civil rights issue of the 21st century." In particular, this was because of the stark contrast in performance between African-American and Latin-Hispanic children, who, on average, perform much worse academically than their white peers. And there's also a stark contrast between children of families on low incomes and those from higher-earning families. All current educational reform movements have closing these education gaps as their "*raison d'être*": it's what motivates them, and it's by these metrics that they will be judged.

On these metrics – closing the achievement gaps between America's different ethnic groups and between America's rich and poor – the two oldest SABIS charter schools are unequivocally a success. Here are some headline findings:

- At SABIS Springfield, at Grade 10, *African-American students are outperforming white students* in Massachusetts. That really is closing the achievement gap, an extraordinary result.
- On the 35 state standardized tests taken by students in the two SABIS schools, on thirteen of the tests (37 percent) the gap between African-American and Caucasian students was completely closed (that is, either the black students have overtaken their white counterparts, or they are within five percentage points of their scores); on a further twenty of the tests (57 percent) the gap had been significantly narrowed compared to the state norms. In other words, on fully 33 out of 35 tests (94 percent), the two oldest SABIS charter schools have either closed or significantly narrowed the black/white achievement gap.

- The SABIS schools are also successfully narrowing the gap between rich and poor. In SABIS Springfield, the socio-economic gap averages twelve percentage points, compared to an average of 32 percentage points in the state of Massachusetts. In SABIS Flint, the students who are economically disadvantaged outperform those in Michigan state in twelve out of fourteen exams.

Let's delve into these findings in more detail. Both SABIS schools are similar in many respects. Both serve Grades K–12. SABIS Springfield opened in 1995, SABIS Flint four years later. Both are large schools – SABIS Springfield serving 1,574 students, while SABIS Flint serves 1,178 students. Indeed, SABIS charter schools in general are much larger than the national norm. In the school year 2009/10, there were around five thousand charter schools in the USA, serving around 1.62 million children – with an average size of around 320 students. That means that the two schools we're considering here enroll the equivalent of nearly nine conventional charter schools.

Both SABIS Springfield and SABIS Flint have a preponderance of minority students – 67 and 88 percent respectively. Both schools are heavily oversubscribed and use a lottery to admit students. *There is no selection by any other criteria*, including academic, in either school, in common with the policy at all SABIS schools across the world. And their success is not because they expel students either; in general, they don't. We'll explore this more in the next chapter.

In both schools 100 percent of graduates are accepted to college – SABIS Springfield has been doing this for ten years, while SABIS Flint has achieved this for the past six years – both since they started their graduation classes. Both schools have received state-wide and national recognition for their educational excellence, including featuring in the *US News & World* "America's Best High Schools" list (SABIS Springfield for two years and SABIS Flint for three years in a row), and in *Newsweek* as a top American school (SABIS Springfield in 2007).

Both Springfield and Flint are similar cities – mid-sized cities facing severe economic challenges and high crime rates. Flint was ranked the fourth-most dangerous city in America by the FBI in 2010, up from sixth the previous year. Springfield was in the top ten in 2006.

The ethnic mix at SABIS Springfield is similar to that in the district of Springfield, although significantly more diverse than in the Commonwealth of Massachusetts in general. The SABIS school has 33 percent white, 31 percent African-American, 29 percent Hispanic and 7 percent other races, compared to 68 percent white, 8 percent African-American and 15 percent Hispanic in Massachusetts schools in general. In other words, the SABIS school proportionately has nearly four times as many African-American students as an average school in the state, and twice as many Hispanic students.

The percentage of SABIS Springfield students from low-income families is 47.9 percent, compared to 34.2 percent in Massachusetts as a whole. In other words, the SABIS school proportionately has 40 percent more low-income families than schools in the state in general (see Figures 1 and 2).

Figure 3 gives more details on the remarkable result that the *African-American students at SABIS* are outperforming the *state's white students* in ELA and mathematics at Grade 10, and equalling their performance in science and technology.[1] This outperforming appears to begin in Grade 6 in English. The figure also shows the achievement trend of the SABIS African-American students (as a solid line) and the state's white children (the dotted line). The improvement trend is much more marked for the SABIS children than for the state-wide white children, another important achievement for SABIS.

Next, we see from Figure 4 that the SABIS African-American students are outperforming the state's African-American students in every subject and grade as tested in the 2010 MCAS, apart from Grade 5 science/technology (where the SABIS and state students are equal) and Grade 4 mathematics (where the SABIS students lag behind the state). In the higher grades, e.g. Grade 10, the SABIS students are hugely ahead of the state students: in Grade 10 ELA, they have

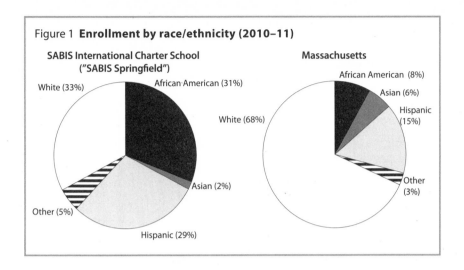

Figure 1 **Enrollment by race/ethnicity (2010–11)**

SABIS International Charter School ("SABIS Springfield")
White (33%) · African American (31%) · Asian (2%) · Hispanic (29%) · Other (5%)

Massachusetts
White (68%) · African American (8%) · Asian (6%) · Hispanic (15%) · Other (3%)

a 36 percentage point advantage (a 60 percent advantage), while in Grade 10 mathematics, it is a 40 percentage point advantage (a 75 percent advantage). In science and technology, the advantage is again 36 percentage points (in this case, a 97 percent advantage over the

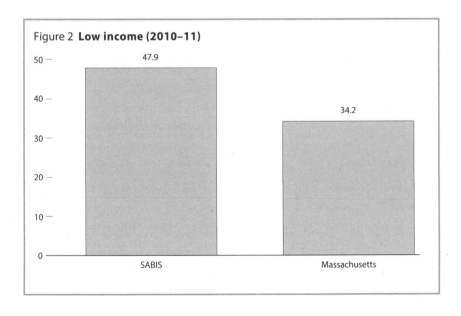

Figure 2 **Low income (2010–11)**

SABIS 47.9
Massachusetts 34.2

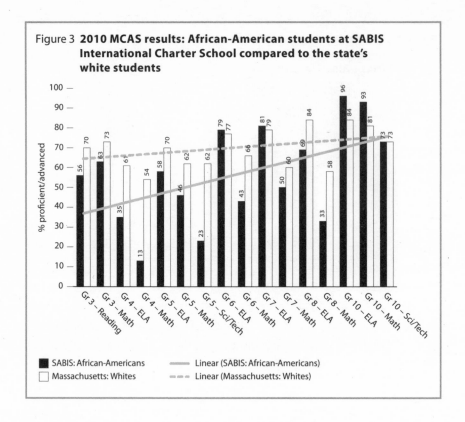

Figure 3 **2010 MCAS results: African-American students at SABIS International Charter School compared to the state's white students**

average state scores). Again, we can see that the trend line is much more advantageous for the SABIS students compared to the state-wide children.

Moreover (Figure 5), the gaps between African-American students and Caucasian students at SABIS Springfield are in general much narrower than the gaps between African-American and white students in the state of Massachusetts in general. In Grade 10, for instance, in ELA, the gap is actually in favor of African-American students; they are two percentage points ahead in the 2010 MCAS. In the state at large, African-Americans are 24 points behind. In Grade 10 mathematics, African-American students are four percentage points behind their white peers in the SABIS school, compared to 28 points behind in Massachusetts generally. In general, the gap between Massachusetts

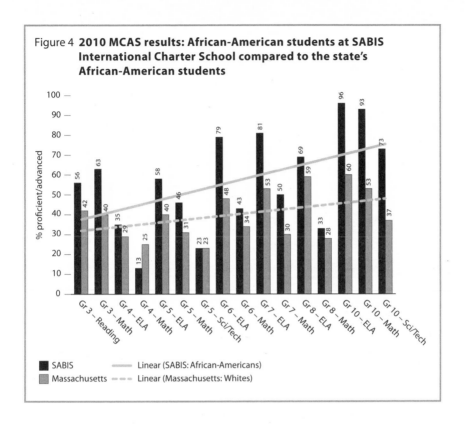

Figure 4 **2010 MCAS results: African-American students at SABIS International Charter School compared to the state's African-American students**

African-American and Caucasian students is 30 percentage points; in SABIS Springfield it is only fifteen percentage points.

Finally, Figure 6 shows us the proficiency gaps between students from low-income and those from families of higher incomes ("non-low-income"). In every subject at every level, there is a significantly smaller achievement gap between those SABIS students from low-income and those from non-low-income families with than students from the state in general. In Grade 10 mathematics, the low-income children even outperformed the non-low-income students at SABIS schools. In general, the average gap at the state level between low-income and non-low-income students was 32 percentage points; for SABIS students it was twelve percentage points, a hugely significant difference.

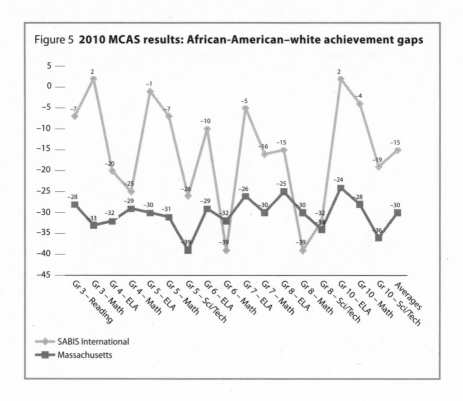

Figure 5 **2010 MCAS results: African-American–white achievement gaps**

A similar story can be told about closing the achievement gap between Hispanic/Latino students and their white peers, as well as when comparing Hispanic/Latino students at SABIS with their state-wide peers. In all subjects and at all grades, SABIS Hispanic students achieve significantly higher proficiency levels than their state-wide counterparts. By Grade 10, SABIS Hispanic students are performing 42 percentage points better than those in the state (98 percent compared to 56 percent) in ELA, 46 percentage points higher in mathematics (95 percent compared to 49 percent) and 41 percentage points better in science and technology.

Similarly, by Grade 10, SABIS Hispanic students are outperforming the state's white students in all three subjects – 98 percent to 84 percent in ELA, 95 percent to 81 percent in mathematics and 74 percent to 73 percent in science and technology. And the Hispanic/white gaps in

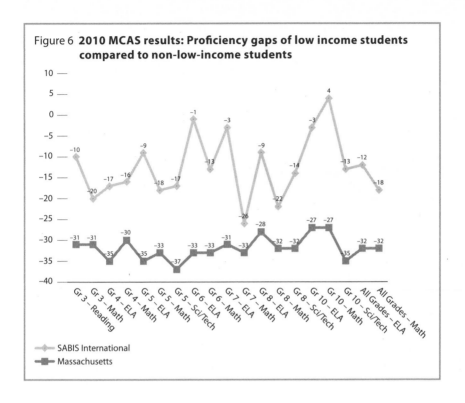

Figure 6 **2010 MCAS results: Proficiency gaps of low income students compared to non-low-income students**

the SABIS schools are in all but one case dramatically smaller than the Hispanic/white gaps in the state. In Grade 10 ELA, the gap is actually in favor of Hispanic students at SABIS – four percentage points in favor – compared to a state-wide average of 28 percentage points in favor of whites. In Grade 10 mathematics, Hispanic students are only two percentage points below their white peers, compared to a massive 32 percentage point difference state-wide.

In short, starting as the second-worst-performing school in Springfield, SABIS Springfield is now a veritable high-flier, challenging schools across the state to do better. What about Flint?

The International Academy of Flint ("SABIS Flint") has a student body made up of 88 percent minorities – 78 percent African-American, 1 percent Hispanic and 9 percent other – compared to the student body in the state of Michigan in general, which is 71 percent white and

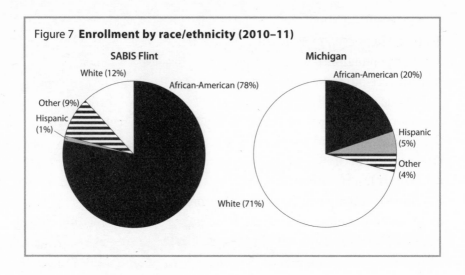

Figure 7 **Enrollment by race/ethnicity (2010–11)**

20 percent African-American. In terms of low-income families, SABIS Flint has 82 percent low-income children, compared to 41 percent in the state of Michigan in general. Clearly it's serving a very deprived population (Figures 7 and 8).

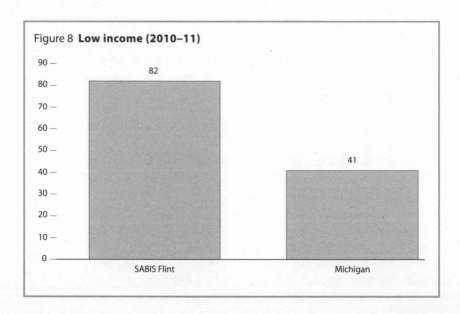

Figure 8 **Low income (2010–11)**

Figures 9–11 show comparable achievements to those of Springfield – perhaps even more remarkable as they're serving an even more deprived population. Figure 9 shows that SABIS Flint African-American students are outperforming African-American students state-wide in all but one grade and subject tested (that is, in Grade 3 reading, where the difference is narrow, 78 percent compared to 81 percent). Moreover, they're not far behind Michigan's white students either – actually surpassing them in Grade 4 and Grade 6 mathematics, and coming almost equal in six tests (mathematics in Grades 3, 7 and 8, and ELA in Grades 6, 7 and 8). Notably, while the trend line for African-American students in SABIS Flint is more or less flat (the solid line), for African-American students across the state it declines dramatically (the dotted line). African-American students in the SABIS school escape the terrible problem of steadily declining achievement that is a severe problem state-wide.

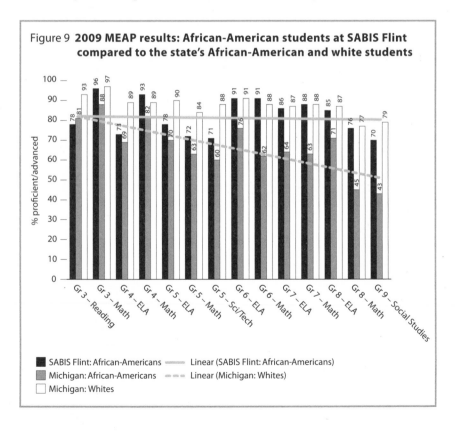

Figure 9 **2009 MEAP results: African-American students at SABIS Flint compared to the state's African-American and white students**

Figure 10 looks at the African-American/white gap at SABIS and state-wide. It shows that at every subject tested and at each grade, there were smaller gaps between SABIS African-American students and their white counterparts than in the state as a whole. Indeed, in some grades and subjects African-American students outperformed their white counterparts – in Grade 6 mathematics and Grade 3 reading, for instance. In general, the average African-American/white achievement gap across Michigan is 23 percentage points; in SABIS Flint it is only nine percentage points, a huge advantage.

Finally, Figure 11 shows how children from low-income families at SABIS Flint are outperforming children from low-income families in Michigan in nearly every subject and grade level. In Grade 8 mathematics, for instance, SABIS Flint low-income children attain 75 percent, compared to 56 percent state-wide. In Grade 8 ELA, the comparable figures are 83 percent and 75 percent.

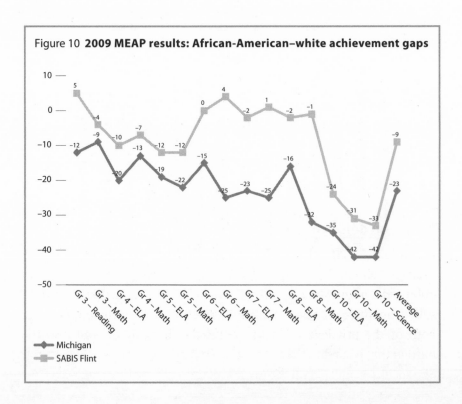

Figure 10 **2009 MEAP results: African-American–white achievement gaps**

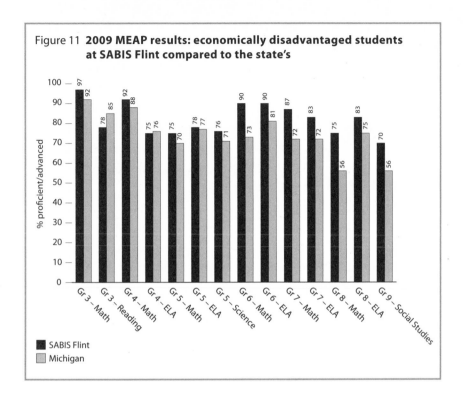

Figure 11 **2009 MEAP results: economically disadvantaged students at SABIS Flint compared to the state's**

It's all a tremendous success story. The two oldest SABIS charter schools, in Springfield and Flint, are quite dramatically succeeding in closing the achievement gaps for ethnic groups and between rich and poor. SABIS schools are key players in solving the major civil rights issue of the 21st century.

Kids who don't go to jail

Karen Reuter is the third and current director of SABIS International Charter School, SABIS Springfield. Coming from years of service in public education, she is sophisticated, polished and intelligent, with a silky-smooth voice. She took over in 2010 from Maretta and is aware both of the privilege of heading this flagship school, and also the burden that it carries, to continue these fine traditions of achievement. She speaks proudly of all the achievements of her school, including the

100 percent acceptance to college – this seems to be a natural feature of the SABIS terrain and it is too easily forgotten how remarkable it is, given the student body intake. And she's proud too of the elite destinations that are awarded to some of the children – alumni have gone to Harvard, MIT and Smith College; many of the students progress on full or large scholarships to a range of other reputable colleges. But when you hear these stories, it's all too easy, she says, to miss what she thinks might be the really important thing about her school. She tells me the story of Jane[2] to illustrate her point.

Jane graduated in 2010 and is now in college studying occupational therapy. She began her graduation speech to Springfield by saying, "Students live many secrets that are not always obvious to their peers, adults, or teachers. Over the past few years, I have kept secrets: I have been homeless and abandoned." She was abandoned by her mother; her sister gave her space, but it "was not a stable environment for a teenaged girl. There were no rules to obey; I made my own ... No consequences were given when I came home late or when I went out on a school night ... I saw no reason to attend school when I was feeling lost, begging to be found."

But, says Karen, that's exactly what SABIS does; it finds kids with cards stacked against them and gets them back on track. "That's what SABIS is all about," she told me. "Its essence is about serving kids that would otherwise not have a chance." Yes, of course, the school can feel proud when its graduates are accepted at Harvard or MIT or Smith. But sometimes "I'd like to talk about the kids that didn't go to jail." In the end, she says, "That's why I'm here."

Perhaps Jacob is one of those kids. He graduated in 2007, another student with a difficult home life. The family was homeless from time to time; his father, a drug addict, was in and out of the home, frequently in trouble with the law. He would often beat his wife, and Jacob and his siblings. One day, Jacob came home from school and found that his father had sold his bed for drug money. Not surprisingly, Jacob didn't take to school easily. He'd leave the building during school hours; teachers would chase after him to bring him back – not to punish him, but to try to help him. "Over time," says Tom Campagna, the affable and avuncular guidance counselor who played a major role in steering Jacob's life back on track, "Jacob began to see that the lessons he learned at home and the neighborhood did not have to rule the rest of his life, that there were people who cared for him." And eventually he pulled himself around too, "became a starting and contributing member of the state championship basketball team, applied to college, got his GPA up to over 2.0, graduated high school, took one Advanced Placement course, and enrolled in Mitchell College." Tom said: "One of the things I really like about this school, and it showed itself with Jacob, is there's a culture here that kids learn to value, of the need to go on and become the best that they can be."

Or there are students like Trevion, whose parents came to the USA at the end of the 1970s; they split up and his mother brought him up along with his two sisters and two brothers. Like many inner-city black kids, Trevion really didn't like school. He was always in trouble, often in fights. Trevion is a very big kid, but the way he holds himself makes him look vulnerable. "Every time we went to a new school," he said, "it was like everybody thought, 'Oh, I'm going to beat that big kid up.'" Or, because he wears glasses, "Let's beat up four-eyes."

He tried to avoid fights, but in the end succumbed and was often kicked out of class. By the time he was sixteen, he'd been to six different schools and never got a chance to settle. Then his mother eventually got him into SABIS Springfield – his name in the lottery, he was one of the lucky winners. "She heard it was a good school; they're strict; they don't tolerate bullying or nothing like that. She thought that would be good if I came here."

When he came to SABIS it was different from the start. Instead of having to fend off bullies, he was sitting at a lunch table by himself, and "a whole bunch of other guys came up to me, everybody just came and asked me my name and was greeting me and just welcomed me, and I started hanging around with them, even till now they're still my friends." This was one aspect of the Student Life Organization in action, welcoming newcomers and integrating them into the school.

After being the troublemaker all his life, he was asked to be deputy head of the Discipline Department, sorting out troublesome younger kids. "I just tell them that you only live life once, and you want to have everything set right now. Don't get to senior year and think, 'Oh my God, my grades are not good.'" Some of them listen, he says, others just say, "Oh yeah, sure." But he's set himself up okay now. He wants to own his own mechanics shop, "A big mechanics shop." He'll go to college first for two years to study business, then mechanics. He'll stay in Springfield: "I'll stay around my mom; I've got to help her."

Every member of staff, says Karen Reuter, will have stories like this, of children they've helped from less than promising backgrounds get back on track. But sometimes there are near-misses. Sometimes to a young teenager the way of life at SABIS can seem too demanding, the freedoms at other schools too tempting. Some children do leave – last year it was 23 out of the total student body of 1,574, although five of these moved cities and another went to an early college program. So only 1 percent of students leave of their own volition or are expelled.

Mitchell was one of those who left, tempted by the apparent freedoms enjoyed by his friends in Springfield public schools. It was December of his Grade 9 year. He didn't like "all the test taking, the constant push-along" at SABIS. So he left and enrolled at an apparently good public school in Springfield. It was a shock to his system: "There were a lot of discipline issues; it was rowdy; there was a lot of gang violence, that stuff you definitely would not see here [SABIS Springfield]." And he'd learned about how discipline issues ought to be handled during his time at SABIS Springfield: "They didn't go about it in the right way. They'd suspend the kids, which would make them more angry, and they'd come back and do the same things, and there were no repercussions. There was no sitting them down and speaking to them, clearly setting a way forward for them." It was all so different from his earlier experiences: "I left here because I didn't like the rigor, and then I went to a place without rigor and realized I needed it. And liked it."

But it was not just the lack of rigor which shocked him; it was also the attitude of teachers toward the students. At SABIS he was used to teachers who wanted to help him understand things – and the constant test-taking, he began to realize, was in fact all part of teachers and the system trying to make sure he had understood. In the public school, the teachers "really didn't care much at all. It was basically, 'I gave you the information, you do what you need to. Sink or swim. Do what you want.'" In contrast to SABIS, "the first thing I noticed was the lack of caring." Being at the public school was "like being downgraded"; the teachers seemed indifferent to what he wanted to pursue or how he would get there. That was very different from life at SABIS.

After a couple of months, he could take it no longer. He plucked up the courage to talk to his mom, a single mother who worked as a secretary in the local medical center. She had "not been thrilled" that he'd wanted to leave SABIS in the first place. She'd given him "a rough time about it for a while. I guess she figured I had to learn the lesson for myself." When he came back to her and said he couldn't bear the rowdiness of his new school, her response was predictable, if fair: "I told you you shouldn't have left." But Mitchell had learned something from SABIS, the lessons of determination and perseverance. Every day, he went back to SABIS Springfield, and asked whether he could return. "I came back every day for four months, trying to speak to whoever I needed to speak to, to be admitted again. Every day for four months." And finally, he was readmitted, Beth Conway says, on the grounds that he had siblings still in the school and he was an exceptional case – but he had to repeat the grade that he'd already taken at the public school. "I wasn't too happy to do that," he said, "but I didn't think twice about not coming back."

Springfield 2, or the school that never was

So SABIS had created an immensely successful school in Springfield, Massachusetts – in academic terms and in terms of being able to cope with the kinds of youngsters who were especially needy. It had also created other successful charter schools across America. Given its success, and given the waiting list of nearly three thousand, an obvious next step might be to open another SABIS school in Springfield.

Springfield School District has 21,141 students in total. That means that around 14 percent of Springfield's children are on the SABIS waiting list! Or, to put it another way, fully 20 percent of Springfield's children, one in five, are choosing or would like to choose SABIS – combining the 3,000 on the waiting list with the 1,574 at the school itself. And, of course, others in the community may also prefer SABIS but don't think it's worth going on the waiting list. That's a pretty remarkable endorsement from the community of a particular school model. A second SABIS school in Springfield seems an obvious next step.

The Springfield Prep Charter School was to be that second SABIS school. The story of this school that never was is a salutary tale, however. It cautions against anyone being too optimistic about using the charter school route to effect change in American education, or against reforms which seem likely to bring about charter-like reforms elsewhere (as with the current "free school" academies in Britain, for instance).

The new SABIS school was the brainchild of the president of Springfield Technical Community College, who contacted Jose Afonso, the SABIS US Business Development Director, saying that the college had space available and was interested in doing something for the community. Furthermore, they had always been very impressed with the SABIS system; could they apply for a charter in partnership for a second Springfield SABIS school?

Jose Afonso is a dynamic and shrewd 40-something executive. We've met him before – he had worked for the state government as the senior person involved in authorizing charters, and was the guy who approved the first SABIS charter in Springfield. He had been very impressed by the SABIS model, their vision and academic success. They seemed to have the best track record and the clearest vision of all the education management companies that he'd come across: "They were way ahead of their time," he says. After about eight years as "a state bureaucrat," he'd done "pretty much all I could do." He wanted to have a hand in actually creating and launching schools, instead of just overseeing them as a government bureaucrat. Udo

Schulz invited him to join his department at SABIS, and he worked under him for ten years or so, before taking over his position when Udo semi-retired.

Given SABIS's reputation in the city, it was easy convincing the board of directors of the college to sign off on the concept, and the board of the trust that controlled the college property also voted unanimously to endorse the new SABIS charter school. The city mayor endorsed it too, as did a range of business and community leaders.

SABIS helped an applicant group – who would become the board of trustees of the charter school – of local professionals submit the application. SABIS had done this many times before successfully. Jose's early role as state gatekeeper for charter schools also meant that he knew a thing or two about how charters get approved. So the documents were prepared with their usual care and thoroughness.

In the normal way, it went before the Massachusetts State Department of Education. The review process took some weeks. At the end of this process, the Department of Education rejected the application.

How could that happen, given what we've said about SABIS's unequivocal success in the city?

SABIS was given a summary of the six reviewers' positive and negative comments, neatly laid out in columns. Somehow, the Department of Education judged that the negative comments outweighed the positive; it's impossible for an outsider to see how.

For instance, in the section entitled "Organizational Management," the "strengths" of the application are clearly listed:

> The two current SABIS charter schools [in Massachusetts] are viable and sound organizations as evidenced by their charter renewals, their independent audited financial statements, full enrollment (and extensive waiting lists), stable staff retention, high parent satisfaction on surveys and high graduation rates. SABIS's record is strong in management.

That sounds pretty persuasive; a pretty strong endorsement of what SABIS has done and can offer the community. The weaknesses? In full, these read:

> Many assumptions can be made about the organizational manage-
> ment provided by SABIS, but they do not give any detailed information.

This reads like bureaucratic pedantry. Reputation is nothing, unless all the details are faithfully recorded.

Or there's the section "Link of Proven Provider to Program Success." The positive SABIS features listed are many, and include the fact that the huge success of SABIS Springfield in graduating 100 percent of its seniors with 100 percent acceptance to college for the last ten years is clearly down to the SABIS model itself: "The proprietary SABIS program is the only program being implemented, therefore, directly tying the results of these schools to the SABIS educational program and model." Again, this all sounds pretty persuasive. But again, the weaknesses of the application outweighed these strengths. In full, the weaknesses are:

> Inflexibility of program model (adaptable to local conditions and student needs?)

Given that SABIS had been running successfully in Springfield for some sixteen years, successfully graduating everyone to college accep-tance for the last ten, then this would suggest a resounding "yes" in answer to the question posed in parenthesis. Curiously, inexplicably, the Department of Education concluded otherwise.

Perhaps the worst section of all to read is the "Description of the Communities to be Served." The strengths listed here are again many, including, of course, the observation that the total of 3,000 students on the waiting list for SABIS Springfield alone would suggest a pretty strong case for the desirability of a second SABIS school in Springfield. But this aspect was clearly not enough to sway several of the nega-tive reviewers: "Does not make a compelling case why a second SABIS school will serve the specific needs of Springfield," said one. Clearly having 3,000 children who are desperate to get into the first school is not a "compelling reason" for opening a second. "A long wait-list at the existing SABIS school isn't enough – I want to see that they know HOW and WHY the methods used by SABIS are helpful to the kids in their district." I'm baffled as to what detail this bureaucrat might require to prove that.

At least these reviewers appear to have read SABIS's application. Another reviewer sails in with the observation that "I am looking for a much more detailed description of how the SABIS methods and curriculum will help students reach the founders' stated goal of 100% admission to college. I want to know why they think this program is best suited to help the children in their community reach that very admirable goal." This reviewer doesn't seem to have noticed that the reason why SABIS has adopted this goal is because, well, it's what their program had already achieved just down the road, with similar students.

It's clearly all down to politics. I had some of the state and district politics explained to me by Jose Afonso, but it all seems much too tiresome to relate. Because in the end, to an outsider, it's completely bewildering why a disadvantaged community like Springfield should be denied a replication of its successful school. As an outsider, you'd think the state of Massachusetts should be begging SABIS to open more schools, given their success so far and their willingness to risk their own capital for the benefit of the state's disadvantaged youngsters. Instead, their attempts to open more schools are being thwarted by this petty politicking.

Talking to Jose about this, I felt something like this: okay, perhaps going back fifteen years or so, you could understand or at least sympathize with those objecting to the first charter schools in America and to SABIS's first charter school in Springfield, Massachusetts. The model was unproven. How could you know that it would work? Indeed, in terms of SABIS in particular you could be forgiven back in 1995 for wondering whether a model that had been explicitly designed for children of the elite in an international setting could be applicable to inner-city kids from diverse and less supportive backgrounds. And again, you could probably be justified wondering whether a for-profit organization based in faraway Lebanon could really be expected to act in the interests of American citizens and not be tempted to profiteer at their expense. All these objections might be understandable back in 1995.

But in 2011, it should be impossible to hold on to such attitudes. There are no unknowns, all is known. And *yet still* SABIS finds it hard to make progress. Organizations like SABIS have proved that their interventions can work to raise standards and enhance opportunities for disadvantaged children. SABIS has proved – among other things by its own investment of $20 million – that they're not interested in profiteering at the expense of the community, but rather are interested in reinvesting profits for the community's benefit.

Any perceived dangers back in 1995 turned out to be false alarms. But the fact that today an organization like SABIS can still be turned down in the way that it was over Springfield 2 makes one feel rather despondent.

Listening to Jose Afonso's story of the SABIS school that never was and the political intrigues that accompanied other SABIS charter schools, one realizes that his own tongue-in-cheek characterization of how he saw himself somehow makes a lot of sense: "Sometimes I feel like I'm a Che Guevara, a beret-wearing revolutionary fighting against the system, fighting the blob." But what keeps him going is that he believes he's fighting on the right side. Yes, he says, his role with SABIS is of "a traveling salesman." But this business description doesn't preclude a deeper dimension to his work: "I have a genuine mission. It's to go to the neediest communities, with the worst schools, where the kids have the least opportunity, and find those communities, and open up schools. That's the mission that SABIS wants me engaged in."

Would they go to a district like Springfield again and ask for its worst-performing school? "Don't tell anyone. But I bet we would."

The problem, though, is that, if they did that, if they went out of their way to try to make a difference in America and succeeded, there's no guarantee that those with power and influence would so much as acknowledge what they've done; there's certainly no guarantee that their work would be rewarded with a second school in which to make a difference. That, to an outsider, is the conundrum of the politics of American charter schools.

CHAPTER 5

American antidote

Flint & me

I traveled to America to see SABIS charter schools for myself. I ended my journey in Springfield, Massachusetts, just days before Christmas. The first school I visited, however, was the International Academy of Flint, in Michigan – SABIS's second-longest-established charter school after Springfield, whose successful results in closing the achievement gap we looked at in the previous chapter. I visited in a bitterly cold mid-December.

In my interviews with senior staff, teachers, parents and students, I was on the lookout for positive, heart-warming stories. Let's be honest, I'd read books like *Work Hard, Be Nice*,[1] the *New York Times* bestseller about the creators of KIPP, the Knowledge Is Power Program, which runs 99 schools serving 27,000 disadvantaged children in America. I wanted the kind of stories of children that were in that book – you know, of the kid who came from a really bad background, father absent, mother on drugs and welfare, who is rescued by the charter school, and eventually gets a full scholarship to Harvard and is now doing a PhD in astrophysics at Yale, that sort of thing. All very uplifting, the kind of stories you want from a book about charter schools serving deprived neighborhoods.

Indeed, there are many success stories like that in SABIS – some are highlighted on SABIS's own website. But the more I spoke to staff, students, and parents, the more an unexpected kind of story came to the fore, a story which in the end seemed more important to relate.

There's a mythology built up against charter schools in general, and those run by for-profit companies like SABIS in particular. They get the glowing results they do only because, first, they cream the crop of students, taking only the best. Secondly, they are ruthless, expelling students at the drop of a hat for any petty misdemeanor; with only the best-behaved students left, their good results are a shoe-in. Furthermore, because a company like SABIS is *for-profit*, it won't be concerned about individual children's welfare; the profit motive will make it *uncaring*.

I've already given some vignettes from SABIS Springfield in the previous chapter which should start to dispel the last point, but because it's so commonplace an objection I think it's worth focusing on it a bit more, in another context, to show how completely off the mark it is. The first criticism is also entirely wrong: oversubscribed SABIS charter schools use a lottery to select students. They don't cream the best, period. They're not allowed to by law, and they don't. But what about the second criticism, that charter schools like SABIS expel their disruptive students, thus enhancing their academic results? In the previous chapter we noted that only 1 percent of SABIS Springfield students leave – either of their own accord or by virute of being expelled. So clearly the objection isn't valid statistically. But because the figure is so low, perhaps people will think that the kids must be angels in the school – reinforcing the sense that they're not really dealing with deprived neighborhoods. The more time I spent in SABIS Flint – and in their other schools – the more I wanted to convey the reality of what I found: far from wanting to do this at the drop of a hat, SABIS *goes out of its way not to expel anyone*. But the children are not angels, far from it.

Flint achieved notoriety in the late 1930s as the site of a major sit-down strike which led to the unionization of the US automotive industry. More recently, Michael Moore's 1989 film *Roger & Me* chronicled the devastation wrought by the closure of General Motors' automotive plants. The Roger in the title was Roger Smith, then CEO of General

Motors, whom Moore confronts at the end of the film, also just before Christmas: did he know people were being evicted from their homes on Christmas Eve because they'd been fired by General Motors? Job losses at the time of the film were around 30,000; they're probably 80,000 now. Unemployment in Flint is 27 percent, compared to the state of Michigan at 15 percent and the national average of 10 percent. Flint was a one-horsepower town, as it were, dependent on jobs in the automotive industry, and GM in particular. When GM closed its plants, the city collapsed with it.

Since 2007, the FBI has ranked Flint in the top five US cities with the highest rates of violent crime. In 2007, it was ranked the second-most violent city in America; by the time of my visit in 2010 it was fourth, but on track to beat its record of 61 murders, set in 1986, the year crack cocaine hit the city (by the time of my visit, in mid-December, there had already been 61 murders that year). "I don't think there's a kid in this school," Art Wenzlaff, the Director of Community Relations at SABIS Flint, told me, "who hasn't been involved with some kind of yellow [police] tape around a tree or a car or something."

High crime and deep social problems – and a public education system that makes no positive mark – made it exactly the kind of place where SABIS wanted to make a difference in America.

Traci Cormier is the director of SABIS Flint, joining in 1999 as the school was opening. She had previously worked at SABIS's private school in Minnesota. But then when the opportunity to come to Flint arose, she loved the idea of getting back to her roots in public education: "It was the idea of a public school and SABIS together. SABIS was embarking on this challenge to serve students in need and I just knew it would be a good fit. I just knew we had our work cut out for us, but we had a great support system."

She recalls her first visit to Flint: "I remember thinking even though I was in my thirties, 'My mother is going to kill me.'" She was single and the environment was one of boarded-up and burned-out homes, graffiti and general inner-city neglect. Indeed, her mother thought she was crazy; as luck would have it, having accepted the position, while back in Minnesota Traci had picked up a magazine which said Flint was "the number one most dangerous place for single women in America." She said to her mother, "It's too late. What can I do?"

It wasn't only her mother who was causing her grief. Just as we saw in Springfield, the unions had provoked a lot of anti-charter school feeling in the city. Every time they wanted to do something with the district, such as getting a food service or transportation or even information, "we basically hit a wall."

Traci makes no bones about it – the early years were incredibly difficult. They had to train teachers who weren't used to high demands, and they had to impose discipline on children who weren't used to systems, period. "It wasn't as simple," Traci says, "as saying to students, 'Sit down' or talking to them after school. You know, these kids had life-shattering experiences that they were dealing with. They were staying home all evening caring for their siblings. You know, they were being evicted in the middle of the night."

One story from early on was a formative experience for her: a young man in Grade 5 had urinated in another student's lunchbox. Traci put him on Saturday detention and brought his mom in on Friday evening to explain: "She seemed incredibly supportive, just telling me how good it was to have me in her life and working with her." It seemed like "the perfect situation, the young man had learned his lesson, the mother was supportive, and so be it." The following Monday morning Traci saw the young man had a deep welt on his arm. On further inspection, it transpired he had been beaten all over his body with an iron bar. His sister was also in the school; she too had deep welts all over her back. They called the mom back in and a fracas developed; in the end police had to be called.

It was very sobering, Traci recalls, coming to realize the kind of community you were dealing with: "How do you go forward and keep that strong outer skin that allows you to deal with these situations, but yet at the same time do right by the kids?"

Someone at the sharp end of student behavioral problems is Kendra Giles, the Student Management Coordinator at SABIS Flint. Hailing from Ohio, by coincidence she'd lived in Eden Prairie, Minnesota, prior to moving to Michigan, and so she used to drive by the SABIS private school there every day on her way to work. She joined SABIS Flint in 2004.

When I interviewed Kendra, she first told me about a former student, D'Andre. She remembered the boy as a regular visitor to her office. He had come from a single-parent home – his father had disappeared someplace. He was often disrespectful to staff; one time he was brought before her for punching another student in the face. Slowly she and others worked with him, and "he came right; he went to college; he was captain of the basketball team." But a couple of weeks earlier he'd been killed in a car accident. "To see someone on their way, on the right path and their life to be cut so short ..." She welled up with tears. "There's a picture of him in the hall ... where the mailboxes are," she told me. She is crying; we stop the interview for a while.

The families in general, Kendra told me, are so different from the ones she was used to in Minnesota. "Let's just say they don't come from homes where education is priority number one. They come to us with so much other baggage. They deal with some things that I as an adult don't know that I would be able to handle." Many of their children have only their mother at home; many are being brought up by their grandmothers. Fathers have disappeared or are in jail, mothers are often on drugs. Some of the children "are in homes where there is no heat, no lights; they don't know when they'll get their next meal; they're taking care of younger brothers and sisters. So they come to us in the morning with so many issues."

One of Kendra's roles in the school is to act as a buffer between the children and the teachers, allowing children to talk through their feelings and frustrations and explore the reasons if they've gone off the rails in class. She is the person to whom children can turn in school in confidence, knowing that she will hear them out.

She told me about a couple of cases that had come to her recently. Two Grade 10 boys – fifteen years old – were in the building after school hours for basketball try-outs. At around 7 p.m., they had left the group and walked through the building, checking doors to see whether any were unlocked. They found one, walked in, rummaged around the teacher's desk, and stole the teacher's laptop. Next morning, the teacher came in and noticed her computer missing. With help from the IT Department, Kendra and Traci were able to look back over CCTV footage and identify the students – both known to them as kids who were often in trouble.

Traci and Kendra called one of the boys to the office. "Initially," says Kendra, "he was not going to comply." Eventually, he admitted taking some potato chips from the teacher's desk. Kendra told him he'd better think about it some more because this was really serious. The other boy was called. He said he'd taken some candy from the desk – the teacher had confiscated his candy during class, and he was just reclaiming what was his, "by right." Anything else? "Some chips, too," he said. Kendra said, "What else? And he just kind of calmly said, 'and a laptop.'"

They asked him where the laptop was now. He said it was not at his house, but "up the street somewhere." Traci asked him to go and get it, giving him a time limit of twenty minutes. "Well, he didn't come back that day." The young man in question was not living with either of his parents, but an aunt. Traci called this aunt but "she hadn't seen him." The next morning, he strolled in, "and is sitting out there waiting for me like nothing had happened." "You were supposed to come back. What happened?" He said, "Oh, I got caught up doing something." Like what? "Oh, I was helping my dad move into his new condo." And the laptop? It was in his backpack. "He got the laptop out; it was in perfect condition, the same way it was taken, and that was the end of it."

When I was told this story, my assumption all along – and my interjection at this point – was "And so he was expelled." His offense seemed serious enough, even without the reputation of for-profit charter schools, that one would assume it would have to result in an expulsion.

"No," Kendra said. "He wasn't expelled; we try not to expel." She saw my puzzlement and tried to explain: "Even in our most serious situations, we try not to expel because that means they can't go to any other school in the state of Michigan. If you're expelled, no one else is going to take you. We can't let that happen, that's a whole year of their life wasted. If we have to, we'll suspend them, for a specified period." The school has the authority to suspend for up to ten days; for offenses which require more severe punishment, the kids go before the board.

In this case, the two boys were suspended until after the Christmas break (the event had happened in November). And then they'd come back. Surely they'd rather go to a less demanding school? I ask. "They always come back," she said.

What was their parents' response? One of the mothers, Kendra told me, "was very thankful, because the boy could have been expelled and we chose not to go this route. She was very grateful." For the other young man, who was living with his aunt, the school spent a great deal of effort trying to persuade her to come to the board hearing when the young man's case came up, "because it's always good that the board sees that they have some type of support outside of school." The aunt refused to come, saying how embarrassed she was by his actions. "I ended up telling her," said Kendra, "that it looks a lot better in front of the board if he comes with someone than if he shows up by himself. I understand you're embarrassed, but you need to be there to support him." Kendra knew the woman; she had other kids who had been through the school. In the end, she said she'd come.

For Kendra, and the school, the priority was making sure that the young man was adequately defended at the board hearing, so that they could ensure he was not expelled. This, recall, was a young man, a known troublemaker in the school who had just been caught red handed stealing his teacher's laptop, and who then had not cooperated with the inquiry, but had absconded from the school. Very definitely, this was an expellable offense. And the boy, the sort of miscreant, in other words, that, the common myth goes, charter schools in general, and charter schools run by for-profit companies like SABIS in particular, would be very keen to expel, in order to keep their achievement performance high. But not at SABIS Flint (and the same stories applied at each of the SABIS charter schools I visited). The truth, as so often, is very far from the myths that are perpetuated.

But why did they bend over backwards trying to make sure the boy was not expelled? "Because," said Kendra, "I think he's a good kid; he just makes bad choices. And he didn't choose his parents. Unfortunately, he doesn't have the luxury of having a mom and dad who live together and can make sure he does the right thing. So if we expel him then where does he go? Even if we long-term suspend him, where does he go?"

Traci answered her question: "If he's not here, he's not going to be in school; he's going to end up in jail." I recalled Karen Reuter's suggestion at Springfield that glowing stories of success were important, but stories about the kids who don't go to jail are not often shared. But they are a key part of what all SABIS charter schools do.

This was one story. There were many similar ones, all illustrating the school bending over backwards to try to ensure continuity of learning opportunities for children who were not playing by the rules at all. But surely they have zero tolerance when it comes to *some* offenses? I asked. What about drugs or weapons? Surely offenses like that would mean expulsion? Well, on paper, maybe. A case of drug possession recently came to light. And again, the outcome was not what I expected.

A couple of weeks before my visit, a student's cell phone had gone missing. In trying to locate it, "we came across some marijuana." Someone must have dumped it, knowing teachers were searching for something. Kendra immediately said they would search the lockers of all the students who were in the area at the time. By the time they got to the last of the lockers, one of the girls had gone into the exam hall, "so obviously we waited until she was done." The student, let's call her Gladys, was called into Kendra's office: "This young lady can be very disrespectful so I wanted to let her know that this is what's going on and this is what I'm going to do: I said I am going to search her locker, and she was fine with it," said Kendra. On the way to the locker, there was some interaction between a boy whose locker had already been searched, Gladys, and another female student. "When I got there, Gladys was handing something to the other young lady. The other young lady attempted to walk off and I just said, 'Give it here.'"

She turned around and put three small bags of marijuana in Kendra's hand. "'Nickel bags,' they're called on the street."

In the office, the girls were in tears, recognizing that they could be in serious trouble. The parents were called in. One of the girls' mothers was very upset: the girl was a freshman in the school, and her mother had actually brought her here because she was "jumped by a gang at her previous school; Mom was devastated that she got herself into any type of situation again." But eventually the boy admitted responsibility. He told his mother – again there was no father in his life – over the phone, while Kendra listened. It was his marijuana and he'd tried to get the girls to help him out. He was guilty, not them.

The school could have recommended expulsion, no question about it. Instead, they recommended a suspension, which was what he got.

While suspended, children get work sent home and can still take tests to track their progress. "They just can't come to school or to other activities." But does it have any impact? Does suspension work? Kendra said, "They hate it." She had spoken earlier in the day to the mother of the suspended young man: "I said: how is he doing? She said he hates being at home. They hate it at home because everybody else is at school."

It takes a lot of hard work, and, most importantly, a lot of *rigorous systems*, to get to the point where the school functions as well as it does. An important part of these systems originates in the Student Life Organization. One of Student Life's departments is "Discipline," through which students are tasked with the ownership of creating a social environment conducive to learning – and which we'll explore thoroughly in Chapter 10.

A final story from Kendra: two first-grade boys, six years old, were found with knives in the school. Big knives, ten inches or more. "I think I still have one in my office," Kendra said, laughing. One of the boys "had an issue with a student here at school in his classroom; he thought the best way to handle the situation was to bring a knife." His mother was "beside herself. She had to leave the house earlier than he did, and he was left with his grandmother to get ready." As usual, there was no father on the scene.

Another mom who might have felt entitled to be a little upset was Kendra herself: this story seemed particularly poignant when I discovered that, although Kendra lives in a very good school district, with top-quality public schools, her daughter not only attends SABIS Flint, but was in the same class as the boy with the knife. It shows a particular kind of dedication and commitment to the school to keep your daughter there. I suppose above all it shows *trust* in the school too – that you know the systems in place are good enough to protect your own daughter, should anything like that arise again.

***

Flint was Michael Moore's hometown, which is why the demoralization of the city hurt him so deeply that he made a film about it. An inspiring person I met on my visit was another native of Flint, and a contemporary of Moore's, Art Wenzlaff. He had been recruited as the director of SABIS's school in Flint some seven years earlier, but was now Director of Community Relations, a position in which he was much more comfortable, totally in his element in fact.

As Michael Moore still is, Art was initially skeptical about charter schools. His background was in community education, working out of a Flint public school to get parents and the communities involved in their children's education; later he moved into the central office administration, mainly involved in parent advocacy. He was doing this work when the charter school movement hit Flint. Art recalls the reaction: "Didn't want you here," he says, "you" being the charter school movement. Given its history, Flint is a very strong union town. "The teacher unions," he said, "played on those heartstrings." The charter schools wouldn't be unionized, which was a "burr in their saddle." Even in the local churches, Art said, the message about charter schools from the pulpit was, "They're taking our kids, taking our money; they're no good; they're the bad guys."

In 2003, the city of Flint was undergoing budget reductions, and Art was let go in June. For four months he was looking for opportunities, but could only find them away from Flint, which he didn't want to leave. Then the Student Life Coordinator, Chris Matheson, and a long-time friend of Art's, tried to interest him in the role of director at SABIS Flint. "He would only visit at night," Chris joked. "I kept trying to get him over; Art would phone and say, 'What are you doing tonight?' and I said, 'Art, its nine o'clock already.'" Art quipped back: "He goes to bed at nine fifteen. This ain't Bart Simpson." But seriously, Art really didn't want to be seen at the school during daylight hours: "I didn't under-stand charters and I'm indoctrinated all my life into a public school district and 'they're taking our kids and we don't like them.'"

Finally he came to the school, learned more about what it was doing, saw it didn't seem to contradict his beliefs about how to help improve the community, and decided to accept the offer. He points out that the school is not like a typical inner-city school: there are no graffiti, no broken windows, no "messed-up doors." Art said: "I think that part of that might be due to the fact that the neighborhood respects us." And that's part of his job description now, to engage with the neighborhood and ensure that the respect goes both ways.

On my last day in Flint, the school had a food distribution session; "Free Food Available at International Academy of Flint," said the flyer. And following this was the "Warm the Children Luncheon" – a free lunch (sandwiches, soup, chili, salads, croissants, pasta, desserts, etc.), provided you brought something with you to "warm the children; any size will do," because "We have school and neighborhood children of all ages with clothing needs – and some will not get toys for Christmas."

As you get to know Art, you get to hear more of his infectious laugh, but also more of his deep involvement with the community, which overwhelms him with emotion when he tells some of his stories. He was wearing a tuxedo and bow tie, dressing up for the luncheon. I felt underdressed beside him. He told me, "I do this for Thanksgiving dinner and this event. It just adds a little something; people like it that you make a special effort for them." Later he would dress up as Santa and give out the presents.

Art is clearly well known in Flint; his years of involvement in the community have made him a key figure whom people turn to when in need. Just before I met him, for instance, he'd been approached by an African-American guy to help him get the bus to Mississippi. The guy is a paraplegic, has prosthetic limbs. "He'd gotten into a fight with his girl-friend," Art said, "and she took his legs and threw them in the street. Now that sounds either funny or ghastly. But this guy's trying to get to his legs and his neighbors see that and they call me." His girlfriend had also stabbed him in the hand, "not severely, thankfully." Eventually, Art got him his bus ticket to Mississippi, where he has family. "It's a grue-some story," he says, "but the point is, we – the SABIS school – really are embedded into this neighborhood."

Being embedded in the community often means going the extra mile for them. One family uses the school showers at night "because they don't have any water and their water bill is thousands ... they've been without water for a long time. I found out about that recently; they've been going around to different homes to shower, so I let them shower here at night." Mother and the kids come to shower at night. As so often, there is no father around.

Art is totally committed to going the extra mile in cases like this: "So those are some of the things that go on here. But by doing that we really are literally building community, building faith in what we do here. And I think we pick up people because of that. Just because the family is poor doesn't mean they don't have good kids that will learn. I think we are in a kind of oasis here for education." It's an oasis with flowers – in the summer it boasts a beautiful flower garden that is tended by Art and student volunteers. "Many stop by and compliment me on the school grounds," he tells me. "Sometimes I invite people to help me tidy up, 'Weed with Wenzlaff,' I call it." As usual, his laugh is infectious and genuine.

We go outside to the food distribution event. In the bitter cold, a line of some three hundred people winds along outside the school. People, black and white, old and young, wait patiently in line to receive a food box from the table, staffed by volunteers from the school. In my work, I'm used to dealing with very poor people, in the slums and villages of

India and sub-Saharan Africa. It was odd here in 21st-century America seeing food parcels given out in this way. Certainly it was very different from what I was used to – the poor people here looked pretty well dressed, for instance. I spoke to a couple of people in the line and they said, "Once you've paid all the bills and filled up the car with gas, there is no money left for food." And Art commented to me, "I carry the food for them to the car, and oftentimes they're not getting in an old beat-up jalopy." In the end, I couldn't quite understand the event; perhaps poverty realizes itself in different ways in different contexts. But I knew it exemplified the heart of the organization and the people within it. Whatever one thinks of this initiative, it is absolutely clear that it comes from the heart of people, like Art, like Kendra, like Traci, in this school. That caring heart of the organization is what I'll always think of when I think about this SABIS charter school in Flint, Michigan.

After Katrina

From Flint, I went down to New Orleans, Louisiana, spending some uncharacteristically cold and wet December days there – Bourbon Street was windswept and quiet; the street jazz musicians sheltering from the rain. The state of Louisiana provides an antidote to the deflation I felt after the description of Springfield 2, the school that never was. Perhaps in Louisiana it may be possible after all for companies like SABIS to make a difference, without the political grief that hits them elsewhere. But even there, it's been a struggle getting to that point, as I'll relate.

My guide in Louisiana was George Saad, the 38-year-old great-grandson of the Reverend Tanios Saad, the co-founder of the village school in Choueifat that evolved into the SABIS global brand.

George is an important figure in American SABIS, now in charge of operations there. In common with each of the cousins in his generation who are active in the company, Victor Saad, and the two Kansou brothers, he's very close to its roots. For his first ten years, George lived in Beirut, and every Sunday his parents would take him to the Saad (extended) family gatherings at the mother school. George's parents traveled a lot, and so he would often stay with his great-uncle and aunt, Charles and Leila Saad, at the school. Over meals and at the Sunday gatherings, the school was always "the talk of the table." The school, George said, "was kind of the center of the family. I grew up in the school basically."

The growing violence of the civil war was sometimes not as troubling to a young boy as it was to adults. When bombs came at night that meant school was going to be canceled the next day. It was just like getting a heavy snowfall in the USA. The boys would go into the bomb shelters and think, "Cool, no school tomorrow."

His parents weren't so sanguine, however. In 1983, troubled by the effect of the deepening civil war, they enrolled George at the new SABIS boarding school just opened in Bath, England. Cousin Victor had earlier been enrolled. George graduated in 1990 and went on to McGill University in Montreal, Canada, graduating in economics. He then signed on for a two-year master's in economics.

In the summer, Mrs Saad and Mr Ralph Bistany asked whether he would go to Bath to work in the summer camp. For George it was a life-changing experience. He spent two months teaching mathematics and also acted as houseparent. "Really," he said, "I just completely got hooked." He returned to Montreal to finish his master's, but now knew that his future lay in the SABIS schools. In September 1996, George closed up his life in Canada and went with Ralph Bistany to Springfield, Massachusetts, to help strengthen their first charter school, which had opened the previous year. George stayed a month, then went on to spend a year in Dubai, being inducted into the range of areas that SABIS was operating in, before returning to the USA, initially for a three-month visit. He's still there thirteen years later.

One of SABIS's charter schools in Louisiana is Linwood Public Charter School, in Shreveport, serving Cedar Grove, one of the poorest and most crime-ridden areas of north Louisiana; in 1988 there were riots there which made international headlines. Gard Wayt, a delightful Southern gentleman, semi-retired from business and very passionate about education, is the chairman of the board of trustees. Shreveport is his adopted hometown. Years previously, he had run for office in the House of Representatives. He's a Democrat, and in those days Democrats typically won in Louisiana, but: "I got caught in a sweep and everyone on the ballot that was elected was a Republican, for the first time in history." He was completely broke as a result of this, so he had gone out and built a business in insurance, "had some amazing success ... At one time I had five offices in three states; traveled all over the country and finally realized that all that travel time was crazy." So he consolidated his offices, took a backseat to his sons in the business, and gave himself more time to give back to the community: "I began to realize that Shreveport will never be what it can be if we don't educate our people."

The school is in a really deprived area: it opened in 2009 and now has 489 students in Grades 6–8; 98 percent of these are African-American and 91 percent are eligible for free or reduced-price lunch. It was Gard's initiative to seek to create a charter school: "I applied for that school because it was available and it was one of the worst, and if you want to do a turnaround then you want to do a turnaround where it's really bad."

He chose SABIS to partner with, after having looked at other groups, including KIPP. He was greatly impressed by KIPP, no question about it. But his need was more urgent: "KIPP builds their school around a person. They hire that person a year ahead of time and they train that person for a year and that's expensive. It would take a couple of years and at least a couple of hundred thousand dollars to even start a KIPP deal. You had to hire that principal ahead of time, send them to a year's training and then build the school around them and recruit the people ahead of time." Gard simply didn't have that time: he was awarded his charter and school in June and wanted to open the school by August. SABIS was able and willing to move as quickly as he needed to. Indeed, SABIS loaned the board a quarter of a million dollars to get started: "They *lent* us the money to get started. We signed a promissory note to be paid back through the proceeds that came from the charter. They put themselves out, they trusted us and we trusted them. So we have developed what we think is a very good working relationship."

Gard is inspired by what he's heard and seen of SABIS Springfield. "They turned the second-worst school in the entire system in Springfield, MA, into a pillar of excellence," he said. But as in Springfield – indeed, as in charter schools all over the country – Gard has come up against the system, which is trying to impede his work: "The school district took a variety of actions to try and draw students away from us. Because they did not want to see charter schools do better than them."

A new superintendent had arrived at the same time as Gard's board was granted the charter. He had come from Saginaw, Michigan, where "he had fought tooth and nail to keep SABIS from succeeding with their school there." The school district was supposed to be providing bussing services for the new charter school. This "has been a nightmare," Gard told me. Linwood had given the district a list of all the students that had applied to the school; the school district then apparently sent all those same students information that they'd been enrolled in other schools. "And when the day came for them to pick up our students at their bus stops, they denied that those students were enrolled with SABIS. So we came probably about 'that close' to suing them, but we got a lot of very favorable publicity on TV stations by objecting to the way they were handling it." They worked it out with the district so that the same "misunderstanding" wouldn't happen again.

But at the start of the second year, just a few months before I met him, there were more problems. This time the start of their term, publicized in advance to the school district, was a couple of days earlier than at the other public schools. The day came. "We found out that the school district drivers were not working that day." But Gard is nothing but resourceful. The board arranged with a local church that had a number of buses to provide emergency cover. And they managed until the school district drivers were working once again.

It's been an incredibly hard first year for the school, he tells me. A failing school like that in such a deprived community takes some time to turn around. "The discipline problems were overwhelming, absolutely overwhelming," Gard said. Fights between kids in the classrooms were "daily occurrences"; teachers were being intimidated to the point where they would become physical. When they had to fire a teacher "because a kid pushed him against a wall and then the teacher lost it," the board decided that they were going to put CCTV cameras into the classrooms. "Time has shown that that was exactly the right thing to do because it has improved the discipline and reduced the number of incidents significantly."

But Gard feels that they have begun the process of starting to improve. People come up to him now and say that they can tell SABIS is making a difference, "without even walking in the school." How so? "Last year, before you took it over, at school closing time, you would not drive down East 70th Street." The kids flocked on to the street, stopping traffic, intimidating and threatening passersby. But today, "now you can drive down that street again. When you drive by, you can't even tell that school is out. They're all going out the back door; they're all getting on the buses; it's orderly." It's true that once a week there is a fight. But last year there was one a day. "Already you can see the discipline showing."

And they've started the process of turning the school around using teachers quickly recruited from whoever was willing to come. Gard stresses this point: it's the SABIS system which is providing the structure that is leading to improvement, not the fact that they've somehow managed to find brilliant teachers out of nowhere. The charter school approval was granted only in June, so they couldn't start recruiting teachers until then. It really was a question of "grabbing for teachers," anyone who was willing to come and work with this new system. That didn't include many of the old Linwood teachers, however. "They were unionized and offered positions elsewhere," reported Gard.

The other SABIS charter school in Louisiana is Milestone SABIS Academy of New Orleans (MSANO). It's in a rented building in a relatively upmarket neighborhood, but the children are bussed in from outside: 96 percent of the 396 students are African-American, and 92 percent eligible for free or reduced-price lunch. There had been a SABIS charter school in New Orleans since 2003, but in effect it was starting all over again after Hurricane Katrina hit in August 2005, just ten days after the school had opened for the new school year.

The school closed for two and a half months. It was the second school to reopen in New Orleans after Katrina, in mid-November 2005. Just eight of the previously enrolled students turned up: the majority of their children had come from the Lower 9th Ward, which was flattened by the hurricane and the flooding aftermath. More than 90 percent of the students had lost their homes and were forced to move out of town.

But the school was going through difficulties – in effect two charter schools had been amalgamated into one by the Board of Elementary and Secondary Education ("BESE" to its friends). But vestiges of the two school boards remained and threatened to tear it apart. BESE was agitating to close the school completely. It was clear to SABIS that only a new school leader could save the situation.

Catherine Boozer was the smart, go-getting deputy director of SABIS's charter school in Arizona at the time. She'd joined SABIS in 2001 as a fourth-grade math and science teacher, and then been rapidly promoted to Academic Quality Coordinator and then deputy director. When she'd come across the methods SABIS were using in the school, it was her eureka moment: "This was exactly what I'd been looking for!" she told me. The methods of "teach-practice-check" and peer learning with prefects in the classroom really impressed her: "I loved the structure of the lessons and the structure of the classroom procedures, being a structured person myself."

In the summer of 2006, Catherine had been invited as one of a select group of Americans to the SABIS annual directors' meeting, held that year in Beirut, Lebanon, to celebrate the 120th anniversary of the mother school's opening. She told her friends she was going to Beirut; they scolded her, saying it was not a safe place to go. Catherine replied, "The same Jesus that is in the United States is in Lebanon! I said I was going and didn't mind, and I'm glad I went." It was her first time in a foreign country: "I had a ball," she said. We'll hear more about that directors' meeting in Chapter 8.

In early 2007, when things were getting particularly desperate in New Orleans, Carl Bistany, president of SABIS, asked whether she would come for three months to be temporary director of the New Orleans school. She seemed a natural choice – her leadership qualities had been noted, and she was a native of Louisiana, so would understand something of the politics and environment. She arrived on 4 March 2007, with the goal of returning to Arizona in June. But she soon got a sense of the "political ripples" that were about to close in on the school. Catherine Boozer chose to stay and fight.

A letter arrived indicating that BESE was going to close the school with immediate effect. Catherine Boozer took the bait. SABIS quickly hired lawyers in Baton Rouge, the Louisiana state capital. All schools were accountable for year-on improvement. But if a school had suffered severely because of the hurricane, then it could be allowed to start again – the post-Katrina year's performance would not be evaluated against past years. One of the criteria was that if a school lost more than 75 percent of its student population then it could start afresh. SABIS had lost 92 percent, so that certainly qualified them. Somehow the Board of Education had disregarded this in its notice to close the school down.

So SABIS sued. Catherine Boozer and George Saad went back and forth to Baton Rouge to meet with their lawyers and prepare the case against BESE and to attend board meetings whenever their school was on the agenda. Eventually, the process led to a mediation which took the form of a court trial, held in the Department of Education. The case didn't get far. As the first day got underway, Linda Johnson, the board president, became increasingly puzzled by the case that was brought before her. After an hour or so, she asked for the hearing to be adjourned, and came across to speak to George Saad and the SABIS lawyers, who agreed to let the case drop in exchange for a commitment to finding a way to work together.

A further twist in the story was that at that time in the state of Louisiana, charters were granted for a minimum of five years, but then when renewal came up, it was for ten years or nothing. Given the perceived mood of BESE as regards SABIS, they were reluctant to reapply under these conditions – fearing that the ten-year-or-nothing clause would lead to SABIS getting nothing. Coincidentally, however, at the same time a local politician was championing a bill in the house that would make the rigid ten-year renewal more flexible. This was signed in by the governor and allowed SABIS to reapply with more confidence.

SABIS was eventually granted a three-year renewal, and within those three years its performance started climbing. When the school reopened after Katrina, 52.7 percent of students were performing at grade level or above. By the time BESE allowed the school to renew its charter, its score was 61.9 percent. The following year it was 74.3 percent, in 2010 76.3 percent.

As the three of us had dinner together in St Charles Street, and the bass and piano duo supplemented their jazz standards with arrangements of Christmas carols, George Saad filled in the details – emphasizing the pivotal role that Catherine Boozer played in changing BESE's ideas: Catherine made a "personal connection with every BESE member in Baton Rouge." Right up until the point where they wanted to shut down the school, "not one of those board members had been to the school. Really what Catherine was brilliant at doing – I have her on my phone listed as Senator Boozer – she made that connection with every single board member and had them come to the school, sit in on classrooms, really put a face to this name. Now everybody knows her up there."

Catherine Boozer would go every month to the BESE board meeting, "working the floor." She tried to meet with the very influential appointed (i.e. not elected) board member Leslie Jacobs, who was clearly an important source of dissatisfaction with SABIS. It's not clear on what grounds. "Ms Jacobs, I'd really like us to have a meeting," Catherine said. Leslie replied: "No, I don't want to meet with you." "But Ms Jacobs," said Catherine, "I'm the new kid on the block." And a few months later, said Catherine, "Guess who was sitting right in my school? Leslie Jacobs."

Now Louisiana is one of the most favorable charter school states in America, post-Katrina. The state recognized that the only way to rebuild their education system was to bring in school choice and allow favorable terms for education management organizations like SABIS to provide alternatives. Louisiana is attractive for charters; it has great needs. It is one of the lowest-performing states in the country, academically.

George drove me to Baton Rouge to meet with Linda Johnson, who had played such an important role in the SABIS saga and was now influential in the more positive environment for charter schools.

Linda Johnson is a wonderfully practical, down-to-earth woman. With a degree in microbiology, for 28 years she was human resources supervisor for a chemical company. She's now retired, spending time raising her grandchildren. She has a direct manner of speaking, but can be warm and friendly, with a ready chuckle. Importantly, she showed what I was struggling to find in Springfield, Massachusetts – that it is possible to go from being very skeptical about an organization like SABIS based on genuine worries to being excited about the organization based on empirical evidence of performance and approach. On this level, meeting her provided exactly the more optimistic antidote that I needed to counter the Springfield 2 experience.

In 1999 Linda Johnson was elected to BESE. As in Springfield, there were two charter school management organizations looking for contracts, Edison and SABIS. She looked at both, but was worried about the tremendous amount of negative publicity that Edison was having in the media. And she was concerned that most of SABIS's experience seemed to be outside of the United States, and in elite private schools at that. She wasn't convinced that they'd really understand the difficulties of working with poor urban populations in Louisiana. In short, "I wasn't supportive of them."

But Linda Johnson is not someone who is bigoted or prejudiced. Nor were SABIS the kind of people to give up easily. "They were very persistent; they sent me information a lot, and I'm the kind of person who will look at the information and try and make a decision based on the information. And the information kept getting better and better." She began to see that SABIS's school in Flint, Michigan, was beginning to deliver great results, with populations not that dissimilar to those in Louisiana. So Linda Johnson began to look at SABIS a bit differently. She came to realize that "undoubtedly what they were doing in their more affluent model could carry over to the less affluent. That's what I've seen."

Linda Johnson reaffirmed what I'd heard about Catherine Boozer's persistence: "They must train their people to be 'in your face' people because she just would not leave me alone." In the end, Linda went to see the school. "You know, I really went; I spent a whole day. Looking at the program, the academic program. Talking to the teachers, talking to the students, trying to really get a feel of what was going on there. And I was impressed. And so, I gradually grew to like the SABIS model. And I really like it."

What does she like about it? First, she likes the fact that SABIS is engaged in "formative" assessments, "to see where the children are almost on a weekly basis, so they know how to intervene with those kids." That's a great innovation that isn't in place in many schools. Because they get this formative data, "They know what needs to happen. I do like that."

Secondly, she likes the discipline model too: "I think they have a really good way of dealing with discipline. Once they set up the discipline model in the school, the teachers and the students seem to understand it and to follow it. That seems to be a big help."

The third point is related to this: because the discipline model seems to work, she really likes the fact that no children get expelled and few suspended. "In most of our schools in Louisiana children are suspended, expelled, suspended, expelled. You know, kind of frequently. But that was not happening at Milestone SABIS at all." This reaffirmed what I'd found in Flint and Springfield: "Parents really don't like being called to the school, to take care of minor kinds of infractions, so they have a really good model for the way they are. It's so different from the public schools, and different from other charter schools too."

In fact, Linda Johnson says, "I judge when a charter school is doing what it says it's going to do by one criterion – that the children who entered in September are the children who finished in May. Because if all you're doing is entering kids and taking them out, then to me you're wasting my time." In other words, she's not interested in schools that make great claims about their performance based on their ability to expel children who are not up to scratch or to otherwise encourage children to leave. Only if you can show that you kept children for the whole year, "then to me you're doing something worthy with those kids." In New Orleans, she says, it's been a huge issue with a number of charter schools, "the suspensions and expulsions and canceling out. That did not happen with Milestone SABIS."

She elaborates on what she sees as a very important point. She knows what parents are like in the predominantly African-American community that Milestone SABIS is serving: "If you're a parent raising a child, there are a number of things that you don't want. You don't want them calling you to the school every week. You really don't want to do that. You don't want anybody telling you this program is not for your child, you need to move them. Because if it's in your neighborhood that's where you want the child to be. Or if you put the child there for whatever reason, that's where you want the child to be." The data for Milestone SABIS show very low turnover; only 1 or 2 percent of students who enroll at the beginning of the year are not there at the end of the year – the same as I saw in Springfield. "So I was very impressed by that as well," she tells me. "How they seem to just try and try and try again. To avoid even suspending or expelling a child." Exactly the impression I got from Flint and Springfield. "Well, it's crucial to your education. Because if you're not there, you can't learn. It's crucial. I'm very impressed with that."

Perhaps swayed by similar evidence, BESE has gone from being dead against charter schools to having the six votes required (out of eleven) to approve further charter school applications. That was the first piece of good news Linda Johnson conveyed. Another was that Milestone SABIS will get an automatic renewal this time, "unless something serious happens. I don't see them being in any danger because they have just done really tremendous work at that school." Another was to confirm that Louisiana no longer has a cap on the number of charter schools that can operate, so theoretically there's no upper limit on the number of charter schools that a company like SABIS could operate there.

Moreover, Louisiana operates what they call a "Recovery School District" (RSD). Schools will be graded A, B, C, D, and F according to their performance on standardized state tests. Schools graded F are allocated to the RSD, which can either directly manage them, or allow them to become charter schools, managed by organizations like SABIS. Linda Johnson thought that there might be 81 schools put into the RSD, theoretically available for charter status. "It's going to be a lot of schools," she says.

The downside of this, the only bit of bad news I heard from Linda Johnson, is that the appetite for charter schools doesn't extend below BESE. "Of the seventy-one districts in our state, I don't believe any of them would say we are out here seeking charter schools." All of them would try to block them. This news was reinforced by the fact that SABIS's second application for a charter school in Shreveport by Gard Wayt's board had just been turned down. Linda Johnson was clear that there would still be an uphill struggle in the school districts.

It was a strangely perplexing few weeks in America. My overwhelming sense was of an organization, SABIS, committed to improving lives in really difficult conditions, always keen to go to the most difficult places, such as Shreveport, New Orleans, Flint, and Springfield; yet at every turn, this organization was seemingly being thwarted by politics, by vested-interested groups.

In the end, I felt an extraordinary respect for the organization and the people within it – I really felt it my duty to catalog how SABIS is making a difference in places like these, with people like those, which I've tried to do in these two chapters. George Saad put it succinctly: "It's almost like a challenge to us, to prove a point that every child can learn when they are given the proper learning environment. If the proper structure, the proper building blocks are in place, then they can learn. They can succeed, whatever social and economic demographic they're from."

I was pleased, but not surprised, to hear him say that. But something really did surprise me. At every SABIS school I visited, several of the senior teachers and administrators literally welled up, tears in their eyes, with pride in or concern about some of their children; very consistently there was a message of caring, love, family, in each of the schools. I wasn't expecting this; I was expecting a professionalized, successful international organization doing good work; I wasn't expecting to find so much *caring*, so much heart.

But on the other hand, I didn't know what to make of those who were always trying to get in the way of change, the forces of conservatism, as Tony Blair might have called them – the school districts, those in the school boards opposed to change, the unions. I felt that it seemed all too difficult, too much of an effort for so little *acknowledgment*, let alone reward. In New Orleans SABIS had been thwarted by nature, in the shape of the devastation of Hurricane Katrina. They'd got over that. A combination of human ingenuity, effort and resources, motivated by a desire to care for children in need, made sure they were able to create a school again out of Katrina's ruins. Getting over Katrina, challenging though it was, seemed much more manageable than getting over state and union politics elsewhere.

I put some of these thoughts to George Saad as he drove me in the rental car back from Baton Rouge, after we'd met with Linda Johnson in the government offices. We drove on the completely straight highway, raised above the swamps and marshes that stretched to the horizon, skirting a massive lake. George was surprisingly philosophical – again and again I have been impressed by how the twin families are sanguine in the face of these kinds of adversities; again I wondered how much this had to do with growing up and learning to survive in an environment like that of Lebanon during the civil war.

He smiled when I told him I got an odd feeling going into the Department of Education building in Baton Rouge. It's in a pleasant enough government park, with expansive lakes and clumps of mature trees, but the government buildings seemed cold and imposing, impenetrable. As we walked up the steps, the cold wind seemed to whistle through us. He confessed that he too got a shiver every time he went to the Department of Education in Baton Rouge. For him, it brought back memories of the meeting after meeting leading up to the trial hearing that he'd had to endure to ensure the survival of Milestone SABIS Academy. But the memory of the trial hearing was strongest.

The members of the board, BESE, were sitting six feet above him, as if in a Senate hearing, looking down on him both literally and metaphorically, he felt. George was alone with his lawyer. The details of the hearing seemed weighty; he felt stuck. Then suddenly he felt calm. They would get over this little hiccup. Sitting on the bench beside him, he felt the serene presence of the Reverend Tanios Saad, and Charles Saad too. And he felt: we're in this together, and we've been in it together for a long time. There's a bigger picture. What we are doing together is much greater than this, working to change the lives of so many children, in the most difficult places in America and the world. We'll pull through.

Remembering that feeling of serenity, as we drove into the outer suburbs of New Orleans, past the Louisiana Superdome, home of the New Orleans Saints football team, he told me a story from Lebanon. The Reverend Tanios Saad had a daughter, Venus – the children called her Nisa – who never married. She lived with her brother Charles and Leila Saad in the family home at the mother school. She was a great favorite with the youngsters – indeed, George always used to seek her out when he was back in Lebanon, right up until she died in 2003 at the age of 90. It was she who told George how his great-grandfather, the Reverend Tanios Saad, always had this air of serenity around him. Every evening at dusk, she told the young George, Tanios Saad liked to sit on his balcony at Choueifat, surveying the majestic sweep beneath him, of the olive groves extending all the way down to the Mediterranean, watching the magnificent sun set in the azure blue of the great sea. Drawing on his hookah, contemplating the vastness of the world, he would tell Venus, "When you let your vision stretch so that there is nothing blocking you save the horizon, then your mind can stretch out too." Every evening contemplating the vastness of the sea between the lands, he would let his mind become clear and uncluttered, so that he could see the things that really mattered.

The story helped George through the trial hearings in Baton Rouge. There's a bigger picture. SABIS has been doing something for 125 years now and is empowered to continue the vision of its founders, to make a difference through education in the world's difficult places. Things will get in the way of that vision; there will be distractions and obstructions. But unclutter your mind and the vision will continue. The story has stayed with him and continues to motivate and inspire him to this day.

CHAPTER 6

A school fit for Hêro

Up in the air

The president of SABIS, Carl Bistany, is a tall, slim man in his mid-fifties, with gray-white, neatly flowing hair and a fine white beard and mustache. In 1996, Carl had joined SABIS at the age of exactly 40. His father, Ralph Bistany, and Mrs Saad had invited him to join the company because, as we shall see in Chapter 12, they were keen to ensure the company's continuity. Bringing in family members seemed an attractive way forward.

Carl himself, like all the family members who eventually joined, had graduated from the mother school in Choueifat. His mother was French, and his grandfather was a prominent French doctor working in Lebanon who had wanted his first grandson to go to a French school, so this is what Carl did initially. But he didn't thrive there. So his father, Ralph, director of the mother school, switched his son to Choueifat, where he began to prosper. Carl went on to the American University of Beirut, graduating with a BA in mathematics. He started a master's degree in mathematics there too in 1975, but the civil war put an end to that. In 1977 he left for Syracuse State University of New York, taking two master's degrees in mathematics and computer science in 1979. But he didn't feel inclined to return home then: "Lebanon was often inaccessible, the airport closed; we had all kinds of challenges in the country. I ended up in the Emirates." This is where he successfully ran a computer business for seventeen years, building it up to be one of the largest computer companies in the Emirates, until he joined SABIS.

Carl had grown up in the school and seen the belief and passion and drive of his father and Mr and Mrs Saad. It was – and is – the drive of "making sure we are helping the world become a better place." Mrs Saad and Ralph Bistany wanted to involve individuals from the family "who would carry the torch, carry the passion, carry the mission of the ancestors." Pretty soon Carl became infected: "This drive, this belief in what they were doing – Mrs Saad and my father were able to pass on to me. And I hope that I will be able to pass it on to others."

It's a drive that sends them to serve children in difficult places. Perhaps, Carl muses, it comes from the wars they've lived through – "these difficulties that gave us strength of character and resolve." The adversity that they have been through – "you can have everything one day and nothing the next" – is bound to sharpen you, to "deepen your resolve," he says. And it also deepens your understanding of the need for education as the key to survival through adversity. Carl says: "When my father had to leave Lebanon during the civil war, he didn't take with him the buildings or any physical assets. He took with him his mind only."

One of the "difficult places" where SABIS is involved is Iraq, specifically Kurdistan in northern Iraq.

At around 4 a.m. on the morning of 12 May 2007, Carl Bistany was on a Royal Jordanian flight from Beirut, via Amman, to Erbil, capital of Kurdistan in northern Iraq. He'd been to Kurdistan several times and was looking forward to seeing again the school that SABIS had opened nine months earlier, in this country so recently ravaged by war.

The "Fasten Seat Belt" sign was on, the efficient air stewardess had made all the correct preparations for landing, and the plane was making its descent into Erbil airport. Instead of landing, however, the plane banked steeply, climbed again, circled the city, and then descended for another approach. Carl was not unduly worried. He is a frequent flier – indeed, he is a life-time platinum member of KLM/Air France, an honor he achieved after earning over one million air miles.

When you fly so much, you're aware that these things happen from time to time. The plane came in for a second attempt. Again, however, it banked at the last minute, climbed steeply, and circled the city. This time Carl exchanged glances with the passenger next to him. Is something wrong? Has there been a coup? Have terrorists taken over the airport?

The third attempt was also unsuccessful. The captain came on the intercom. In his polished, reassuring voice, he told them that, contrary to impressions, nothing indeed was unusual about what was happening. For "operational" reasons they had been diverted to Baghdad. Carl's neighbor raised his eyebrows: "Baghdad?" he said. "Why couldn't they return to Amman?" The air stewardess was less inhibited than her captain: "There were no lights on, the runway was in darkness. The control tower was not answering. We don't have enough fuel to get back to Amman, so that's why it's Baghdad."

Flying into Baghdad at that time would have troubled even the most seasoned of travelers. Only recently insurgents had used surface-to-air heat-seeking missiles to destroy aircraft coming into land at the airport. Who was to say that they might not yet try it again? If you successfully landed, you then faced the challenge of the airport road, dubbed "Death Street." Apparently you could hire an armored car from the airport to the city for over $2,000 one way, possibly the most expensive airport cab ride anywhere in the world. Once in Baghdad, suicide bombers were a constant threat. Just the day before Carl's trip, car bombs on bridges across the River Tigris had killed a dozen people.

To be redirected to Baghdad, in short, must have been unsettling for anyone. Carl had by now convinced his wife that flying into Erbil, Kurdistan, was safe enough. But Baghdad? The flight to Baghdad was brief; but there was plenty enough time for Carl to reflect on what he was doing in Iraq, and why SABIS had come here.

***

It made perfect sense that SABIS had been one of the first outside education providers to come to Iraq to help the people rebuild after the ravages of war. For SABIS, the education company that had evolved out of a village school just outside Beirut, Lebanon, knew about rebuilding after wars more than any other group.

The initial contact from Iraq came in 2003. A friend of Carl's, a man of Kurdish origin who lived in Lebanon, heard through the grapevine that a party from the Ministry of Education were scouting the Middle East for private education providers to come to Kurdistan. The Kurds met with Ralph Bistany and Mrs Leila Saad, then 71 and 76 years old, respectively. The Kurdish visitors had been overwhelmed by what they'd seen and heard: "You *must* come to Erbil and start a school there," they said.

Father and son, Ralph and Carl, and Mrs Saad, discussed it earnestly, but the images from CNN were not encouraging. After the fall of Saddam Hussein on 9 April 2003, Iraq had witnessed horrifying atrocities from within, atrocities which extended to Kurdistan: around the time of the visit, for instance, on 10 September 2003, a suicide car bomb attack in Erbil had killed three and injured 45. Of course, they had grown sadly accustomed to this kind of violence in Lebanon. But could they really afford to risk the lives of their own people again? And yet, and yet ... Ralph Bistany couldn't stop thinking about the idea. Ralph is a student of world history. He knew the history of the Kurds, the mountain people who for so long had been denied a state of their own, who had suffered injustice after injustice. "Can't we do something for them?" he asked.

Mrs Saad said no. Carl Bistany thought no too. Ralph shrugged. They let it rest for a bit.

But the Kurds didn't let it rest. The team reported back to the minister of education, Abdulaziz Taib. When he heard all they had to tell him about the school and the company, it became absolutely clear in his own mind: we have to get them to Kurdistan. He could see clearly that the company would understand their situation and needs. And the company also had a record of serving children in difficult places, not least Lebanon during and immediately after their own civil war. He wanted them to help him build his own country.

In 2005, the minister of education himself went to meet with SABIS. He explained how they were positively rebuilding their country, and how important education was to this process. He told them that everyone, up to and including the prime minister, Nechirvan Idris Barzani, wanted them to come. Indeed, Mr Barzani was later to tell Carl that he had four projects that he wanted for Kurdistan: an international airport, a power plant, a first-class hospital, and an international school. "With these four," he said, "I'm going to be able to tell all the Kurds who left during the Saddam era: 'Come back and help me rebuild the country.'" "In any case," the minister of education continued, "you don't have to commit now. Just come and visit. And you'll see it is safe now."

That was in July 2005. But by then, nowhere seemed particularly safe. In early July there had been suicide bombs in London, on the Tube and buses, which had killed 56 people (including the four suicide bombers) and injured around seven hundred. Later the same month, the Egyptian resort of Sharm el-Sheikh was attacked by terrorists, who killed 88 people and injured over two hundred. And on Valentine's Day, 14 February, the former Lebanese prime minister, Rafiq Hariri, had been assassinated, setting off a series of bombings across Beirut which lasted throughout the summer. And, of course, in Iraq itself, numerous suicide bombers were killing innocent people day after day.

It didn't feel like the right time to go, thought Mrs Saad. But she saw that look in Ralph Bistany's eyes, the sparkle when he has made up his mind to do something, and knew that she would be on the losing side. "I won't let Carl go," she said protectively.

"No," Ralph said, "Carl will not go." Was this the end of it? "No, *I* will go."

Mrs Saad didn't want to lose Ralph either. She thought he was taking a big risk. But she knew she could do nothing about it.

***

For his scouting trip, Ralph Bistany went with Elie Sawaya, his right-hand man, whom we met in Sharjah. They flew out from Dubai as, at the time, there were no flights from Beirut to Erbil.

The effect on Ralph was almost immediate. From what he saw on that first visit, he committed the company to open a school in Kurdistan, without even discussing it further with Mrs Saad. He talked about his decision later: "I saw Kurdistan in a state that was appalling. I cannot describe the way I felt. I fell in love with Kurdistan and knew immediately we had to help." Part of his induction was being shown places that had been part of the province's gruesome history: "They showed me the only bakery, the huge bakery that was owned by Saddam. They explained to me that when he was angry he closed it. Nobody else was allowed to make bread."

His hosts took him to see some of their public schools. "What they had achieved with the limited means at their disposal when these schools were started was commendable. The children were sweet and very eager to learn in spite of the fact that the schools left a lot to be desired. My hosts were very eager to raise the standards and to raise them fast."

When he came to leave, the airport was busy, and his flight was delayed for around eight hours. His hosts sat with him all the time. Ralph said, "Please go, I can wait with Elie." They said, "No, we are happy to be at the airport." Ralph asked them what was so pleasant. One of them said, "You know, we are enjoying the fact that when we hear an airplane we don't run and hide. We don't have to fear poison gases. It's nice being here and watching the planes in comfort."

Ralph felt terrible. "The Kurds," he reflected later, "were coming out of very hard times and they wanted to progress. They had been treated unfairly by the world for a long time. And I have a lot of sympathy for these people, I don't like injustice. I felt convinced that SABIS could help put this right."

***

The captain's voice came over the intercom again: "Cabin crew, prepare for landing." Although no aircraft had been targeted coming into Baghdad International Airport for a while, precautionary measures were still deemed necessary. The aircraft descended using the 'corkscrew maneuver," starting the descent higher than usual and taking ever lower and narrower spirals down towards the runway to minimize the time spent within range of rocket-propelled grenades. Everyone was immensely relieved when this uncomfortable maneuver ended and they had landed safely. The plane taxied to the gate and waited for news. Finally, the captain came on the intercom: "Well," he said, his cheerfulness now overcoming his stiff professionalism, "problem solved. It seems that the person in the Erbil control tower had fallen asleep and forgot to put the runway lights on. They've woken him up, given him a good dressing down, and the lights are back on now. After refueling, we'll be on our way. Thank you for your patience." Carl eventually landed at a brightly lit Erbil airport at 7:30 a.m., just in time for the school day to begin.

Hêro's story

From a very young age, Hêro had been encouraged to dream.

She is the youngest of twelve children, with six brothers and five sisters. Her closest sibling is a brother, five years older than her. He had been born just three months before the March 1991 uprisings in Iraq. In the aftermath of the first Gulf War, sensing that Saddam Hussein's power was waning, the Kurds in the north of Iraq rose up against the regime that had oppressed them for so long (as did the Shias in the south). Behind the scenes there seemed to be encouragement from the United States. During March, the people took over all the major Kurdish cities. But on 29 and 30 March, the rebellion was quashed; the Iraqi Republican Guard brutally returned, executing on the spot anyone suspected of colluding with the opposition. Perhaps 1.5 million Kurds, one fifth of the entire population, fled for their lives.

The father took his wife and eleven children, including their new, three-month-old baby, and all the possessions they could muster, and joined the throng of people fleeing Saddam Hussein's murderous regime. They left their home in Erbil and made their way across the mountains into Iran. Although officially spring, it was cold and terribly wet, the muddy road crowded with desperate people, walking, or on donkeys, or crammed into the backs of trucks or tractor trailers. Saddam Hussein sent helicopter gunships to fire on the fleeing columns; his aircraft dropped phosphorus bombs. Many Kurds were killed. Every night they went to sleep believing it might be their last.

After three months, the USA and its allies set up a "no fly" zone across Kurdistan to stop these airborne atrocities. The refugees slowly began to return home. By October 1991, the Iraqi forces had left altogether, creating a de facto Kurdish state in the north of Iraq. Could the Kurds, so long without a home of their own, now build a nation?

The family returned to their home in Zanyary, a working-class district of Erbil. Their home was damaged, but not beyond repair. In this time of relative peace and optimism, the family had one last child. They named their daughter, born in December 1996, after the beautiful red and pink flower that blossoms in late winter in the mountains of Kurdistan, *hêro*.

Five-year-old Hêro started public school in September 2002. The school, "Naz Naz," was fine; the teachers turned up and taught regularly, unlike in many other schools in the area. And although operating on a shift pattern, the school was usually open for the whole four-hour session, again unlike other schools, which might operate only from 8 a.m. to 11 or even 10 a.m. Hêro's father was a janitor at another public school, and he told her horror stories of teachers who weren't committed at all; her older brothers and sisters told her likewise. Classes were very crowded – there were 67 in Hêro's class. If children were naughty, they would get beaten; if, as smart, quiet and diligent kids like Hêro, they could work on their own, they could flourish.

Toward the end of her first year in school, in March 2003, the second Gulf War erupted. As the allied forces led by the Americans prepared to invade Iraq, and Saddam Hussein's elite forces prepared to fight back, Hêro's parents wondered whether they should flee again into the mountains, to Iran or Turkey. Many Kurds did leave their homes, but in the end Hêro's father decided they would stay put. Their celebrations for Newroz, the Kurdish New Year, on 21 March, were low key: in awe they watched their television as rockets fell on Baghdad. Occasionally there would be fighter jets screaming noisily overhead; older people would all rush nervously for cover. After Baghdad fell on 9 April and all those who had fled returned to Erbil, Hêro felt full of hope. Spring had begun, new life was emerging and with it their new history could begin.

Hêro began to love learning, and she would work very hard to achieve the highest rank in her class. Her father began noticing her passion for education and would always encourage her with her home-work, although he himself was illiterate, as was her mother. She felt very privileged to be in a good public school. She shared her dream with her father: when she grew up she'd like to help children who couldn't get such a good education as she could.

In the heat of the summer of 2006, during the three-month-long school holidays, something happened which threatened to upset the family equilibrium. Hêro was at home, helping her mother in the kitchen. There was a knock at the door: it was her public school direc-tor. She had good news for the family. She told them SABIS, an edu-cation company from Lebanon, was opening a new, international, private school in Erbil in September 2006. There would be teachers from America, from Britain and Australia, from Lebanon too. The school would have all the top facilities, no expense would be spared. The prime minister himself, Nechirvan Idris Barzani, had personally persuaded SABIS, she said, to open this school in Kurdistan, to help it rebuild after the war. And Mr Barzani wanted the school to be open not just to the rich and privileged, but to all children in Kurdistan, to fami-lies like Hêro's. He'd created scholarships for less privileged children. Each public school had had to nominate their top children. A commit-tee had selected from these names, making sure that it was only the less privileged who were put forward, to take the scholarship exam. One of those chosen was Hêro.

When her father came home from work, he was thrilled. With this really great education, he said, she could live her dream of helping her people and her country. Hêro took the exam with over one hundred children crowded into the temporary premises of the new school. She sailed through the mathematics part of the exam; although the questions were in English, and she was used to questions in Kurdish, she managed to grasp what most of them were about, and found them easy to solve. The English part was more or less impossible. Yes, they studied English as a subject at her current school, but it was an open secret that none of the teachers could speak any English, and their comprehension was very limited. Nevertheless, at the end of the exam, Hêro felt she'd done well enough. Surely, she reasoned, the new school wouldn't expect her to do well at something she'd never really learned, like English, provided she was excelling at things she had, like mathematics? Her father agreed. He was confident that his little daughter would get through all right.

Indeed, that was the way it turned out, although it may have been a closer-run thing than Hêro and her family realized at the time.

***

Thirty-year-old Raed Mahmoud was Lebanese and had studied mechanical aviation in Beirut. He'd begun work in that area but had become disenchanted, feeling that he wanted something more meaningful for his life. One evening, he was having dinner with a neighbor, who told him about SABIS, and how it was looking for new talent. Like most young Lebanese, Raed had heard great things about the SABIS "mother school." Perhaps they could provide the meaning he was looking for in his life? He started working with SABIS in the Gulf. Impressed by Raed's diligence and creative leadership, Carl Bistany had told him about the new operation about to start in Kurdistan. There was no pressure. "Just go, check it out. See if you like it," Carl said. If not, there was always work for him elsewhere. But from his first visit, Raed had been sold on the place. He could see a huge potential to make a difference. He could see people who were thirsty for education, who appreciated all that they could bring and offer. Kurdistan was a place where he could "make a new story." His wife agreed, and they moved together in 2006.

One of the children that Raed immediately saw as part of that "new story" in Kurdistan was Hêro. Fortunately, he'd decided to look through all the applications and test results himself, including those from children who hadn't made it. Hêro's had been rejected because she had scored zero in English. But her math mark was the highest of all the applicants. He personally interviewed her and accepted her on the strength of her character and determination. She would need extra help with her English, but that could easily be arranged.

Hêro was offered a place at the new International School of Choueifat, to start in September 2006. Hers was one of 92 scholarships. Over five hundred had applied.

Not everyone was happy now, though. The director of her public school came around to the family home again. She told Hêro's father and mother she was now having misgivings. Hêro would be sorely missed at the public school. And would she really make it in the new private school, with the sons and daughters of the privileged? Would they appreciate her special talents, or would she disappear from view? "*Berd le cêgay xoyda qurs tire*," she cautioned ("A rock is heavier in its own resting place"; a person will be much better valued among her own people than among those she doesn't know). Hêro's father retaliated, "*Zanetîyê sivik, barê giran*" ("Light wisdom, heavy burden"; it pays to be better educated). Naz Naz was a good school, of course, but look at Hêro's older siblings. One had recently graduated and he hadn't yet been able to find employment. "He's just sitting around at the house," her father said. If Hêro can graduate from the new private school, then she can get a degree from a great university and be properly employed thereafter. Then her burdens will be light.

Hêro's first two weeks were terrible. She cried after her first day at school. Her mother was very disappointed that SABIS had insisted that Hêro repeat Grade 4, rather than continue on to Grade 5 as she would have done at the public school. What a waste of a year for her bright daughter! And the school hours were so much longer – until 3:30 p.m. in the afternoon, rather than 12 noon. And Hêro was also required to attend school on Thursday (then the first day of the weekend) for a couple of hours to learn English. When would she ever see her daughter? Her daughter was so sad, crying all the time, clearly tired and worn out. Mother decided that they would withdraw her from the SABIS school.

Without telling Hêro, her father went to the school and told the administrative assistant, "I want to take my daughter away from the school." The office staff tried to dissuade him, but he was not to be moved. The next day he came back with his wife: "She's going to waste a whole year, by repeating Grade Four. That's very insulting to us and to her, wasting her time. We want to remove her," said her mother.

This time the staff made an appointment with Raed Mahmoud, and her father came back the next day. Raed pointed out that it would be advantageous to her to learn English well and repeat that year. That they were really keen on helping her, that she was very much the kind of child they wanted in the school, but the family would have to believe in them. Raed explained that she would soon get into the routine of the school, and that the education she could get there was second to none. The father didn't look convinced. Finally Raed said, "The prime minister himself has given this scholarship. Do you want to refuse this generous offer from him personally?" The father said he would discuss this with his wife. He came back a fourth time and said, "It's okay, keep her. She can stay."

For two weeks, Hêro was upset. She felt bad about her old friends and her old school. One day, very early on, she started crying in class, because she didn't know anyone and felt lonely and isolated. Suddenly, everyone in the class seemed to be surrounding her, asking her to stop crying, telling her that they were her friends. The teacher was there too; and suddenly, she felt less alone and much better.

Over the next few months, Hêro was to realize that she had been accepted into a quite remarkable school. There were many differences that all the children noticed, whether they'd been to posh private schools before or just to the public schools. It was clearly part of a much larger system, with distinctive ways of learning that set it apart from all other schools that the children had experienced. Hêro had to learn this new system. So did the new staff too.

Flattening the plain

Dr Humaira Bokhari, the new director of the school, arrived at the SABIS campus in Kurdistan at 4 a.m. on 16 August 2008. She had flown directly to Erbil from Milwaukee, USA, via Paris and Amman.

On 31 July, just two weeks earlier, she had been for her interview with SABIS. She was from Pakistan, a Muslim who as a child had gone to Catholic school (so she could recite, among other things, the gospel of Luke by heart). Moving to the United States with her young family, she had soon become, in turn, principal of a Catholic, an Islamic, then a Pentecostal school, all in Milwaukee. Meanwhile, she gained her PhD through distance education from the University of Hawaii. One of her friends was looking for a job in Pakistan and heard about the SABIS school in Lahore. She told her that SABIS's motto was "Students will not be allowed to fail in peace." This caught Dr Bokhari's attention, fitting in with her passion for education and her "no excuses" philosophy. Herself interested in new challenges, she saw that SABIS was also advertising for the director of a new charter school in Phoenix, Arizona. Her husband didn't like Milwaukee very much, and they both felt the south-west would offer a pleasant change, certainly a more agreeable climate.

Returning from the interview she told her husband that she'd been offered a position with SABIS. "That's good news," he congratulated her. "Yes," she continued, "in Kurdistan, northern Iraq. Starting in two weeks." Her husband told her to quit joking. But she wasn't. During the interview SABIS had become convinced that Dr Bokhari was the right person to lead the new school in Kurdistan and had persuaded her that here was a place where her skills and experience could make a huge difference. Here was a place that had been a war zone; the children needed a person like her who cared for their futures. The country desperately needed something like SABIS too: there was a large and skilled Kurdish diaspora, eager and ready to return to their motherland, but deterred by the lack of good schooling. International companies wanted to set up in Kurdistan too, but were finding it difficult to persuade their employees to move, again because there was nowhere for the children to attend school. With SABIS's school opened, this roadblock had been removed. Now the school needed someone like her as director. Should she take up their offer?

She asked her sons. They said: "Mom, do you want to do this?" They knew her passion for education, her desire to make a difference in the world. They heard her reasons, and said, "Go. You've cared for us all the time, Baba can look after himself."

***

It was getting light; Dr Bokhari took a walk around the campus that was to be her home. Already it was incredibly hot, 45 degrees Centigrade. The campus was spectacular. The buildings were new, modern and spacious. There was a magnificent play area, two swimming pools (one almost Olympic size, another for the little ones). The gym looked incredibly well equipped. There was a huge computer lab, science labs, an extensive library. Her own accommodation was comfortable and spacious. Already it seemed like the correct decision to have made. When she met the first children, then she knew it was absolutely the right place for her to be. And parents and children alike appreciated her coming. When she took over, there were 420 students who had been in the temporary campus in Erbil. A month after she arrived, in September 2008, there were 780 students. The total was to grow to 1,400 students by 2010 and to 2,000 a year later.

Dr Bokhari quickly decided that she would make no distinction between different types of students at the school. Whether a child was on a prime minister's scholarship and from a humble background, like Hêro, or from the prime minister's family itself, they were all checked to see whether they had clean and tidy shoes, no matter who they were.

But there was so much to learn about the SABIS way of doing things. She, like Hêro, was learning about a system that had been developed over a long period and had been adopted in many countries around the world.

The structure of the lessons was noticeably different for a start. The teachers were working from a "pacing chart," centrally produced in the SABIS system, from which "points" were derived that guided each lesson. These four or five points were written by the teacher on the side of the whiteboard, enabling all in the class to follow the structure of what was being taught and learned. Any member of the academic support teams could also see immediately where the lesson was going. The "points" were the things that children would be expected to learn in the class that lesson, with the teacher explaining the concept, getting children to practice it, then testing in their groups whether it had been learned.

Teachers in the classroom were supported by three kinds of experts within the school – and these support structures were replicated across the regions and globally. One of these is the "AQCs," the Academic Quality Controllers. The AQCs are employed across particular grades within the school, across subjects. Their focus is to ensure that the academic standard of the grades they are responsible for is of a high level and to do whatever is necessary to make sure that the standard is maintained at that high level. They have offices outside of the classrooms, but visit classrooms frequently, observing lessons, talking informally to teachers and children, ensuring that academic standards are maintained. They are also major communicators with parents, whenever necessary informing them of where improvements need to be made. And they train teachers, both formally and informally, wherever help is needed. The AQCs meanwhile are supported by Regional AQCs – based in the regional headquarters of Cairo, Egypt, for the Kurdistan school. The Regional AQCs have full access to all the data from each of the schools and can follow up any AQC in any school in their region to explore why particular children, classes or teachers are not doing well and suggest follow-up work.

A key focus for the AQCs, at local and regional levels, is data. And getting good data on the children's performance is an absolutely crucial part of the SABIS system that Dr Bokhari and Hêro were being initiated into. To a new student like Hêro – as to any child, whether from a public or a private background – the extremely rigorous testing regime initially seemed onerous. Dr Bokhari realized its significance early on, however, and was ready to explain to the students its crucial importance: "In your other schools," she would tell new students,

> you were only tested at the end of your school year, your finals. But by then, it's far too late. If you didn't understand your math concepts from your first week, what good is it to find that out at the end of the year? Because math is a hierarchical subject; if you didn't understand week one, then you probably will be lost in week two, and by the end of the year, you've failed. And it's just as true in other subjects too. We don't want that to happen. That's why we test you every week. We want to know what you are learning every week, and if you're not learning, where your gaps are, and how we can help you fill those.

In SABIS schools, there is a purpose-built computer hall where the testing takes place, the SABIS Integrated Testing and Learning® (ITL®)[1] hall. For a student like Hêro, it took a while to get used to going to this place. In the Erbil school, you went down into the basement under the main hall, to a room packed with 400 computers. The first few times you felt nervous. After a while, however, it soon became normal practice. It meant that the exam room had no fears for Hêro in the end, unlike in her old school, where finals at the end of the year were the only time they were formally assessed, so the stakes were often terrifyingly high.

In each subject they take, children sit a SABIS Academic Monitoring System®[2] (AMS) test each week. The system has twelve versions of each test, and children are seated so that no one can cheat. Then every few weeks, there are "periodic" exams that are in roughly the same format as the AMS, but are more comprehensive, covering material taught over a longer timeframe. So almost every day children are being tested in something. Teachers are not involved in either setting these tests or marking them. Hêro soon realized that she liked this system – for teachers didn't know exactly what the students would be tested on, and so had to make sure that they were being taught well in everything. It seemed like a good system to her. And, of course, it meant that this further freed up teachers' classroom time, if they didn't have to be marking. Clearly teachers seemed to like that freedom too.

For the AQCs, the subject teachers, heads of department and the school director, the data collected from all the various tests were crucial for their analysis of the success of the school. They spent a lot of time poring over the data and deciding what actions to take as a result. But for a student like Hêro, there was a more immediate kind of feedback and follow-up, which was unique to the SABIS system.

Hêro was very good at mathematics, so she could finish these tests quickly. In a 45-minute period, she might get all the questions done in 25 minutes. The result would come through instantly as it was all marked by computer. Often she would get 100 percent right, but sometimes she would make one or two mistakes. For each question she got wrong, the software would guide her to the pages in the book where the problems were described – the appropriate pages would come up on the screen. She would quickly read through these and be able to answer the questions she had got wrong (in any case, often it was just a simple arithmetical error that could be put right straight away). Once she'd finished the test with everything correct, something rather interesting happened. The computer software provided her with some additional, more challenging questions. These would sharpen her understanding of the concepts and really test her appreciation and creativity. Sometimes she got a real sense of achievement from having answered these questions. Other times she had to puzzle over them for some time and would not make much progress. All the questions, of course – the standard and the more advanced – were created back in Lebanon and the USA, where the company had its two headquarters. Sometimes it was strange for Hêro to think of people in all these different faraway places being concerned about what went on in her classroom, in this dusty part of Erbil, in a mountain province of a faraway country. It made her feel rather special and connected with the wider world.

For her fellow students, things could go differently in the ITL. If someone was rather weak in a subject, they would get their mark instantly too, once they'd finished the exam. Then they would have time to select their answers again, having been guided by the software to the pages of the book where these problems were discussed. But supposing they still couldn't get these answers right? What happened next was particularly interesting to Hêro. They were assigned a "Shadow Teacher®,"[3] either in the Student Life Organization (SLO) period or during the weekend school slot. The Shadow Teacher was one of their peers, someone who understood the concepts required, and who had been specially trained to help.

This peer learning is used in a couple of ways. First, the top students in a particular subject are invited to become "prefects" in the class in that subject only. It is good for their subject knowledge – by helping others, their own mastery of the subject increases and their communication skills improve. In a regular class, the children sit in groups of four (so in a class of 28 there would be seven of these subject prefects). Once they achieved the right answers to questions given by the teacher, they help anyone in their group of four who has failed to do so. This kind of "peer learning" is a crucial part of the SABIS philosophy. It is good for them all – those who are great at a subject can really practice their skills; Hêro soon realized that the only time she really felt that she absolutely understood something was when she'd taught it to someone else. For those in the rest of the class it provides them with additional help: some prefects are more patient than teachers, and in any case, for a class of 28 it offers eight possible teachers rather than just one.

In this way, this process got over the terrible waste experienced in other schools. Hêro was not alone in having come across something like this in her previous school: the teacher would teach a topic and give out questions. Seven or eight of the children would get the answers right straight away. But then they would sit quietly, doing nothing – it was a virtue to be quiet, because then you wouldn't get beaten or otherwise punished. Sometimes you'd be sitting quietly doing nothing, having got all the answers correct, and sitting right next to you would be someone else who you could see had got everything wrong. But you couldn't help them, you had to keep quiet. To children like Hêro, that seemed an awful waste – it was like pretending there was only one person who knew anything in the classroom, the teacher, when really there were seven or eight or more people who knew the topic: the teacher and those smarter kids who picked it up quickly. In a country like Kurdistan, which was developing and needed all the talent it could get, what a squandering of scarce resources that seemed. The SABIS way made a lot of sense to her.

This practice of "peer learning" had its strongest expression in the process of "Shadow Teaching" that SABIS had introduced. In its simplest form this was simply a protection against time being wasted in the class if a teacher was absent or had to be called away for any reason. Then one of these prefects would be called upon to be Shadow Teacher, and the lesson would continue as if the teacher were still there. But the Shadow Teachers were also called in to help those children who weren't learning so quickly in the extra SLO periods or at weekends.

Hêro herself had been a beneficiary of this in her first year. She had needed help in her English, so was assigned a "support group" in her first year. Her Shadow Teachers were in Grade 5, a year ahead of her – Meena, Pramod, and Allan. The three taught her English, and she improved very dramatically. She now began to read English novels and poetry – and Shakespeare proved to be a particular favorite for her. But reading English didn't make her abandon her native tongue either: she still loved Kurdish poetry. One of her elder brothers wrote poems in Kurdish, about the landscape and weather, and flora and fauna. Once he'd written a poem about the flowers of Kurdistan, the *nergz*, the Kurdish lily, and, of course, the *hêro*. She loved to listen to him recite these poems.

With this year of learning experience behind her, in her second year she herself became a Shadow Teacher when she was in Grade 5. On

Thursdays again, she was assigned to teach math and English, mainly to children in lower grades, but sometimes to children from her own class. Mainly she was assigned students who were having difficulty in math. If they didn't pass their AMSs, then she helped them learn before they took their retakes. She must have helped hundreds of children in this way during the next year or two, and generally she saw improvements in their achievement. So that she could best assist these children, Hêro herself received training from other, more practiced Shadow Teachers. It was very strange to her; she was helping children who were not on scholarships. That meant they were all posh children, children of business people, ministers, influential parents. They didn't find it odd, but she found it strange herself, because this seemed like a reversal of all the normal social roles. But SABIS said this was the way it should be, and she felt pleased that her talents were being used in this way.

Her fellow students weren't the only ones she was helping. Her next-eldest brother, the one who had been born only three months before the family exodus to Iran, was in Grade 12 when Hêro was in Grade 6. The things he was studying in English were exactly the same level of difficulty as she had studied in Grade 4!

One day early in her new job, Dr Bokhari was walking down a corridor and saw Hêro, who seemed to be glowing with a quiet but palpable joy. Dr Bokhari knew each of the children in her care – this was something particularly important to her. And she was especially careful to get to know the scholarship children, from less privileged backgrounds than the others, and had been closely watching them. Dr Bokhari asked her why she was smiling. Hêro said she was "just happy." Did she want to share why? Hêro said, "Okay. I really want to say thank you to SABIS." Why? asked Dr Bokhari. "Because they have given me the same opportunity as the prime minister's son. I am in the same class as the prime minister's son. I am studying the same material as the prime minister's son. I have the same opportunity to go to any university as the prime minister's son. I would never have been able to get this if it wasn't for SABIS." She finished, "They have flattened the plain for people like me."

Dr Bokhari liked that image, creating a level playing field by flattening the plain. Hêro continued walking down the corridor. She *was* happy, truly happy. The school really had flattened the plain for her; all students rich or poor were receiving the same education, from the same teachers, in the same building. Opportunity was knocking on her door as it was on theirs. She was definitely making the best use of the opportunity given to her, now ranking in the top 5 percent of her class. But she hadn't lost her dream, her dream of giving back to others.

Hêro was never totally free of the sense that she had been given a huge opportunity, but that others had been left behind. And this didn't seem totally fair. She was benefiting, but others, even her old friends, and certainly others in much worse public schools than them, were still disadvantaged. She knew that she was now part of a privileged few, even if she hadn't started out with any of those privileges. But, she thought, if only SABIS could open more schools. Especially schools that catered for everyone, not just the elite.

Little did Hêro know that SABIS had been thinking along exactly the same lines. At the same time as Dr Bokhari joined the International School in September 2008, SABIS was about to open the first of a new type of school in Erbil, aimed at closing the achievement gap between Kurdistan's least and most privileged.

CHAPTER 7

In partnership

The governor

The governor of Erbil (or "Hawler," as the city is called in Kurdish, the name which appears on the signboards as you enter the office), Nawzad Hadi, is completely bald with a Gorbachev-style birthmark on his forehead above his right eye. His office is situated at the foot of the Citadel, which Erbil boasts is the oldest continuously inhabited settlement in the world, dating back to around 2300 BC (although, strictly speaking, at present it is not inhabited, given that the remaining inhabitants were removed a few months ago to have their homes renovated).

From the time that the new SABIS international school had opened in September 2006, Mr Hadi had been getting visits from many of his townsfolk. People like the father of Sana, who had even brought his three-year-old daughter to the meeting. His comments were typical: "The people who have good incomes, they can send their children to the SABIS school, but what about us? Not everyone has the opportunity to send their children there. What will I be able to do for my daughter when she is ready for school? What can the governor do for us?"

What the governor realized he could do was to create a model of "public–private partnership" (PPP) with SABIS. In many parts of the world, including in the United Arab Emirates and the USA (in its "charter" schools, as we've just explored), SABIS was involved with PPPs which were designed to raise educational standards in public education. Under a PPP arrangement, the government handed over the responsibility for running public schools to a private education management company, paying them a management fee for doing so and holding them to strict performance targets. Ideally – although in practice it didn't always work out like this, as we shall see later in this chapter – the private company was free to run the school as it saw fit, provided that it satisfied equal access criteria and successfully raised standards. Often a government handed over a failing public school to the management company to do its best. Research from around the world had shown that educational improvements could be achieved by handing over management in this way. Indeed, many development experts viewed PPPs as a kind of panacea, bringing the best of private sector expertise into a system that was free at the point of delivery to the general public.

Given his interest in the SABIS international school, the prime minister himself got involved in the discussions about this possibility with the president of SABIS, Carl Bistany, and the governor. The prime minister's office would provide some additional funding, and the governor would find the school or schools to allocate to the company.

The model they came up with was particularly innovative – perhaps an entirely novel way of approaching PPPs. It was a public–private partnership that would create managerial and educational expertise within Kurdistan, using SABIS to help build this capacity.

The government had already created a wholly owned private company, Froebel, which had partnered with SABIS to create the new international school. Froebel was now to be given three-year renewable contracts with individual government schools to enable them to progressively take over their management in conjunction with SABIS. It worked like this: in the first year, SABIS would subcontract with Froebel to manage classes from kindergarten to Grade 2, while the government kept the remainder of the school. In the second year, SABIS would take over a couple more classes from the government, and by year three SABIS would be managing all the classes up to Grade 5, and the government the remainder. In these three years, Froebel would be holding the management contract, nothing more – apart from learning from SABIS how they were doing things.

After three years, assuming everything had been successful, the contracts would be renewed. Simultaneously, as SABIS took over the management of higher grades from government, so they would hand over the management of the lower grades to Froebel. Froebel would manage the lower classes but would *license* all the curriculum, teaching and learning methods from SABIS, so that continuity was maintained. After another three years, SABIS would be managing Grades 6–12 in the school, while Froebel would manage Grades K–5 under license from SABIS. After a further three years, SABIS would have withdrawn from managing the school entirely, handing it over to Froebel, which would license the whole curriculum from SABIS.

The cost of this would be slightly greater than running an existing public school in the first few years; the prime minister and governor both stressed, however, that there was a better way of looking at this: it was not simply expenditure, but genuine *investment* in the future of education through this partnership in capacity-building to create a viable alternative education system. Yes, the governor told any critics of this new scheme, he could continue spending his funding on public education as before, but this would continue to bring "zero quality and zero results." By spending more initially, the expectation was that this investment would yield much greater returns for minimal cost in the medium to long term. The choice was between "throwing good money after bad into a bottomless pit" or investing more in the short term for enhanced educational and managerial capacity in the long term. He was absolutely clear in his own mind which Erbil should opt for.

SABIS had other innovative ideas about capacity-building too. Initially, the Kurdistan government wanted SABIS to fill the PPP schools with expatriate teachers – the medium for the schools was going to be English, so it seemed essential to have expatriate teachers whose first language was English. SABIS resisted this: it would create a level of instability in the schools that would be undesirable – for if the security situation in Iraq was perceived to be deteriorating, then expatriate teachers would leave. In any case, sustainability required that local teachers should fill all the major roles. So instead of bringing in expatriate teachers, the focus should be on building up the skills of local teachers.

This was to be more of a problem than SABIS had foreseen. The team began interviewing prospective teachers, fresh recruits from the local universities. It soon became apparent that, beyond simple greetings, the applicants' understanding of English was minimal – even though many had been studying college-level English. One young man famously had just one phrase, "I godda go," after four years of English in college. And although he could say it, he couldn't actually explain what it meant.

Although the team's initial reaction was shock ("How are we going to run a school using English as the medium of instruction when a hundred percent of the staff cannot speak English, let alone teach it?"), the SABIS way is to come up with solutions rather than reporting problems. There was still time for a solution. Around nine months before the first PPP school was due to open, SABIS started an intensive training program for staff in English. For at least six months, and for four hours per day, SABIS staff trained the new recruits in English and also introduced the SABIS system – and this training was to continue for two hours every week for the first year of each school's operation. The success of this program led to the creation of the SABIS University in Erbil – initially only as a College of Education to educate young Kurds as potential teachers for the SABIS system. (A College of Business and Management Studies was added in 2010, with more growth anticipated in the next few years.) The English training provided to SABIS teachers leads to certification, so this feels like a great perk for the teachers. They themselves are learners: as Anita Zadook, a new teacher at the first PPP school, put it, "I'm still learning every day. So I'm an educator and at the same time I'm a student, so this helps me to enjoy class every day."

The first SABIS PPP school in Kurdistan opened its doors in September 2008. Named Fakhir Mergasori International School (FMIS), after the Kurdish leader who had been martyred in 1975, the school was housed in a new building created with aid from South Korea. It had opened as a government school less than one year earlier but already it was in a poor state. Filthy and inadequately maintained, it looked as though it had suffered at least ten years' wear and tear, not less than one. When cleaners employed by SABIS came to remove the grimy carpet, they were inundated with mice fleeing for cover. As per the contract, SABIS took over the early grades, while the remainder stayed as a government school. After a successful year of operation, for September 2009 the school was set to offer 50 new places at kindergarten level, for children of four years of age.

Sana's father had heard excellent things about the new PPP school. And the good news was that his daughter was now four years of age, so eligible to apply. He was one of the first in line. The bad news was that he was one of 1,212 applicants. There was no other option, SABIS would have to instigate a lottery for admission – something, as we saw in Chapter 4, they were used to doing in their American charter schools. They made sure that those who were entered for the lottery were on low incomes, getting confirmation to this effect from their employers. Sana's father was certified in this way.

On the date of the draw, mother, father and daughter all went to the school. Mother and father were "really, really hoping she would get in." It was a red-letter day, the date and time ingrained in their memories: 11 a.m., 13 June 2009. Hundreds of hopeful parents and children were gathered in the school hall, sitting on the ground, waiting. The local media had turned out in force – television, radio and newspaper journalists all crowded in to observe this new phenomenon in Kurdistan. On the stage at the front, on a large table, was a clear bowl, in which all the names and numbers of the applicants were written. As the name of a successful child was drawn, he or she was asked to draw the next name from the bowl. Sana's father and mother waited. Name after name was withdrawn; Sana's name was not among them. As children's names were picked out, "parents celebrated as though they had won a million dollars."

Sana's mother was very, very nervous. This meant so much to her.

Her husband had told her so much about the SABIS school, she didn't want anything less for her daughter, having seen what her older children had experienced in the public school system. But she was realistic enough to know that her daughter might not get in. How would they cope if that happened?

Names were called, but not Sana's.

Then suddenly it was her name that was pulled out of the bowl. Father smiled and looked down at his feet, mother hugged daughter, and they left. Father felt bad for the parents remaining, knowing that, as poor families, their options were limited. People were crying. But Sana had won a place at the new school.

The governor, however, could not win. Having stuck his neck out to create the PPP school, he found his office now inundated with people again angry at the unfairness of it all – this time on account of having only one PPP school with such a limited intake. "Can't you increase the size of the school? Can't you open other PPP schools?" When the SABIS representative came to a meeting, the governor joked, "You brought me a real headache." He added: "Please tell me what are you doing in this school. Why do all these people want to go there?"

Some people were trying by whatever means possible to get their sons and daughters into the school. The governor resisted. He told those who were trying so hard, "Even the daughter of the sister of His Excellency didn't get accepted. The system is fair, believe me." And he wasn't the only one under pressure. Ms Jwan Husny, the principal of FMIS, who had lived in London, Ontario, Canada, for fifteen years before returning to her homeland, had parents coming to the school, pleading, "I have one son in the old school, the other daughter or son is in another school. Please, I'll do anything. I want them here. You can do it." And "fathers come crying – in our culture when men cry it's a big deal – pleading that they want a better opportunity for their sons than they had."

Clearly, one PPP school would not be enough to satisfy demand. Carl Bistany showed photographs of the lottery to the prime minister at their next appointment. Soon it was decided to open their second

PPP school in Erbil, this time aimed only at the sons and daughters of martyrs. This second school, Sarwaran International School, opened in September 2010, together with the third, Sardam International, in Dohuk, the mountain city toward the Turkish border.

(And these developments won't stop there. Four more PPP schools will open in September 2012, in rural areas of Kurdistan, to serve some of the most deprived children in the country. And SABIS is being approached by delegations from other parts of Iraq too, including Najaf, Basra, and Al Anbar. "Can you imagine how much work will have to be done?" Carl Bistany asked me, thinking through these options.

> Not only on learning math or English, but the kids' reality has been guns and war. We will be dealing with kids who for ten years have been through war, who've seen their parents killed in front of them, who've seen the damage inflicted by suicide bombers day after day, night after night. It will not be an easy task at all. But working in those places will be such a wonderful reward, even compared to what we are doing in Kurdistan. When we expand into other parts of Iraq, we will be serving some of the neediest places on this planet. It will be a big challenge; it will not be easy. But our staff are very motivated and committed. We'll even go to Baghdad if we can.

A few days later, when I was meeting with Ralph Bistany and Mrs Saad back in Lebanon, I asked, innocently, about further development in other parts of Iraq: "Would you be happy for SABIS to expand into other parts of Iraq?" Ralph Bistany replied "Yes" simultaneously with Mrs Saad's "No.")

Each of the new PPP schools in Kurdistan soon had to initiate lotteries, such was the demand for places, just as the SABIS charter schools had to do in America. At Sarwaran International School, the director, Nabil Ismail, a Kurdish national who had also lived in London, Ontario, for 23 years before deciding to return to Kurdistan in 2010, joked that the school's popularity was "like a curse." "I hate to turn people away," he says, "but what can I do? If I had the liberty to register every pupil who applied, with no problem I would have registered three thousand students in two or three weeks. More than five hundred people have phoned asking, 'How should I get my son in? How should I get my daughter in?'" This lobbying is incessant. When he attended a function organized by the prime minister's office, people high up in the government approached him, asking, "How can I get my kids into your school?"

East/West

What is the answer to the governor's question? Why do many parents want to send their children to the SABIS PPP schools? One parent at the Sardam International School in Dohuk put it like this: "Why we are confident to enroll our kids here is that we know this is an organization; it is not only individual people, depending on unknown textbooks, unknown programs. This is a known education institute and this makes us confident for the future of our kids." It's the known brand which is now part of the attraction for parents. But, of course, that brand recognition and popularity have to be built on substance. What is the substance?

It's not the buildings. Usefully, because of the way the first two PPP schools were set up, an existing public school was divided into two sections, with SABIS taking one half and the other remaining with the government. The buildings of both public and PPP schools are in fact the same. Someone once joked to Carl Bistany that this provides a neat little natural experiment. Just as at one time you were able to compare socialism and capitalism by comparing East and West Berlin (or East and West Germany), so you can make a comparison between government and PPP schools by comparing the two halves of the FMIS and Sarwaran schools. The SABIS side, the person remarked, is very definitely West Berlin; the government side socialist East Berlin.

The teachers are also predominantly the same kind of person on both sides of the East/West divide. As we've seen, the majority of teachers at the PPP schools are local, often newly recruited from the government teacher training college. Only a few are expatriates, so this is unlikely to explain the difference. In Sarwaran International School, for instance, there are five expatriates out of 37 teachers in total. The teachers do get paid more in the PPP schools – perhaps $200 more on top of their existing $350 monthly salary. But then they work much longer hours – from 8 a.m. to 3:30 p.m., rather than the 8 a.m. to 12 noon or earlier that is the norm in the public schools. It's also common for a teacher in a public school to take on an extra job, which pays a similar amount, in the afternoon or evening when they are not in school – so the pay is in effect not much different for teachers in both public and PPP schools.

The reason for parental preference is the SABIS program – and here it is very important to realize that SABIS introduces its *full program* into the PPP schools. All the concepts and processes we encountered in the SABIS International School, in Chapter 6, are present in the PPP schools too. Whether it's the huge range of books used, the system of AQCs, the Student Life Organization, Shadow Teaching, peer learning, testing in the ITL hall (albeit a mobile one in the case of the PPP schools, using laptops carried from one class to another, but featuring the same software and concepts), or the support structures, these are identical in the international and PPP schools. When they realize this parents are very impressed – at no cost to them, they can be getting an identical education for their children in the PPP school as richer parents pay for in the international school. This must be attractive to poorer parents and one reason for the exceptional demand.

Also, in both types of school the medium is English, which is another important factor for parents. English in Kurdistan, as in many developing countries across the world, is a key to accessing the middle classes for the less privileged. As Nabil Ismail, director of Sarwaran International School, put it, "English is a great equalizer. If you're rich or have great political connections, then corruption and nepotism can get you employment, so the poor and/or less connected lose out again. But anyone can learn English, rich or poor. There are no short cuts just because you are rich or politically well connected." In this way, "SABIS helps the poor compete on equal terms with the rich, which is a key reason why it is so popular with parents."

One area we didn't discuss earlier, however, but which is seen as absolutely key by the poorer parents who use the PPP schools, is the SABIS discipline program – again common to both private and PPP schools, but developed in some of its details out of SABIS's experiences with PPP (charter) schools in America. For low-income, less well-educated parents, discipline is another great equalizer. If their children are disciplined, then they can work hard, gain good results, and get better jobs. They can impress at interview and rise quickly in their chosen employment. And putting all this in the context of the classroom, parents feel that if their children can be quiet when necessary, focus when necessary, walk in a straight line quietly, and can defer gratification, then this will help prepare them for the world of work and adult life.

The discipline difference is quite obvious to see across the East/West divide. In the second PPP school in Erbil, the Sarwaran International School, the school for the children of martyrs, East/West becomes Upstairs/Downstairs, for the SABIS school is downstairs and the public school upstairs. It's the same building, built to the same standards throughout. The children are also the same – many of the children from both upstairs and downstairs play with each other on the streets after school. But go upstairs and the first difference you notice is that it is filthy, stinking. There is the same number of students, around 450, in each school, but the difference in behavior is stark. Upstairs, during lesson times, you'll see many children roaming around in the corridors, and teachers who don't seem to control their classes. Perhaps you'll see the headteacher himself standing outside his office, smoking. But downstairs, the behavior of the children is usually impeccable. In the classrooms, they are all focused on learning. If they are moving between classes, they walk in neat, silent lines along the corridor. (It has nothing to do with badly behaved children being expelled either: just as we saw in the chapters on charter schools in America, SABIS is reluctant to expel any child, however badly behaved, in Kurdistan.)

If you compare the disorder in the public school with the orderly atmosphere in the PPP SABIS schools, then it really is easy to see why parents would want to send their children downstairs rather than upstairs, West rather than East. That would be enough reason in itself. But how, using the same kind of teachers with the same kind of children, is this huge contrast possible? For Nabil Ismail, the director of Sarwaran International School, it is absolutely clear: "It's the system that SABIS brings. The fundamental difference is that our focus from the minute we are in the school until we leave is the students. And when we say that, it's not just a slogan, it's a program, it's the timetable, it's the follow-up, it's the checks and balances, it's the carrots and sticks we have with teachers. And we see the difference in children very quickly. Parents tell us after only a couple of months their children are different ... It's the difference of the atmosphere that SABIS brings, the moment you walk into the building."

So what is the system of discipline that SABIS brings? It has two particularly distinctive elements. First, through the Student Life Organization (SLO), the students themselves are active in keeping behavioral standards high, so that learning is not impeded. One of the eight specific "departments" of SLO is discipline; students themselves are involved in setting and policing standards, they are the ones who roam the corridors and playgrounds, enforcing standards. They are the ones who stamp out fights and act preemptively to prevent bullying; they are an important part of what ensures compliance.

Secondly, there is the important factor that teachers themselves only rarely have to get involved in disciplining students. Azhaan Jaff, a teacher at Sarwaran International School, put it like this: "Upstairs [in the public school] they do have academic materials, but they don't care about discipline. Here there are *specialized people* who deal with discipline, the supervisors. So the teacher mainly focuses on the material to teach, while others help create the disciplined environment." Sure, SABIS trains all its teachers in methods of classroom management, and stimulating children to ensure they are kept on task. But when things go wrong – in small ways or large – the teacher doesn't have to get distracted from the business of teaching. Instead, just as there are specialized people helping with the academic side, the AQCs, so there

The Founders

Louisa Procter

The Reverend Tanios Saad

Excerpt from the first register in Louisa Procter's handwriting.

The building where the school started. It was previously a silk factory that its owners wanted to close down.

GENERAL ACCOUNT, 1900,

July 1st, 1899, to June 30th, 1900.

─✳─ BUILDING FUND. ─✳─

RECEIPTS	£	s.	d.
Acknowledged in Report for 1899	230	0	0
Interest, six months, on £200	5	0	0
A Friend	0	1	6
Andrews, Miss	0	3	6
B. D.	50	0	0
Cory, Mr. J.	50	0	0
Corry, W. F. C. S.	1	0	0
Lyster, Miss, the late, Legacy, 2nd inst., per Mrs Penrose	50	0	0
Pease, Miss	2	0	0
Perry, Miss	5	0	0
Williams, Colonel	5	0	0
Per Miss C. de C. Willis :—			
Harpur, Mrs	0	15	0
Harpur, Miss	0	2	6
Harpur, Miss C.	0	2	6
Per Miss Amy Procter —			
Brayne, Mrs	0	5	0
Heywood, Mrs	0	10	0
	£400	0	0
Cory, Mr J. (second donation to enable the School to be opened quite free of debt)	50	0	0
	£450	0	0

EXPENDITURE	£	s.	d.
Masons and Stone	90	2	4
Flooring	30	10	6
Iron-work	43	17	6
Tiles for Roofing	29	15	3
Wood	131	12	3
Carpenter	23	18	8
Plastering	26	7	9
Glass	14	12	4
Painting	35	4	5
Desks, Forms, and Bedsteads for 15 extra boys	23	19	0
	£450	0	0

Balancing the budget was always part of the operation.

One of the oldest photographs of the staff and students, taken circa 1895. The Reverend and Mrs Saad are at the far right in the back row. Miss Procter is at the far left in the second row from the back.

An informal photograph of infants, teachers, and helpers taken circa 1900.

A formal picture of senior girls with their teachers. The Reverend and Mrs Saad are seated at the center of the third row from the front.

From the earliest days of the school, physical education was part of the curriculum for both the boys and the girls.

The girls always looked forward to the annual May Day display.

Senior students with their teachers. The Reverend Saad is at the center of the front row; his elder son Fouad is at the center of the second row; and his younger son Charles is at the center of the back row.

Charles Saad (at center) with his wife Leila Saad and Ralph Bistany at the opening of the 1974 graduation ceremony in Choueifat, at which he was awarded the "Commandeur de l'Ordre des Cèdres" to mark his 50 years of distinguished work in education.

Supported by extensive IT systems and tools, SABIS® schools use technology to help students achieve their full potential.

SABIS® students engaged in group work as part of a typical lesson using the SABIS Point System®.

SABIS Shadow Teacher® explaining a concept to her classmates.

Students at a SABIS® US charter school reaching for new heights of achievement.

Children at one of SABIS®'s public-private partnership schools in Erbil, Kurdistan, in northern Iraq.

SABIS Student Life Organization® prefects engage in teamwork.

SABIS® students, epitomizing the diverse, international environment in schools in the global network.

Graduation day at a SABIS® school.

are specialized people ready to assist with student management and discipline issues. These are the supervisors.

SABIS believe that punishment should take into consideration the total behavior, past and present, of the student, and that it should be given after objective, third-party assessment of the infraction, not on the rebound. Within the SABIS School Management System (SSMS), there is an elaborate system of codes for various student infractions. Mohammed Omer, Student Life Coordinator of the PPP school for martyrs, is up on all these codes:

> If a child is talking in class when he shouldn't be, the code is B16. The student's name is written in the discipline sheet with this code, together with the time of infraction. By three p.m., the supervisors will collect this from all classes and enter it into the SSMS software. The next morning, the "Daily Infractions" record is printed out, which shows suggested actions for the supervisors to take. It's an accumulating process, with the SSMS showing patterns of behavior that need to be dealt with. If there's one infraction, the system will give suggested actions to the supervisor. If infractions increase or show some sort of pattern, the system will suggest other, more involved actions required.

And if there are serious infractions in the classroom, such as fighting or other disruption, the teacher can call on the Student Life Organization prefect or the supervisor immediately to get involved. It's the prefect or supervisor who takes a disruptive student away and implements a plan for dealing with disruption, not the teacher.

The system clearly seems to be working well in the PPP schools. So SABIS is providing scholarships to some of the poorest children in Kurdistan, like Hêro, to enable them to be on a "level plain" with the children of the elite. And the PPP schools further level the plain, by providing a high-quality, international-style education to even more of the less privileged.

But it doesn't feel as if they've reached the end of all they can do – not least to people involved in SABIS itself. There is still a feeling that they could help so many more children, the need is so great. Nabil Ismail, the director of the Sarwaran International School, put it like this: "The children down here are getting something so much better than the children upstairs; the majority of the public schools are like the one upstairs." But this upsets him: "I am Kurdish at the end of the day. It is a very sad when you see kids who go to school and don't learn anything. And on the other hand, you see a school like mine. I'm happy that I'm part of that change, but on the other hand I'm sad and I want to do more."

Everyone in SABIS wants to do more. How can they reach more children with methods that have proved their worth in difficult places like Kurdistan? An important dimension of the way forward is the idea of moving from public–private partnerships to licensing, something we'll address toward the end of this chapter and take up in full in the next.

Toward a model public–private partnership

It's not only in Kurdistan and America that SABIS has been involved with public–private partnerships. The experience in the United Arab Emirates, however, has not in general been as promising, although it has led to important lessons that have helped influence the work in Kurdistan and elsewhere in terms of what kind of public–private partnership can really make sense for SABIS.

Different people at SABIS have been involved in the development of PPP projects. The person who has been at the forefront of the evolution of these ideas on PPPs is Victor Saad, the 42-year-old great-grandson of the founder of the mother school, the Reverend Tanios Saad. Victor joined SABIS as a three-year-old in kindergarten. During his early childhood, his family was included in the regular Sunday gatherings at the mother school at Choueifat with Mr and Mrs Saad.

Victor remembers many cheerful times with the extended family, but he also has a very clear image of one Sunday in June 1981, which was less happy. That day he woke up to see his father – whose closet was in Victor's bedroom – putting on his black tie and black suit. The eleven-year-old Victor knew what had happened. His great-uncle,

Charles Saad, had been very ill and had been hospitalized. Victor recalls: "I began crying. I will never forget that moment because we took it for granted ... Charles Saad was *the* man of the family. If there was any trouble, if there was any request, he was the man to approach. And in an instant it would be solved and nobody would argue with him. So that morning when I woke up and I saw my father putting on those clothes, I immediately realized what had happened."

His family had left Lebanon as the civil war broke out in 1975, the same year that Ralph Bistany had established the first SABIS school outside of Lebanon, in Sharjah. His father and his brother – the father of George Saad – went to set up business in Riyadh, Saudi Arabia. Meanwhile, Victor was sent to the SABIS school in Bath, England, as a boarding student. He continued with a mathematics degree at University College London, and then went on to study engineering at McGill University in Canada.

Like Mrs Saad, Victor confessed to having a "very sentimental attachment" to the mother school, even though he'd been a student there only until he was aged thirteen. In 1986, after eleven years of civil war in Lebanon, but during one of the lulls, he and a classmate decided to revisit their old school. "That day I can never forget," said Victor. They went to their old dormitory. It was completely devastated. Underneath some rubble, Victor found one of his friend's copybooks, which he retrieved and still has to this day. They walked over to the basketball court, which the militia had converted into a berth for a tank, covered with camouflage and defended with cement blocks. Where they had played as children, all you could see now was the looming and menacing barrel of a massive gun.

After university in Canada, Victor worked in his father's business in telecommunications for three years in Saudi Arabia. But then came the defining moment in Victor's life, the decision over whether or not to join SABIS. "It was a very difficult decision for me because I am the only son. In our part of the world, if your father has a business you are expected to work and help and eventually take over. So that was a pivotal time for me."

But SABIS was growing, and Victor was being enticed by Mrs Saad and Mr Ralph Bistany "very discreetly, but very clearly" to join – because they had decided that their succession planning should involve family members.

In 1995, Mrs Saad and Ralph Bistany suggested that Victor should come and spend a month in the International School of Choueifat in Dubai, in one of the rather well-appointed apartments now used by the senior SABIS staff. He took leave from his father's business for this period. For a month, he shadowed the director, getting to know every aspect of the managerial side of the business.

After the month, he went back to Riyadh, to talk to his father. He was very good, very wise, very calm, remembers Victor: "Okay, so you need to decide, did you discuss all aspects? Are you reassured? Is it something you want to do for your future?" Victor then traveled to England to meet with Mrs Saad and Mr Bistany to get his final questions asked. He was 25. He put to them his final concern: "I just want to make sure I have a future with SABIS; that I can become something." He remembers the answer very clearly: "You'll go as far as your efforts take you." Back in Dubai, he had to make the decision. "That is the only time in my life that I remember I had insomnia, two to three days I would not sleep, it was that tough." But his heart was with the school. He chose SABIS.

It obviously helped smooth things with his father that in a way he was simply moving to a different family business – for, of course, it was the grandfather of Victor's father who had started the school in the first place. Perhaps it helped too that Victor's father's childhood sweetheart had also been at Choueifat; she became his wife and Victor's mother.

Victor joined SABIS in December 1996 and has been with them ever since. He was inducted into working for the company in Dubai, UAE. His background was in mathematics, so he started work in that area: Ralph Bistany asked him to summarize the algebra books they were using for the "classic questions" we met earlier, developed initially by Ramzi Germanos – defined as the minimum number of questions needed so that the student can absorb the whole book. "I remember we were able to do it in twenty-nine questions – the whole book."

Having completed this mathematics project, on 25 April 1997 he got a call from Ralph Bistany: "How do you feel about going to Jordan?" he asked. Victor said, "I have never been to Jordan. I would love that idea." Ralph said, "Okay, please book for 1 May. We are opening a school. You'll find out what to do. Don't worry, just hop on the plane."

Four months later, on 2 September, the International School of Choueifat in Amman, Jordan, opened with 128 students enrolled. Everything from staffing, to marketing, to follow-up on site construction, to furnishing, to registration, to training and induction, was done in those brief months. With this baptism of fire, Victor had been initiated into the SABIS way. For the next two years Victor spent half his year in Jordan and half working in company head office in Lebanon. The school has flourished ever since – now it has 1,364 students. Then he helped open the International School of Choueifat in Damascus, Syria, in 2001. This started with 425 students and again has prospered. Victor was also very closely involved in opening the private schools in Oman, Bahrain, and Abu Dhabi, as well as their third private school in Lebanon, at Adma, also the site of the company headquarters.

Five years ago, SABIS was invited to bid for the public–private partnership (PPP) schools in the United Arab Emirates. Worried by low standards in the public schools, the Ministry of Education had invited school operators from around the world to bid to take over the management of these schools. In the first year, they selected four operators: SABIS, two British companies (CfBT and Nord Anglia) and the American company Mosaica. Each was given six schools to manage. In year two, further operators were invited in, more again in year three to make a total of nine operators. In 2011, SABIS had partnership agreements with 35 public schools in Abu Dhabi – sixteen in Western Region and nineteen in Eastern Region – but in 2012 this was reduced to fourteen schools (five in Western and nine in Eastern). The project will be phased out altogether in 2013 – for all companies involved. It has not been a resounding success, and it may be useful for any organization or state getting involved in public–private partnerships to ponder the reasons why.

Victor was involved in the negotiation process, making up the triumvirate with Ralph and Carl Bistany. It was clear why the Ministry of Education in Abu Dhabi approached them. As we saw in Chapter 3, SABIS had been running private schools in the Emirates since 1976: "We were the only group who had such a presence in the UAE. So they looked at us as a group that understood the local heritage and culture yet could bring a modern and global outlook. The combination of that was very important to many countries in the area."

Victor recalls that Ralph Bistany in particular was exceedingly excited about the possibilities this opened up for SABIS. The Request for Proposals that they responded to was very clear that the school operator would be free to manage everything: curriculum, testing, staffing and school organization. In its turn, it would then be fully accountable for results. That's exactly what they desired. Unfortunately, "it turned out to be a bit different," Victor said. Again, just as we saw in the chapters on American charter schools, SABIS's experiences here offer a salutary lesson, revealing some of the problems that can arise in public–private partnerships.

Instead of the *carte blanche* to introduce all they wanted to in order to raise standards, as they'd been led to believe, once they'd signed the contracts and been given their schools, it was clear that things weren't quite what they'd hoped for.

First, there was a frequent shifting of the goalposts. SABIS brought native teachers from the UK, the USA and Canada to teach English. "Within the same comparable budgets as other providers, we were able to bring in these teachers from overseas. After the first year we were told, no, that system cannot work; we do not wish you to have teachers at all, just advisors. So we had to comply." But then in the second year, SABIS was told that they could bring in these teachers after all; then in the third year, the personnel could be there, but not as teachers, only as teacher assistants. It all made planning very difficult.

Secondly, they had to take over the schools with existing staff, over whom ultimately they had no power: "We thought we were going to have *authority* over principals and staff." Instead, they were asked to *influence* rather than control. It was all a big headache for Victor: "I am responsible for the results at Grade Twelve. But it's the principal who decides whether or not she wants to send her team to be trained. I can't do much about it. I can write letters to the authority in charge or to the principal asking, cajoling, but it's the principal who still decides." Victor added, "It's very hard to manage through influence alone, to have no authority."

Finally, SABIS could not implement its whole program – which for SABIS undermines its whole *raison d'être*. As we are beginning to see in this book – and as will be spelled out explicitly in Chapters 9 to 11 – SABIS has a coherent logic of learning, embedded in a community of learners; to take only parts of this is not going to bring the benefits of the system at all. The biggest problem for SABIS was the desire of Abu Dhabi Education Council (ADEC) – the organization within the Abu Dhabi government responsible for the PPP – to want to standardize the project. Hence, all the schools were provided with the same curriculum and required to use the same methodology, some of which contradicted the SABIS approach.

All this meant that the company was frustrated in what it wanted to achieve: "The results are not what we wanted them to be," said Victor. This is particularly galling because SABIS prides itself on fulfilling its contracts – and has refused to go into places where it did not believe it would be given the freedom to make a difference. This happened just before Abu Dhabi created the PPP process. The Qatar government had previously invited tenders from companies to be involved with PPP schools, again worried about low standards and wanting to influence their schools in a global way.

Initially, early noises coming out of Doha seemed promising, so the triumvirate – Ralph and Carl Bistany and Victor Saad – plus the SABIS regional director put in a preliminary statement of interest and went to a series of meetings with the Supreme Education Council, along with other prospective bidders. The Qataris were guided in all they did by consultants from the RAND Corporation, one of the largest think tanks in America. In their final meeting, it soon became clear that there would be an important political constraint. Again, rather like the situation with the charter schools in America, companies like SABIS were not going to be allowed to apply to run the schools themselves. This would have to be done by a local Qatari – and there were a whole host of educational and residential requirements for that person to satisfy too. The person holding the contract would then be able to choose from the approved operators, but also consultants, and would be able to mix and match these as he or she wanted. But then, "the funny part," as Victor put it, "he or she would have the final say on how things would run in the school, yet you would be accountable as a consultant or an operator for standards!"

When Mr Ralph Bistany heard this, he stood up in the meeting, and said, "Okay, we stop." The other SABIS members tried to mitigate this abruptness, but they all knew the game was over. "How can three captains run a ship?" said Ralph Bistany. They were surprised that other education companies were still interested, but there was no way that SABIS could get involved with so many constraints.

Clearly Abu Dhabi had been monitoring the Qatar experience, which was why initially they seemed to offer much more to companies like SABIS. But in the end, the promised freedoms did not materialize. "It's been difficult, a challenge. Instead of focusing where we needed to focus, a large portion of our time was occupied trying to convince and influence," said Victor.

But there are positives. First, Victor believes that they've had a positive impact on local students: "We actually were able to benefit them, although not to the extent we wanted or anticipated. But we introduced self-discipline, good teaching habits, solid English into their classes."

There are also positives in terms of the processes that SABIS has developed, and the lessons they have learned from these processes, which could be replicable in other areas. SABIS was accountable in four subjects, English, math, ICT, and science. In English and math they designed, *from scratch*, books specifically for the Abu Dhabi schools. These books were designed in the company headquarters in Lebanon, based on the outcomes desired in the UAE. So again, the usual SABIS process was followed: starting from the outcomes required, working back to decide all the concepts and points needed, the essential knowledge, the pacing charts and so on, to design entirely new books. But the math and science books also have the additional aspect that they have pages in Arabic and English alongside each other – just as in US charter school materials books feature Spanish and English. The medium of the PPP schools is Arabic, but in the last two or three years they have been trying to change to English for maths and science. The dual-language texts "ease the transition for students from various local backgrounds." The textbooks are then linked to computerized testing in the ITLs, as in other SABIS schools.

That seems to be an "extraordinary commitment," I point out – and "only for thirty-three schools: did that seem worthwhile from SABIS's point of view?" Victor responded that they did all of it for their first six schools in fact. The investment was worthwhile to them "because SABIS plans long-term. We wanted to make an impact; we wanted to add value. Only in this way did we know that we can promptly plug knowledge gaps. That's why we invested." This experience, of course, can be replicated in other places too – and it's already being done for the Kurdistan PPP schools. Again, starting from the desired outcomes there, materials have been developed, with books in math, for instance, having Kurdish and English pages.

Other evidence of extraordinary commitment was the fact that, at its peak, SABIS had 400 employees in its Abu Dhabi PPP office. It acted as a SABIS regional office all of its own, featuring its own Regional Academic Quality Controllers and director of operations, a core director, a deputy director, as well as subject coordinators and licensed teachers. Now these 400 people will have to be redeployed – some into SABIS private schools and regional and head offices.

Thirdly, even though SABIS was unable to do what it wanted to do in the schools, Victor still feels they had an important and enduring impact. Even as they withdraw from the schools, the feedback from many is that they are still trying to maintain many of the SABIS ways: one principal I met said that she was going to follow the pacing chart and Point System, exactly as SABIS had taught her to. Another was adamant that she would continue to use the SABIS books and continue where possible with the ITLs, which would be left in the schools, although the software would not be updated. In a third school, the principal insisted that the Student Life Organization model would be maintained because it had had such a huge impact on student responsibility and morale.

Lest anyone think that the failure has anything to do with the environment in the Emirates, it's worth pointing out that Victor also oversees a very successful public–private partnership, the Military High School in Al Ain. This project began for SABIS in 2003, when they bid for the first five-year contract, which has now been extended for a second term of four years. For the first couple of years it too was a rough ride – particularly in terms of convincing those involved that the assessments they had previously been using were inadequate and needed replacing. But for the last two or three years it has been a real success. "The secret of the success is our ability to communicate with our partners and to agree to objectives and processes. When we are able to achieve that with people who really care, the project succeeds," said Victor. SABIS is able to bring most of what they want to the school. The Student Life Organization is working well. They have a fully functioning ITL, with all student assessments carried out in the normal way. Shadow Teaching and peer learning are all functioning very well. Indeed, in Chapter 11 we'll see that the school is also one of the pilot schools for one of SABIS's most revolutionary innovations, the Integrated Learning and Testing model.

Learning from this success, and the ongoing developments in Kurdistan, as well as the lessons of the disappointment in Abu Dhabi, has led the SABIS team to develop a model of their ideal public–private partnership for the region. The idea proposed, as in charter schools in America, is to take over existing, failing schools, in the worst educationally performing areas – such as Silaa in Abu Dhabi, on the border with Saudi Arabia.

So what is the ideal PPP model? The "Operating Parameters" that SABIS wishes to see include:

- SABIS must be allowed to use *all* of its educational system, including its textbooks, SABIS School Management Software (SSMS), student and staff tracking modules, Student Life Organization, and so on – all the features that we have and will encounter throughout this book that represent a complete system for SABIS.
- SABIS must be allowed to have decision-making authority in the recruitment and staffing process. Any ministry staff assigned to the charter school would have to be selected by SABIS from the pool of teachers sent by the ministry. Those who joined the school would be contracted under the SABIS employee system. All teachers would undergo diagnostic tests to give an indication of their level of English. Following on from this, they would be required to undergo a three-month training period before being assigned to the PPP charter school. This would include a detailed focus on English and allow for continuous practice and improvement for teachers in their skills. Furthermore, each teacher would receive five to seven hours training per week – with attendance mandatory.
- SABIS recognizes that its curriculum, teaching methods and student assessment may be different from those currently in place; hence it would undertake to provide a "Transitional Curriculum design, implementation and student assessment" model, to allow students to move easily between the two systems. In order to provide immediate baseline data, however, they would quickly bring in assessments that could "measure progress ... using international benchmarks."
- SABIS would want flexibility over the length of the school day and academic year – to extend both if required.
- SABIS would require that there should be "No third party interference." This again repeats the need for SABIS to be free to use its *proven* model as it sees fit. Accountability would come in terms of student results, not through outsiders judging the processes and inputs.

With these parameters agreed, SABIS would admit all students on criteria agreed with the ministry. Placement in particular grades or classes, however, would depend upon initial diagnostic testing (in mathematics, English and Arabic) of students, as is customary in the SABIS model. The transitional curricula that would be created for every grade level would be refined on an ongoing basis. Indeed, all aspects of teaching, testing and ongoing follow-up would be refined based on analysis of the progress of students.

Interestingly, as in the Kurdistan model, SABIS sees its PPP charter schools ideally being transformed over time into licensed schools. Hence, the suggestion that the initial contract with the ministry should be for five years only, following which the model would switch to the licensing program. Once the licensing program was introduced, only one senior administrative representative from SABIS would remain in the school.

In a retreat, the company decided (after Jim Collins) to create its "Big Hairy Audacious Goal" of reaching five million children by 2020. Most of this expansion in terms of student numbers envisaged will come from this licensing model. SABIS's most interesting licensing model to date has been in the United States, specifically in Brooklyn, New York. We'll journey back to America, to finish our exploration of the range of business models SABIS is engaging with around the world, helping to make a difference in difficult places.

CHAPTER 8

Licensed to ascend

New York meets Beirut

In one of the toughest districts of New York City, Brownsville in Brooklyn, young children at a charter school are getting the results of their
state exams. I know it's a tough district: when I first visited, my Ukrai-
nian taxi driver initially refused to take me there from the more upmarket parts of town. Speaking in broken English, he shook his head:
"They kill somebody every time. They stab each other. They even kill
their brother." The crime statistics would not allay his fears. In 2008,
Brownsville gained the gruesome title of the "most murderous" neighborhood in New York City. Crimes of robbery and burglary were also
up. One resident was reported as saying, "It's like a war zone here. It's
like a little Iraq."[1]

Steven F. Wilson goes through the results of the children's state
exams. He is the founder of Ascend Learning, which is managing this
and two other charter schools serving some of the most disadvantaged
children in America. He's reasonably happy that the children in this
tough inner-city environment are doing so well. Although barely a year
old, his school has outperformed other, more established schools in the
neighborhood. He feels he could be on the right track.

He's not the only one perusing the children's state results. Five
thousand, six hundred and twenty-two miles away, in Adma, a small
town perched on cliffs overlooking the Mediterranean north of Beirut,

Lebanon, the SABIS team is also poring over the exam results. Again, they are happy enough with what they see, but realize there is room for improvement in the English examination. For instance, when asked to do an extended piece of writing, the New York children do not respond well. The team call in the head of the English Department in Adma to examine how this, and other areas, could be improved. For three months, fourteen people work nearly full-time in the Lebanon offices, preparing materials and electronic assessments that will be used to improve the performance of these poor children in New York. Eventually the new materials, electronic back-up, assessment systems, and training materials were sent back to New York. The next year, children were able to perform even better in the New York state exams.

Thus, a for-profit education company tucked away on the shores of the Mediterranean endeavors to make a difference for deprived children, irrespective of where they live in the world. Crucially in this case, SABIS does not own or even manage this school – it's managed by Ascend Learning, a completely separate organization. Instead, both are piloting SABIS's new system of *licensing*, one of the two major ways in which SABIS hopes to achieve its big, hairy, audacious goal of five million children served by 2020.

To run good schools at scale

In 2006, after publishing his prize-winning book *Learning on the Job*, Steven Wilson was at a crossroads in his life. In his late forties, he had been at the forefront of the movement sweeping America, to "create a new generation of outstanding public schools that would enable students – regardless of their socioeconomic background – to reach the heights of academic achievement."[2] In the beginning he'd been a policy wonk, advising Massachusetts governor William F. Weld in the early 1990s on education reform and drafting the Massachusetts charter school law, which would lead to one of America's first and most successful charter school programs, and, of course, directly to SABIS's first and most established charter school in Springfield.

But his policy work had whetted his appetite for more hands-on involvement: in 1996, he co-founded a company, Advantage Schools, a for-profit education management organization that would create a large chain of charter schools across America, improving the educational opportunities of many thousands of disadvantaged children. In four years, the company grew to educate 9,000 students in twenty schools. This was just the start. But like many engaged in this adventure, he soon began to realize the difficulties of running good schools at scale: "Turning a profit running schools had proven much more difficult than any of us had expected. To cover our costs, we needed to open still more schools. When the dot-com bubble burst, however, further growth was the last thing our long-patient investors were willing to fund." His investors sold the company; he was out of a job; "the adventure was over."[3]

His desire to explore how to run good schools at scale, his abiding passion for almost a decade, however, had not left him. Writing his book may have been an attempt at catharsis; while researching it, he saw clearly a possible, more effective way forward. He analyzed seven leading organizations that had been part of this movement, including his own: what had gone wrong? What, if anything, did these companies do right? It soon began to become clear to him that one company above all had something which none of the other organizations had and which increasingly he saw was one of the essential, missing ingredients for success. The company was SABIS.

"It actually had intellectual property," he told me, as we discussed his book and all he had done since, sitting in his Brownsville office in the attic above his first SABIS-licensed charter school: "A lot of others claim to have it, but if you went rustling around you couldn't really find it." It was true that Edison, one of the companies he'd explored in the book, did create something, but they were unlucky in that much of what they'd developed, such as a set of curriculum standards and the electronic meeting place for parents, "The Common," became commonplace soon afterwards, as state-mandated standards and social networking sites. "But SABIS with its sequential curriculum, its notion of points, its testing to mastery, the whole idea of gap filling, is something completely different. To actually have a proprietary set of products is really something that no one else had."

That had caught his attention. But as he had further researched, the success of SABIS's first charter school, in Springfield, Massachusetts, got him really interested. He was impressed by the evidence we discussed in Chapter 4, that every child who graduated from high school was offered a place at college. Significantly for Wilson, "this was not occurring at a boutique level." Other successful networks of charter schools all featured small schools, as in the highly acclaimed KIPP ("Knowledge Is Power Program"). But SABIS was achieving this "in a school with over fifteen hundred students." In SABIS's one school, almost as many children were enrolled as in *all* of the other seven top-performing Boston charter schools *combined.* "This was impressive," he said.

The more he researched the SABIS model and explored the challenges facing other operators, the more he realized that SABIS seemed to have solutions to two of the major inhibitors of growth facing new players trying to run good charter schools at scale. Both concerned how to economize on scarce resources. The first was to do with teaching staff. Highly performing charter schools required what could only be called "heroic" teachers – they even celebrated this fact. But where were all these heroes going to come from as you moved from boutique to scale?

No need for heroes

I mentioned in an earlier chapter that when I started visiting the SABIS charter schools, I was looking for heart-warming stories of children's success. But readers of books about schools for poor kids in the inner city will also be used to stories of *exceptional* teachers doing *heroic* things for children who have previously been abandoned. That's the theme of *Work Hard, Be Nice*, the *New York Times* bestseller I have already mentioned in the context of the creators of KIPP. It subtitle spells it out clearly: "How Two Inspired Teachers Created the Most Promising Schools in America."[4] Certainly, how these two young teachers, Mike

Feinberg and Dave Levin, created their network of 99 schools in twenty states and the District of Columbia is a truly inspiring story. It's all wonderfully uplifting; inspired teachers can make a massive and transforming difference.

Perhaps readers of this book have also been expecting something similar. When are we going to be introduced to the heroic teachers who are making a difference in SABIS schools around the globe? While I could regale you (although with nothing of the panache that Jay Mathews brings to the job) with stories of some wonderful teachers I saw on my travels – quickly coming to mind are the Spanish teacher in Flint, Michigan; the phonics teacher in Brooklyn, New York; and the mathematics teacher in Springfield, Massachusetts – to focus on them would be to miss the whole point of what SABIS is trying to do. It would also miss the point of what Steven Wilson found so attractive about the company and its system.

Steven Wilson set out the problem and its solution in an excellent article for the American Enterprise Institute.[5] Like many others, Steven Wilson had been very impressed by the performance of top charter schools following what has been dubbed the "No Excuses" model – promoted energetically within the KIPP schools, for instance. This is the model of schooling in inner-city America that focuses on "driven and highly educated teachers" who "lead their students in a rigorous academic program, tightly aligned with state standards, that aims to set every child on the path to college."[6] The name "No Excuses" is apposite: "teachers adopt high expectations for their pupils and stoutly reject explanations for low achievement from any quarter, whether from a child for failing to complete an assignment or from a district apologist's appeal to demographic destiny."[7] Certainly these schools were getting good results. But could they be replicated to serve all those children in the inner cities who needed them? Could they be replicated *with the available teaching manpower?*

Steven Wilson examined the seven top-performing charter schools in Boston, which, together with a couple of hundred similarly high-performing schools, "are the bright lights of the charter school movement."[8] Fully 57 percent of their teachers were graduates of the "most competitive" universities and colleges in America (using *Barron's Profiles of American Colleges*, the definitive work which categorizes US universities and colleges in terms of their selectivity into categories ranging from the most competitive to the least); moreover, 71 percent were in the top two categories, and the vast majority – 83 percent – had attended colleges in the top three *Barron's* rankings, that is, at least "very competitive" colleges.

But compare these to the teachers in ordinary public schools in America: one study showed that *Barron's* "least competitive" institutions, i.e. the bottom three sets, provided fully 25 percent of New York City teachers – compared to only 2.5 percent in the high-performing Boston charter schools. Another study showed that only 19 percent of public school teachers attended schools in the top two *Barron's* categories – compared to 71 percent of teachers in the Boston sample.

In other words, teachers in the high-performing Boston charter schools (and Wilson triangulates the results with data from other parts of the USA and finds roughly comparable results) have an educational background that is "markedly different from that of public school teachers as a whole."[9] The "No Excuses" schools that achieve such exceptional results in the face of great adversity have teachers who are drawn from an altogether different labor pool than those in the normal public schools. And it isn't far fetched to believe that it is in large part owing to their exceptional backgrounds that these teachers are able to draw out the best in their children.

The key question then asked by Steven Wilson is: how many teachers are there, or could there be, like those who work so well in the top charter schools in Boston? Consider this: there are 450,000 teachers employed by the member districts of the Council of the Great City Schools (CGCS), a coalition of the USA's 66 largest urban school districts. But only around 142,000 students in total graduated from the top two categories of *Barron's*, the highly competitive and most competitive colleges. Perhaps it's not beyond the realms of expectation to think that one in ten of these top graduates could be encouraged to enter teaching for two years – in a sort of "Peace Corps" for the inner cities, as Steven Wilson puts it. If these graduates stayed in teaching for two years, then only around 6 percent of students in CGCS schools would be taught by these teachers. Even if *half* of the graduates of the top universities went to teach for two years in these schools, this would still mean *only one third* of urban students benefiting at any one time from these teachers.

In other words, Steven Wilson's key insight: "the labor pool on which 'No Excuses' schools rely is too small to meet the needs of all the nation's urban schools."[10]

Indeed, not only is the labor pool too small, it's probably too fragile even as it stands. Recent research has shown that in some KIPP middle schools on the West Coast, teacher burnout is clearly already happening: the teacher turnover rate was two and a half times higher in the KIPP schools than even in the "traditional public schools serving impoverished students" – 49 percent compared to 20 percent.[11] Moreover, in many districts "the biggest competition for teachers" is with other charter management organizations. "Even in places like Boston, a city with one of the world's largest concentrations of top colleges and universities, charter school leaders say that having to compete against each other for talented teachers is the biggest barrier to their schools' growth."[12]

But why do "No Excuses" schools need such exceptional teachers? And could there be an alternative system which relies less on heroic teachers? Once you examine the "job description" of a "No Excuses" teacher, it is pretty clear that some parts of it could benefit from revisiting. One area is the workload: after working exceptionally long school-days – sometimes from 7:30 in the morning to 7 p.m. at night – teachers then have to develop curricula and assessments, as well as lesson plans based on these. Having to do all this as well as teach means that the job becomes incompatible with having much of a life outside of work.

The second major set of problems is faced because of the dramatic demands that the children bring to the teacher in the classroom: "Each child presents his or her teacher with an accumulated array of undiagnosed knowledge gaps that impede the acquisition of further knowledge," Wilson pointed out to me. Children in difficult schools have typically not had their knowledge gaps identified and remedied. As they lag further behind in certain – if not most – subject areas, children become disaffected with schooling. The exceptional teachers in the "No Excuses" schools have to deal with all of this: but "identifying and then filling these gaps across a class of twenty-five or more students, rebuilding their motivation to learn and freeing them of destructive habits, while also ensuring the mastery of new, grade-level material is indeed an extraordinary undertaking." For Steven Wilson it is clear: "it requires the teacher to possess unusual analytic skill, agility in shaping the curriculum, personal drive, capacity to engage students, and, not least, time."

But are both of these challenges really necessary? Asks Wilson: "Can these responsibilities be partially offloaded and the job be made more manageable – one that could be performed by a broader pool of candidates?" Looking at them both, it is clear that they can: why should teachers be writing curricula at ten o'clock at night? And if teachers didn't have to remedy years of miseducation, nor develop their own tools, then "the job would not require heroic educators."

What SABIS had achieved precisely addressed these issues, realized Wilson. They had started with the admission expectations of selective colleges and systematically worked back through all the grades to kindergarten and figured out exactly what has to be taught at each level. They had created pacing charts to show teachers what needed to be taught and when. Then they had figured out how to teach it in an efficient way and provided very rich resources for doing that – including their book series, now standing at 1,600 books, "spanning all grades and academic subjects." They had sorted out which were "essential" concepts that all children should master and created elegant assessments, administered frequently, that would determine whether students had mastered what was required, with further resources for children who had not. These additional resources included a "school-wide system of peer tutoring and school culture-building tools" which encouraged students "to take responsibility for their own learning and that of their peers."[13] All this prevented the learning gaps that so hobble educators from appearing.

All of this proprietary material meant that capable teachers working manageable and sustainable hours could work at an extremely high level, using the powerful intellectual property created by SABIS. Instead of being a job for heroes, unscalable, and unsustainable as the tiny pool of potential recruits suffers from burnout, the role of teacher is turned into a manageable job. "It becomes a job for career educators, who are more broadly available, and who can work at a sustainable pace, can start a family, and can have a balanced life." When you're 25 years old, you can work at the heroic rate demanded by organizations like KIPP: "You did, right? I certainly did." But you can't do work like that when you're 40 or 50 and have an outside life, as most people desire.

Instead of a system for heroes, the SABIS system fosters "excellence without heroics."

Interestingly, SABIS had arrived at this position, coming at it from a different angle. The reason SABIS set out to create its immense body of intellectual property was to ensure *consistency* in the teaching process, to enable standardization – something we'll explore further in Chapter 12. But this need for consistency is precisely what Steven Wilson saw as being especially attractive for the needs of his proposed schools. So it was a happy coincidence of views that led SABIS to create something under different circumstances, for slightly different reasons, which achieved something very applicable to the needs that Steven Wilson found himself addressing.

Back to Steven Wilson's study of where teachers went to university: he conducted the same analysis on the university origins of teachers in SABIS's first charter school, Springfield, as he had done for the seven top-performing charter schools in Boston. Springfield is large – at 1,574 students it has 70 percent of the number of students in all the high-performing Boston charter schools combined – and it is most definitely serving low-income families. Yet the school is hugely successful, as we saw in Chapter 4. In 2008, *Newsweek* named the school one of just three urban "top US high schools" in Massachusetts.[14]

And where did these SABIS teachers go to college? Only 11 percent went to colleges in the top two *Barron's* categories, while 21 percent went to colleges in the top three categories. These should be compared with 71 percent and 83 percent respectively in the top-performing charter schools. The 11 percent in the top two categories is even lower than the 19 percent reported from the survey of public schools in general. In other words, remarkably, SABIS has created an incredibly successful system that is sustainable and scalable. It won't suffer from teacher burnout, but instead can foster career educators – indeed, SABIS Springfield teachers on average have been teaching for nearly nine years, while 28 have been teaching for ten or more years.

It's all done, as Steven Wilson says, by "tapping into SABIS's powerful intellectual property. That permits teachers to achieve exceptional results."

No reinventing the wheel

So these were the reasons why Steven Wilson was led to the SABIS model as a way of solving the problem of creating good schools at scale, which had been exercising him for two decades. But why, having discovered the secrets behind SABIS's success, did he not then go it alone and replicate all that he had seen and learned? The answer to this is simple: "SABIS has created intellectual property that would take years and years, not just one or two but a very long time and an enormous amount of money, to recreate. We'd need tremendous resources to have the kind of curriculum development teams and software writers and all the rest that SABIS has; it's a small army of people doing this work." He wasn't optimistic that he could muster this kind of resource and was wary of the dangers of so doing. But in any case, why would he bother reinventing this wheel, when he fundamentally believed in the model that SABIS had created? "I thought it was extraordinary and I knew that it could be the tool that would bring us the kinds of results that we needed."

Without this level of intellectual property, you couldn't hope to improve the quality of educational provision in the types of school he was considering and with the kind of teachers he wanted to use. And this brings us to the second of the major inhibitors of growth facing any new players in the charter school market: an organization will need to invest heavily in intellectual property. Doing so is very expensive. The level of investment finance required is increasingly hard to obtain, even from major philanthropic players.

Wilson points out that charter management organizations like KIPP, Achievement First and The Uncommon Schools are also now in the business of creating, at least to some extent, intellectual property: KIPP, for instance, "has begun building a Web-based network that will enable teachers to share instructional strategies, lesson plans, and homework assignments."[15] These kinds of organizations, Steven Wilson observes, are recognizing "that in order to be able to have outstanding results at any kind of scale, they need to have unique intellectual property – in part to reduce the dependence on scarce or extraordinary teachers. They need to have information systems. All this requires a lot of writing curriculum and a lot of software development. They're beginning to pour millions of dollars into this, millions that they don't really have. So what this does is that it pushes back endlessly the point at which the organizations are financially self-sustaining."

To see what he means, take a typical charter management organization, Aspire: in order to cover the costs of this intellectual property creation, the company "has had to ratchet up the number of schools it would need to run ... Its original business plan, written in 2000, predicted that the organization would operate in the black with 35 schools in 2012. Its second plan, written in 2004, predicted self-sufficiency with 52 schools in 2014. And its current plan, drafted in 2007, put the target at 65 schools in 2016."[16] Aspire has a long way to go: it currently manages only 21 schools. Says Steven Wilson, "This is what is happening quite consistently in charter management organizations across the country."

The elusive goal of sustainability was not something that Wilson wanted to get caught up pursuing again. Without sustainability there could be no scalability, period. Without scalability, Wilson's vision of good schools at scale could not be realized. But he had another key insight – an insight he took to Carl Bistany at SABIS to see whether they were interested from their side.

From *his* side, he realized that he didn't have to reinvent the wheel. Having seen SABIS's intellectual property at close hand and witnessed how successful it was in their first and subsequent charter schools in Springfield and beyond, Wilson realized that if he could *license* this IP from SABIS, then he could be saved the extraordinary investment required which was pushing other charter management organizations away from, rather than toward, sustainability. He also realized that if he could lease rather than own physical property, i.e. the buildings, and persuade landlords to invest in conversion to schools, he could in effect have a business plan which was financially self-sustaining "essentially from day one." Unlike his competitors. In effect, not only could he rent physical property – his buildings – he could also *rent* the *intellectual* property too.

But would Carl Bistany agree with this insight?

Signing up to SABIS

Wilson had actually met Ralph Bistany early on in his career – when Ralph had been meeting with William Edgerly, the leading business light engaging with Boston public schools, and Peter Negroni, the superintendent of schools for Springfield, Massachusetts, when Wilson had been the young policy wonk helping to develop the legislation to make charter schools a reality. A few years later, when Wilson was writing *Learning on the Job*, he'd interviewed Ralph Bistany several times, and during these discussions his growing awareness of the relevance and importance of the SABIS model had developed. He had, therefore, had preliminary discussions with Carl Bistany, when he had come to give a lecture at the John F. Kennedy School of Government at Harvard. Steven Wilson was based there while writing his book, so they talked about the possibility of licensing the SABIS model for a new chain of charter schools. Indeed, Carl and Wilson had spent a day together in the conference room thrashing out a memorandum of understanding, for moving toward a potential licensing deal. After the book came out, he went to Lebanon to continue these discussions, in July 2006, arranging his meetings around the SABIS annual directors' meeting and their gala dinner, celebrating 120 years in operation.

Then began months of hard negotiation. "I think," says Steven Wilson, "we were both quite happy with where we ended up." For SABIS, the key questions were, apart from the financials, that "the licensee would implement the model faithfully and would not degrade the brand." Wilson felt that they "needed some level of flexibility in how we use it, and that was the key challenge." The main thing to figure out was "what does it really mean to say you're going to use the SABIS system?" Could they pick and choose from the system, or did they need the whole system to be authentically SABIS? Out of their discussions came the "principles of operation," which itemized the components of the SABIS system that Wilson – and now any other licensee – had to adhere to. This included things like using the prefect system, the Point System, using all the assessments and so forth.

The interesting thing about the negotiations for Wilson now, looking back on them, is that he feels he may have been too cautious: "Now as it turns out we use all of those without any hesitation and much *more*, because the more of the SABIS design that we can exploit, in fact, the better."

Happy that the negotiations were going well, Wilson signed up Jana Reed as chief operating officer. Jana and he went back a long way – both had worked for Governor William F. Weld of Massachusetts, and Jana had risen to regional vice-president at Advantage Schools, having been one of the founding team members. After Advantage, she'd been director of business development at Building Excellent Schools, training aspiring charter school principals. They signed the licensing agreement with SABIS in late 2007. In September 2008, as SABIS was opening its first public–private partnership school in Kurdistan, Ascend Learning opened the doors to its first SABIS licensed school in New York. Jana was the driver behind recruiting the faculty and enrolling the students. "I never doubted that she would do it. We had over a thousand applicants for the first two hundred seats." Just as in Kurdistan, a lottery would have to decide those children lucky enough to attend.

Driving home the reality of what Steven Wilson had described in theory, some of the teachers they were able to recruit were from a nearby, high-performing "No Excuses" school: it turned out that teachers were leaving "in droves." They were frustrated, just as Wilson had predicted, by the need to develop *both* curriculum and lesson plans: "They were eager to join a staff with a similar mission but a ready educational system."

The perpetual motion machine

What Wilson was aiming for was to combine the SABIS system with the best of the "No Excuses" philosophy, to create a hybrid that he could easily take to scale in deprived areas of America's north-east. A key part of the "No Excuses" philosophy is that if the children are not behaving well, "it's not because they are bad, it's because *you haven't taught them*." In other words, the key premise of "No Excuses" is that "*everything is taught. If they're not behaving, I didn't teach them right.*"

This explicit teaching of classroom procedures can take up the whole of the first week of a school. "We might teach parts of it for an entire day. But not in a way where we're getting bitchy about it; we don't get frustrated ..." Can it even be fun? "Fun is a bit of a stretch, but we'll say, looks like we need to do that again, we're not there yet." That way, if it's taught well at the beginning, they don't have to keep coming back to it during the rest of the year, which could well provoke frustration for many.

One of the extraordinary things about the experience of being in the Ascend schools for me was the disjuncture between the location in which the schools were to be found and the behavior of the children inside. Inside, you could only be impressed by the amazingly good behavior of the children. You felt all the time that you were in the presence of articulate, well-disciplined children, clearly from sophisticated, well-to-do backgrounds. Only when you left the school threshold and stepped out of the door did you realize you were back in Bushwick or Brownsville, crime capitals of impoverished parts of New York City.

In particular, in my few days in the Ascend schools, I never saw any expression of anger, either from teachers or students. Wilson thought this was significant: "Partly you don't see anger because they feel successful." The results he is getting make him proud: the second-graders in the first school came in at the 23rd percentile; they are now at the 70th percentile in math and English. "If you're at the seventieth percentile, you feel successful and you know that you are good at what you do. Why should you feel anger?"

The financial model that was finally negotiated between Wilson and Carl was that Ascend Learning would pay a certain percentage (8 percent is the standard licensing rate) of all per-pupil tuition funds received from government or state, local or federal. Now, in New York City, charter schools essentially receive around 70 percent of the district recurrent expenditure that would go into a normal public school. The charter schools managed by Ascend, of course, must also pay a management fee to Ascend Learning. What's fascinating to an outsider is that, although the charter schools get only about 70 percent of the public school funding and pay a percentage of their revenues to SABIS and a further percentage to Ascend Learning – in other words, the charter schools have *considerably less funding* available than a public school serving similar communities – the assumption is that they will be able to deliver considerably better results. Certainly parents seem highly impressed by what they see in Ascend schools, which is why there is a highly competitive lottery for school places.

Perhaps also what is fascinating about Wilson's business model is that "essentially, it's a zero capital approach." Because Ascend does not have to invest anything in intellectual property development, or on capital development, and because the schools operate at a surplus from their very first year, meaning that Ascend can also operate at a modest surplus, "it's as close as you can get to a perpetual motion machine."

In a sense, Ascend Learning can theoretically "expand without limit, without capital." This is what makes his model so exciting.

One reason why Ascend Learning is able to keep its costs so low, and so be this "perpetual motion machine," is that the headquarters is based on the top floor of his first school. Wilson wants to be right where the action is, seeing challenges and problems first-hand, also sharing in successes as they happen, and getting to know the children, teachers and parents too. He doesn't want any "social distance" between himself and the families he is serving. Other education and charter management organizations base themselves in Manhattan, in Fifth Avenue even; this did not seem sensible on many levels to Steven Wilson and Ascend Learning.

Board games

There is one very important impediment to growth – for Steven Wilson's Ascend Learning as much as for SABIS. The problem is finding people to staff the boards of trustees required for each school and to maintain trust with the boards once people are found.

For each board, five trustees are needed. The authorizer of Ascend's charter schools has taken the position that two out of five of these trustees can serve on other boards. Currently, this means in Wilson's three schools, "our boards are highly interlocking; on each board two are serving on one other board of the three." This is a very helpful arrangement, "in terms of governance and getting a stable environment." But even so, the thought of how you get people on the board of your tenth and fifteenth school, let alone your 50th school, is challenging. If the rules were changed to allow one board to manage *multiple* schools, then this would be "very good public policy, because you could recruit a much more sophisticated level of trustees, with a larger enterprise that they're responsible for."

Getting the right people on board, as it were, is crucially important. In *Learning on the Job*, Steven Wilson shows that disputes between the charter school boards and education management companies are a constant source of problems. SABIS has certainly had its history of problems with its charter school boards.

In Chicago in 1997, for instance, SABIS had opened a two-campus charter school. There may have been some initial teething difficulties; nevertheless, the Chicago International School, as it was called, was eventually unambiguously successful. During the second academic year, 1998/99, however, the charter school board, the Chicago Charter School Foundation (CCSF), decided to rescind its contract with SABIS. As their action seemed entirely unreasonable, SABIS felt they had no option but to sue. The resulting litigation resulted in an agreed statement, this being essential for SABIS to combat any impression that poor academic performance was responsible for their being let go:

> Litigation between SABIS® Educational Systems, Inc. ("SABIS") and the Chicago Charter School Foundation, Inc. ("CCSF") has been resolved pursuant to a settlement agreement. SABIS is a company with an international reputation in education and a proven track record of running charter schools. CCSF contracted with SABIS to operate the Chicago International Charter School, and SABIS operated the Charter School during the 1997–1998 and 1998–1999 academic years. The lawsuit arose out of disagreements between the parties regarding their contract.
>
> The terms of the settlement agreement, including the amount of money to be paid by CCSF to SABIS are confidential. All claims asserted by the parties against each other have been withdrawn and will be dismissed.
>
> In accordance with the Settlement Agreement, CCSF also states publicly as follows:
>
> SABIS met the challenge of starting up one of the first charter schools in Chicago. The charter school operated by SABIS at two campuses, with an enrollment of approximately 1,600 students, was by far the largest charter school in Chicago, and among the largest charter schools in the nation. While many other charter schools struggled greatly with start-up problems, SABIS successfully opened the Chicago International Charter School on time under a very tight schedule.

SABIS implemented its educational system in Chicago, and achieved academic results consistent with SABIS' high standards. The unique SABIS system of education focuses on core subjects such as English and Math, in addition to providing a well-balanced liberal arts curriculum and physical education. The SABIS teaching method utilizes a detailed and well-defined curriculum, as well as proprietary educational materials and computerized systems. CCSF believes that the SABIS educational system and philosophy are sound.

During the first academic year, the Chicago International Charter School operated by SABIS performed very well compared to other charter schools in Chicago. Both campuses had the highest percentage of students at or above national norms on required external standardized tests compared to other charter schools in Chicago, and one of the schools even beat citywide averages in its very first year in operation. During the second academic year, the students continued to perform at a similar level academically. In elementary math, one campus again beat all other charter schools with the highest percentage of students at or above national norms, and the students at both campuses beat the citywide average. In addition, the students at both campuses received the highest student performance classification from Chicago Public Schools for the average amount of academic growth over the prior year in both elementary math and elementary reading.

Both SABIS and CCSF are pleased that they were able to resolve their dispute without further litigation.

When I was in Lebanon, Ralph Bistany showed me an old faxed copy of this statement. He pointed to all the agreed elements of success that SABIS had achieved in extremely adverse circumstances: "And they still fired us!" he added ruefully.

Indeed, the seeds of the conflict were sown in the fabric of the legislation. It all comes down to control. Boards are by law responsible for the allocation of large budgets, multimillion-dollar budgets. But boards are likely to be made up of people who haven't any particular experience in managing large budgets – even in managing small budgets. Nor do they have experience of managing complex organizations like schools. Organizations like SABIS – and all these considerations apply equally to Ascend Learning – have experience in both finance and school organization. They feel they should be left in charge of day-to-day operations. And an organization like SABIS cannot afford to be flexible – its whole *raison d'être* is that it is a chain of schools with a model that needs to be replicated in full if it is to be successful. So it can't bend to the whims or concerns of a board about the ways in which the school is run.

Add in personalities and local politics, and sensitivities are likely to emerge. Sometimes local figures want to grandstand for effect or for personal aggrandizement. Sometimes people from SABIS or similar organizations really don't have the time to nurture the relationships required to keep things moving along nicely. Furthermore, add children and their parents – and the fully understandable self-interest of many parents when it comes to their own children's lives – and you're in for a truly toxic mix.

This is not to say that it is always a disaster. In the Springfield case, for instance, "the board didn't try to micromanage SABIS," Beth Conway told me. "They realized that SABIS had the means, the intelligence and the background to provide for the school. So they really truly acted as a governing body." But finding people who are willing to act in that way, and in a voluntary capacity, may be exceedingly difficult.

Through licensing, SABIS can get out of the complexity of dealing with boards and focus on the academic essentials. But, of course, that's not a solution to the problem of the boards – it simply moves it on to someone else, in this case Steven Wilson. In the end, there can only be a political solution to this issue, if organizations like Ascend Learning are to be allowed to flourish and prosper.

Quality control at a distance

How will SABIS maintain quality control as it expands its number of licensed schools? Thirty-year-old Ayham Ayche is the manager responsible for licensing at SABIS's Lebanon head office. Ayham is what you might call part of the SABIS *extended* family. Although not related to the major families, he was "born into SABIS," as he likes to put it: his father started working with SABIS the year Ayham was born – indeed, Mr Ayche senior was recently presented with a 30-year service loyalty award from the company at their annual directors' meeting in Warsaw in 2009. (He wasn't the longest-serving member of the SABIS staff – at the same meeting there were also awards for 40 and 50 years' continuous service.) When he was aged seven, Ayham's parents left war-torn Lebanon and took charge of the SABIS boarding school, Ashwicke Hall, Bath, in England. His parents still live there now.

After taking his degree in computer science at Oxford (his college was Somerville, which had only recently changed status from an all-girls' college to admit boys: "An ideal situation," Ayham mused) and after a brief stint in a software company, Ayham joined SABIS in Lebanon.

One of his key concerns is how to maintain the quality of the SABIS brand, as the licensing project moves from its close connection with its trusted colleague, Steven Wilson, to bring in more and more partners as it seeks to dramatically expand this part of its business.

So what elements of quality control are there? In fact, as Steven Wilson points out, quality control elements are built in as an integral part of the SABIS system from the outset. In particular, four elements of quality control are available, independent of any additional controls SABIS might want to exert over its licensee schools (or indeed schools that are simply part of the SABIS international family).

First, quality control is built around the Academic Quality Controllers (AQCs). Licensing schools are free to name staff roles as they see fit, so the AQCs become Deans of Instruction at Steven Wilson's Ascend schools. The Deans of Instruction are responsible for "the high fidelity implementation of the SABIS program," says Wilson; he or she is the key to ensuring that the program is implemented accurately and well. Because the SABIS system "is so specific and so granular," the Dean of Instruction knows exactly what needs to be tracked, what needs to be looked for, and when. "You can tell very, very readily whether or not the system is being used correctly," says Wilson: and if it's not, "then the system itself triggers an immediate set of interventions, designed to bring it back on track."

Secondly, quality control is made easy because teachers are not inventing their own curriculum, not using their own pacing chart, and so are not teaching different things at different times. This means that teachers in a subject or age-related team can easily plan their lessons together, using the SABIS lesson books and other resources, which provide the foundation for the quality of learning. Teachers use lesson templates that are not only school-wide, but network-wide too, which show very specific expectations for what a lesson will include and what it will look like. Lesson plans are submitted in advance to the Dean of Instruction, who reviews and approves – or offers suggestions for improvement for – these lesson plans.

Thirdly, every week children sit the Academic Monitoring System (AMS) tests, providing the most important information that will enable the Dean of Instruction to monitor the quality of the learning that is taking place. Every week teachers meet at grade level to discuss these results and challenges to their teaching arising from them. Says Wilson, "The real father of that discussion is the results; that's what drives it forward." These are SABIS tests, not based at the school or even Ascend network level, and SABIS feeds "very rich information" back to the school. In particular, the reports look at each "essential concept," and show the mastery level for that concept. If a significant number of the students didn't do well on the test items checked for that concept, "then you didn't teach it right," and your team must think of different ways of teaching it. If only a small number didn't get it right, then those students need extra help – usually through the Student Life Organization and peer tutoring. If all students mastered the concept, "then you are green; you are good to go."

This system of testing, with real-time, computer-provided results and reports, is an immediate quality control feedback loop which, says Wilson, "no other school system I've encountered has." It's a key reason, as we've noted, why Wilson was attracted to the SABIS model.

The AMS system is used across all of SABIS's schools, nationally and internationally, with only minor variations (such as the addition of Kurdish in northern Iraq and some adjustments to different state requirements in the USA). This means that Steven Wilson and his quality team not only get data on the performance of his network of schools, he can compare these across all of SABIS's schools. SABIS delivers what's called a "scoreboard," software that combines the results across a set of schools, showing at a glance any performance problems. It's just one of the regional software management tools that SABIS uses. "It's modeled on the analogy of a traffic light," explains Wilson, "so you can see if everything is green, all the schools in the region are on track. If there's yellow or red, it highlights a problem where a particular school, or grade, or section, is underperforming." You can click on that problem, and click down all the way to an individual student if you want, to explore how and where the problems with conceptual understanding are taking place. "It's quite remarkable," says Wilson, and only possible "because the SABIS system is so granular. You'd never be able to make those comparisons across schools in any other system because you wouldn't have enough consistency about what is being deployed." With SABIS's common curriculum and shared assessments, attention can thus be directed to where it is most needed.

Initially, Carl Bistany had thought that a licensee of the SABIS system wouldn't want to be part of these regional quality control systems. But Wilson absolutely wanted to know how his schools were doing as part of the larger system of SABIS schools, and to be able to respond accordingly.

In addition to these quality control components that are integral to the SABIS system as a whole, there are other elements that are more formally part of the licensing agreement. These include formal visits from the SABIS team – with George Saad and Ayham chief among those taking part. As part of the SABIS network, they have access to the e-mail help desk and hold a week's training every summer in Minnesota for all the school directors. In the Ascend three-week-long summer school, SABIS has sent their subject specialists in the past to help train the teachers – now SABIS trains the trainers and provides indepth training materials for each subject and method. Lastly, the licensing agreement itself is focused on quality issues: the licensee has to achieve certain outcomes on the state tests and in terms of "Adequate Yearly Progress" – something that came in as part of the No Child Left Behind Act – for the contract to remain in place. SABIS has the right to terminate the agreement if a school is lagging behind. SABIS can also terminate a contract if the licensee is not abiding by the "Principles of Operation," specifying those aspects of the SABIS system that have to be used, such as the Point System, prefects, AMS, etc.

The system of quality control seems rigorous and extensive. But as I heard of the licensing system, I became concerned about an opposite problem – not so much schools not working to the quality standards, but doing so and then deciding that they could do it alone – "reverse engineering," if you like, what SABIS was providing to avoid having to pay the licensing fees and going it alone.

Neither Steven Wilson nor the SABIS team were particularly worried by this possibility. For Wilson, as we've implied, the key issue was the "huge volume of materials and tests" that SABIS provides. "You could decide to imitate some aspects, but that wouldn't get you very far. The amount of work you'd have to do to develop the software, curriculum, assessments and so on would cost an enormous amount, and take up an inordinate length of time."

Ayham agreed that the expense of replicating the materials would be a considerable burden. He also pointed out that SABIS will become a significant brand name in this market, so "it would be shooting yourself in the foot if you abandoned the brand." A non-SABIS charter school would lose its competitive edge if it abandoned the brand, even if part of what it offered was similar to what was on offer in a SABIS school. One of the things that SABIS is using in its marketing for potential licensees is that Wilson's Ascend schools have been very heavily oversubscribed. "We think associating with a brand that has very rigorous academic results will be popular. And having just a small increase in enrollment will more than make up for the licensing fee," Ayham points out.

But Ayham brings a further angle to this issue. "We're constantly improving what we do," he says. "Three years ago, our product looked nothing like it does now. We've improved the IT and the academic side of things. In three years' time, it will be completely different again, more advanced. We are competing internally with ourselves and will make our product obsolete long before anyone else can do so." Because of this constant striving for improvement, Ayham doesn't believe that it would be in the interests of any licensee to try to simply copy what they have at one moment in time. It would not be as advantageous as sticking with them. One of SABIS's core values is "we never become complacent. This will keep our licensing model ahead of its competitors."

Ayham gives a small example to illustrate what he means. Inspired by the potential challenges in new licensee schools – but as applicable to any school that is part of the SABIS brand – the Academic and Technology departments back in Lebanon are exploring some technological innovations, with specific content in math, English and science, to streamline and reinforce their teaching methods (we'll discuss this further in Chapter 11). If it works in their pilot experiment in Lebanon, then this feature may become part of the product that is licensed. But even if it doesn't, there are plenty of similar innovative features being explored that will become part of the licensed package.

Another example came from Steven Wilson. One of the areas that Ascend Learning is collaborating on with SABIS is the development of a lesson plan bank – with a difference. On one level this will work to make lesson plans searchable by teachers, who can find plans developed within the SABIS framework to use with their classes. Once they've trialed them, teachers will be able to rate the quality of the lessons – so a subjective aggregate perception of the quality of lesson plans will be built up on the website, along the lines of perceptions of quality of books on Amazon. But SABIS will take this further. The lesson plans will be correlated with *student outcomes* for children who have been taught. In this way, teachers will be able to see patterns emerging of which lessons seem to be more or less effective for children's learning. "It will be an extremely valuable resource," believes Steven Wilson. "It's been great to be part of the ideas that led to it."

"Powered by SABIS," the brand used by licensees, is a key part of the company's growth strategy. In the last chapter we saw how Carl Bistany envisages this rolling out in Kurdistan and Iraq. And in the Middle East, Victor Saad suggested that there appears to be a big market for private schools to license the SABIS model. But in America, an important market looks likely to be charter schools, whether stand-alone, or networks like Steven Wilson's Ascend Learning. In three years' time, SABIS aims to have 25 to 35 licensed schools. In the current academic year, the target was three to five licensed schools – the upper figure has already been achieved. Next year, SABIS aims to add seven to ten schools, while the following year a further fifteen to twenty new schools will be added.

Does Ayham want to be part of this growth? I asked him where he saw himself in ten years' time. He remembered what he'd heard about someone giving a novel answer to this question at an interview: "I'll be at your competitor's, drawing a much higher salary." Seriously, he told me, "I want to be with SABIS; I want to be part of making a difference through education in whatever way I best can."

Escape from Beirut

Steven Wilson was the keynote speaker at the SABIS annual directors' meeting in July 2006. His summary of the challenges of running charter schools at scale in America in *Learning on the Job* had impressed father and son, Ralph and Carl Bistany, so they had invited him to present his ideas. They also wanted to continue their discussions about the potential of licensing their system to him. Because 2006 was the 120th anniversary of the founding of the mother school, the directors' meeting was held on the company's home turf, Beirut.

Following his talk, Wilson attended the 120th anniversary gala dinner, on the evening of 12 July. It was a splendid affair, as directors and senior staff members gathered from all over the world to celebrate the company's long history. There was a big alumni reunion too. The prime minister of Lebanon spoke, warm in his praise of SABIS's contribution to his country; he had his picture taken with all those present.

There were fireworks. The banquet was sumptuous; the wine flowed freely. As the evening came to an end, George Saad led a small and only partially rehearsed group of the less inhibited directors in singing jazz standards a cappella, as had become the tradition. Mrs Saad listened reflectively, remembering evenings around the piano as Charlie had played to their gathered extended family.

Many of those making a difference with SABIS in America – people like Maretta Thomsen and Karen Reuter from Springfield, and Catherine Boozer from New Orleans – had to leave the party disappointingly early, at midnight, to catch the 3 a.m. plane to Paris, and then on to the United States. But Wilson was going to stay on for a couple more days, exploring the details of the possible licensing plan with SABIS.

Perhaps some were still revelling even at 6 a.m. If so, they would have been greeted with fierce flashes and thunderous noises in the near distance. Not more fireworks, not the breaking of a summer storm; Israeli fighter jets were bombing Beirut airport. It was the beginnings of yet another serious conflict. At least 1,200 people were to be killed, and a million Lebanese displaced. The early morning plane to Paris was in fact the last to leave for five weeks.

When Wilson had first said he was going to Beirut, he had to overcome the usual flurry of misgivings from family and close friends. The name "Beirut," he said, had become for Americans a figure of speech, a synonym for dysfunction, disorder, state of war. "People imagine this bombed-out place. It's literally an expression in our language signifying that." Wilson had been thrilled and fascinated by the opportunity to go, however, having never before been to the Middle East. Now he was faced with having to write a collective e-mail to his family, including his mother, and close friends, spelling out that, while he was not in any way in danger, "Israel bombed airport. Leaving through Syria. Don't expect contact for some time." "It was a wonderfully Hemingway-esque style," he says, laughing as he reflects on it now. "You know, our lives rarely get that interesting." To him, what was most extraordinary was how easily and readily SABIS set out dealing with this inconvenience: "It was amazing the way the SABIS folks leapt into action to come up with a plan to get me out of there." In the end, the plan was to "spirit me out across the border to Syria." Wilson laughs at how, to an American audience, this really was from frying pan into fire: Syria was part of George W. Bush's extended "Axis of Evil."[17] Exiting Beirut via Syria wouldn't be the ideal conclusion to many Americans' holiday plans.

The SABIS team drove him to the border with Syria, although they had to abandon their vehicles and walk the last stretch. Wilson waited there "fully twelve hours," as the SABIS folks negotiated his exit. "They had to go up into a second-floor room of the building, which was in a state of complete pandemonium, with people literally coming in and out of the windows. There was a lot of jostling and fighting." An American wishing to cross the border without a Syrian visa posed something of a problem: "It was not an easy project; it took a very, very long time." Across the border, he was met, after a short walk, by people from the SABIS school in Damascus. It really felt like an extended family taking control of the situation, wherever he found himself. They drove through the night, stopping for refreshment at a roadside restaurant at 2 a.m., where the regulars were enjoying hostile anti-American videos on the flatscreen. From Damascus, he was driven to the Jordanian border, again to be met by another SABIS team, this time from the Amman school. And from Amman he flew back to Paris and on to America. Everything was "so beautifully organized, and nonchalantly executed," said Wilson, "that I never felt at one moment that this wouldn't succeed."

How did it make him feel about SABIS at the time? He hadn't yet signed with them – didn't it give him misgivings about working with such an organization, based in such a volatile part of the world? "On the contrary, what was so impressive was that SABIS had planned for this kind of eventuality. It had detailed back-up plans for everything, even moving its data centers to another country. Everything like this is *prepared* for." Far from making him nervous about signing on, "It only increased my respect and regard for them."

I could see exactly what he meant. He's working now in some of the toughest parts of New York, where taxi drivers fear to tread. But working with SABIS, you know that they've been through worse challenges than you will ever have to go through, in worse places than you'll ever find yourself in. But each time they've come out on the other side. Seeing them in action in Lebanon when some adversity struck could only make you more keen on having them alongside you, as you try to make a difference in some of the world's difficult places.

PART 3

The enterprise of education

CHAPTER 9

The logic of learning

Three themes

Chris Whittle, as we've seen, dreams of "changing the education paradigm,"[1] challenging the shibboleths that keep public education inefficient and uncompetitive. One of these is the idea that "adults must run all aspects of the school – and do the work within it. Students are there to be 'served.' Schools carry students; students don't carry schools."[2] "Children," he notes, "can teach as well as learn." He also notes that work itself "is a great teacher," but "are we employing work as an educational strategy in our schools to great effect? ... Is it possible that permitting students to play central roles in the actual operation of our schools could enhance not only their own education but that of other children as well?"[3]

Chris Whittle is thinking radically; but much of what he is suggesting in his futuristic school design is already in operation in SABIS schools worldwide.

SABIS's design is truly revolutionary. When I set out a preliminary outline for this book, I made a list of the aspects of the educational model that I could glean from the SABIS website and other publicity materials. The list probably covered all the ground. But after I'd spent time in Lebanon and the Emirates with Mrs Leila Saad and Mr Ralph Bistany, I realized that the list conveyed nothing of the coherence of the whole. There's an underpinning educational philosophy, supporting a system of secular humanism, with knowledge as hierarchical, children as responsible individuals in a school construed as a community, and where time and efficiency matter for educational reasons (as well as for business reasons). There is a "world according to SABIS."

Importantly, the educational model is rooted solidly in practice. It has evolved into the whole over decades of trial and error, modification and refinement – we've seen some of this evolution in Part 1 already. The richness of the SABIS model is that each one of its key educational components has been crafted as part of a coherent system over a considerable length of time. The outcome is an educational program that is unique and evolving, distinguishing SABIS from every other player in the enterprise of education.

In this and the next two chapters, I will discuss the SABIS education model as being made up of three themes, which can be disaggregated into twenty components:

Theme 1: The logic of learning

1. Starting with the requirements for college entrance, SABIS has broken down all that is required into a logical curriculum sequence. From kindergarten upwards, this logical sequence is embedded in the curriculum materials created by SABIS, including 1,600 textbooks and associated assessments. (Where appropriate, the college-preparatory curriculum is adapted to different countries' and US states' requirements.)

2. The logical sequence brings out the concepts to be taught and the steps in which these need to be taught.

3. The concepts are further broken down into "essential" and "non-essential" concepts. The former are those which are essential to master before moving on to other concepts in hierarchical disciplines. The latter provide for more extensive understanding.

4. Memorization is an integral part of learning. Retaining the essential concepts is a minimum requirement for further learning.

5. All children can learn: SABIS schools are deliberately non-selective, taking children of all abilities (apart from those with extreme

learning disabilities). Students are assigned to classes based on their aptitudes as measured in diagnostic assessments.

6. Children are individuals and can learn at different levels and rates, so throughout the system there are ways to respond to this through differentiated approaches.

7. To nurture abstract thinking, an overemphasis on hands-on and other material supports is avoided.

8. Weekly and yearly "pacing charts" are created for the teachers to show the rate at which concepts need to be taught. Teachers build lesson plans based on these pacing charts, using pro forma guidelines.

9. To check on individual students' and the class's mastery of each concept, there is a system of weekly assessments, the AMS, integrated into the curriculum and testing the concepts that have been encountered in the previous week. The periodic exams combine concepts that have been encountered over several weeks. All assessments provide data to inform decision-making at all levels, and are the key first level of accountability within the system.

10. The weekly assessments and some periodic exams are computerized and are administered in the ITL hall. The software is designed to integrate testing and learning. It provides extension activities for some and remedial work for those who need it.

11. The system is data rich and provides the data for school management at school and regional levels to analyze strengths and weaknesses of teachers and students, and to prepare follow-up. The basis of all this data management is contained in each student's "history files."

12. The different roles of the teacher are carefully disaggregated to ensure that teachers focus on what they can do best; other adults take on roles that ensure the smooth functioning of the school and a system of accountability and action. These roles include the AQCs, the supervisors, the heads of department and the exam invigilators.

13. Class size does not matter – small class sizes certainly cannot

guarantee individual teacher attention, so are overrated in that respect. But the logical SABIS system ensures that children are not lost in large classes, but are able to master essential concepts however many children are in the class.

Theme 2: The community of learners

1. There is not just one teacher in the classroom – students who have mastered content are encouraged to take part in peer tutoring and Shadow Teaching in order to help ensure that all students have learned.
2. Cooperation not competition is encouraged between students. Children are grouped in class to encourage cooperation; in particular to ensure that the whole class feels responsibility for each child's learning progress.
3. The Student Life Organization brings students into the school management process. Students help instill discipline, enhance academic standards, prevent bullying and intimidation, and raise student morale, thus ensuring the environment is conducive to learning.
4. The Student Life Organization helps the development of the whole person, building the culture within the school and in the outside world. Organized by their peers, children are initiated into a whole range of arts and crafts, sports and outreach action.

Theme 3: The evolution of the learning environment

1. The learning environment can never be static, particularly with progress through information technology. New and more efficient ways of learning are being pioneered by SABIS, including Integrated Learning and Testing (ILT), which begins to shift many of the teacher's academic roles to information technology.
2. It's not just new technologies that make this possible either – new ideas and realizations about the way learning happens also bring new possibilities, as with the example of students being self-taught on whole courses within SABIS schools.

3. SABIS is exploring ways to bring down the cost of education. SABIS is pioneering ideas wherein information technology and peer learning combine to ensure academic success, while the Student Life Organization creates and manages a conducive learning environment, thus making it possible to bring education to the deprived areas of the world.

Many of the concepts and ideas listed here have already been introduced in the earlier historical and policy chapters. These three chapters bring them together in one place to draw out their interconnections and underlying coherence. To link with the chapter on the business model (Chapter 12), it's important to stress that each of the first two themes (and all of their components discussed below) feature in every one of the SABIS schools – wherever they are found, and whether they are private or in public–private partnership. The first two themes thus define the consistency of the SABIS "brand" – something else we'll be exploring in the business chapter below. The third theme, however, takes us to the cutting edge of developments in educational thought. It features ideas that are being piloted in various settings. If these are successful, then they're likely to be rolled out across the world, becoming an integral part of the global SABIS brand.

In general, schools – public or private – do not follow anything as logical and as well thought out as the SABIS system. There's so much left to the serendipity of who your individual teacher is; and there are no checks on what you've achieved except at best on a termly or even an annual basis, and then these are not in general used to inform your development, but merely to report on your progress or otherwise. And there's much left to chance in terms of your school environment too; if you're unlucky, and many children, especially those most deprived and so most needing a conducive environment, are unlucky, it won't let you work at all. The logic and comprehensive scope of the SABIS system by comparison is very unusual.

The logic of learning

The SABIS system is ultimately, in the academic sense, a college preparation system. So children in the end have to be prepared for externally set examinations that internationally provide the basis for college entrance. Ralph Bistany is very clear on SABIS's role here: "My job is to get those kids over certain hurdles. If the kids don't get over the hurdle, then I've failed them. The parent is not coming to me for me to give him my version of what education should be; they come to us because they want their kids to go to university. That's the job I should fulfill."

From this basis, how are the academic requirements for the system now fulfilled? I met with Ghassan Kansou, Vice-President for Academic Development and Research, based in the company headquarters in Adma, Lebanon, and asked him to take me through some of the ways in which assessments are measured.

Ghassan is a grand-nephew of Mrs Saad's, and cousin to Victor and George Saad, and great-grand-nephew of the founder, the Reverend Tanios Saad. Like all other members of the family now involved with SABIS, from kindergarten he'd been through the SABIS system, doing his A-levels in the SABIS school in Bath, England. Ghassan went up to Oxford, to Lady Margaret Hall, where he studied mathematics and computer science. For one of his projects at the university he asked those at SABIS what it might be useful for him to pursue. Carl Bistany mentioned the need for an automated exam system, and so he researched and devised this. Carl was very happy with it, recalls Ghassan: "Why don't you get on a plane next week and go to Dubai?" Carl suggested. "There's quite a bit to be done in terms of exam generation." And so straight out of college, Ghassan joined SABIS.

In charge of the Academic Development Department, Ghassan oversees many of the areas that we've described throughout the book concerned with education. His department is responsible for the book series, now with 1,600 titles, the "driver behind what we teach." His department is responsible too for testing, immersed in quality control and audit trails. The Academic Development Department links closely with the Information Technology Department, for technology is "an integral part of the system that allows us to really identify what students know, what they don't know, and what issues they may have."

The Academic Development Department employs 120 people globally, some 70 in the head office, with 50 working in the regions. For the SABIS core subjects of English and math there are twenty full-time staff in each subject, working on curriculum development, including writing new books, content development, pacing charts, exam questions and associated support in regions and schools for curriculum and assessment.

Ghassan described to me the process the department goes through in order to create the final curriculum – more or less exactly the same process that Ralph Bistany went through when he was first concerned to help the Yemeni students some fifty years ago:

We're constantly breaking things down. Our end goal is the twelfth-grade curriculum. We break this down to the simplest level: what simple units of information or concepts are needed to be taught within that course? Then we locate these within the school grades. In fourth-grade mathematics, for instance, we decide that these are the skills and concepts that we want students to know. There might be some three hundred concepts within the year, and that is the basis of how we build the program up. And so we break down the specific fourth-grade math program into these concepts. Then we decide which set of concepts should be taught in week one, which in week two and so on. Then we go beyond that and say this is what should be covered in that specific lesson – these four concepts, say. So as the teacher goes in to teach his class on Tuesday in fourth grade, he knows he's going to teach these four concepts. And the teacher walks into class, writes those four concepts on the board, so the children know what is going on too. And the books we provide are there to support the student in learning these concepts.

The "acid test" of the system is: are the concepts being learned? How does the system check this? This is where the AMS exams come in.

The AMS questions are directly linked to the concepts being taught: "So if there were twenty concepts in that particular week, there are twenty questions linked directly to every concept." Every week, these computerized assessments check whether these concepts have been learned. "Are we on pace with a particular class? I don't need to ask a teacher or head of department or the school director, all I have to do is look at the results of the AMS exam." And looking at the results from individual classes, schools and regions is a mainstay of what informs all of Ghassan's and his department's work.

Clearly the AMS questions don't exhaust the possibilities for learning – the further question arises of how children can combine different concepts, integrating them into the larger curriculum. So every three or four weeks, students are given what SABIS calls a "periodic" exam. The AMS, Ghassan tells me, is "gap analysis, but it doesn't tell me if I'm seeing the overall picture within a subject. The periodic exams do." In the periodic, questions include a number of concepts, exploring whether students can synthesize different types of concepts and information. These could also feature longer questions requiring multiple steps to solve.

Importantly, for both types of test, but especially for the periodic, people in the Academic Development Department, in their subject groups, spend a lot of time going through student responses. Here they can see in depth the kinds of problems that students are struggling with – and explore further ways of helping them address these challenges. Tests are created centrally in the Adma, Lebanon, head office. Most tests are marked electronically (see Chapter 11 for ways in which computer correction is being developed by SABIS) or, if there are extended answers, by other professionals within SABIS not directly involved with teaching the particular class.

The question bank now has close to one million questions. These are created by the subject teams – new questions are continually devised to better test understanding of the concepts and the contexts of the concepts. Devising questions isn't a straightforward matter – if questions are multiple choice, for instance, you've got to have the right kind of "distractors" (as alternative answers in multiple-choice questions are called), or you won't get meaningful results. And if questions are badly devised, children can often get the right answers even if they have no understanding of the topic.

A simple example in mathematics – which happens to be my own subject as well as that of most of the Saad and Bistany families – shows some of the potential problems with question design. If a child is asked to order decimals, from smallest to largest, most children can get Set A correct.

A: 0.4, 0.5, 0.1

Most children will get the right answer: 0.1, 0.4, 0.5. But they don't have to understand decimals to do so. A surprising number of children will have successfully ordered Set A simply by treating the decimals as ordinary numbers (this error is called "Decimal Point Ignored"): if you change just one number, as in Set B, you'd soon see whether students have actually grasped how decimals are different from ordinary numbers.

B: 0.4, 0.5, 0.12

Children with the Decimal Point Ignored misconception will give this order for Set B (smallest to largest):

0.4, 0.5, 0.12

With this answer, their misconception can be identified – and remedial action taken.

Another surprisingly common student misconception, however, has been dubbed "Longest is Shortest"; this builds on the correct idea that digits to the right of the decimal point are smaller than those to the left, and get smaller the further you get away from the decimal point. The misconception then distorts this correct understanding to somehow infer that the more digits to the right of the decimal point, the smaller the number, irrespective of what the actual digits are. Now, children with this misconception can certainly get Set A correct. But they will also get a correct answer to Set B too! For they will order Set B as (smallest to largest):

$$0.12, 0.4, 0.5$$

This is, of course, the correct answer. But they will see 0.12 as the smallest because it's got most digits to the right of the decimal point, not because it really is the smallest number.

In order to correctly identify this misconception, going back to Set A, you'd instead need to change the numbers to those in Set C:

$$C: 0.47, 0.5, 0.1$$

The correct answer is 0.1, 0.47, 0.5. Children with the "Longest is Shortest" misconception will write "0.47, 0.1, 0.5," and so can be easily identified. Usefully Set C *also* identifies those with a "Decimal Point Ignored" misconception: they will give a third answer, 0.1, 0.5, 0.47. So asking children to order Set C is a truly diagnostic question – it will identify those who really understand ordering of up to two-digit decimals and cleverly also identify those with two particular and distinct misconceptions about number. (Note that had we changed Set A to Set D, 0.4, 0.58, 0.1, this would correctly identify those with the Longest is Shortest misconception, but *not* those with the Decimal Point Ignored misconception – they'd still get it right, without understanding.)

In other words, it's not as simple as it might first appear creating question banks that can truly identify whether or not children have an understanding of the concept being tested, and provide "distractors" to correctly identify the errors that are likely to be made if differing conceptions of the topic are held, pointing to specific types of remedial attention required.

To address these kinds of issues, SABIS questions in the bank have different "quality control levels," to show that they have been through different quality checks. First, if someone develops a question for a certain section or chapter, this is labeled quality control level "Copper." The next time someone in the department checks it and finds it satisfactory, then it goes up to "Bronze," then "Silver" and "Gold." "Only when it's reached the 'Gold' level is it safe to release it to the regional centers," says Ghassan. Only then can it be used as part of the testing in assessment software. There is one more level, "Platinum," which shows that the question has actually been used – not all questions are used, as they are randomly generated by the exam generator – *and* that a suitable proportion of students have been able to answer it correctly *and* they've been able to answer it in a suitable timeframe. "It's no good having a question in an AMS or periodic which takes an average of five minutes when there are equally suitable ones which only take four minutes," Ghassan explains. Then: "It's tried and tested, it's sealed, it's good enough, that question is 'Platinum.'"

History files

The data collected from the exams – AMS and periodics – are then stored and analyzed in each child's "history file," part of the SABIS SMS – School Management System. This system is very different from anything found in any other school model, I believe. It is true, in most schools teachers and administrators are interested in students' marks or grades. But the way SABIS deals with them is probably unique. Ralph explains: In a grading system as used in many schools, a child might get 85 percent in mathematics, and be applauded for this. Or a child might get 50 percent and at least be applauded for passing the subject. But even for the child who gets only 15 percent of the answers incorrect, and even more so for the child who gets 50 percent incorrect, there are likely to be crucial questions upon which the hierarchical development of the subject depends. For instance, "If he doesn't know how to add two fractions together, it's going to be a disaster later." Indeed, this was how the idea of essential concepts arose for Ralph, when he noticed that children who had equivalent grades in mathematics in eighth grade suddenly went completely different ways in ninth grade – even when both had had the same high grades. Suppose both had 85 percent again. For one, the gaps – the 15 percent incorrect – might be in more advanced areas which weren't essential to know; but for the other, "the gaps were deadly on things that weren't necessarily that hard to learn, but really mattered for progression." Ralph says: "I always give the example that adding fractions is easier to teach than extracting square roots. If you fail to learn the second, no disaster will happen, but if you fail to learn the first you're in for a hell of a lot of trouble." That's where the idea for essential concepts came from, and why they feature so prominently in the history files.

The huge amount of data in the history files is stored electronically, for each child, and for each class. To get an idea of how extensive these are, I was given access to some of the files for one student in Grade 7 at the International School of Choueifat, Dubai, and for another class in full.

For the child in Grade 7, this summary of their understanding in mathematics amounted to 102 pages. Everything had been minutely broken down into the required steps. I could see how the whole math curriculum was broken down into its separate concepts, and the "essential" concepts grouped separately from others. For instance, concepts numbered "MR01046 to MR01050" were as follows:

> Divide by a 1-digit number: 1-digit quotient with remainder
> Divide by a 1-digit number: 2-digit quotient with no remainder
> Divide by a 1-digit number: 2-digit quotient with remainder
> Divide by a 1-digit number: More than a 2-digit quotient and no remainder
> Divide by a 1-digit number: Zero in the quotient (e.g. $1812/6 = 302$)

The data tables show for these, and all the other hundreds of concepts, the number of times, with date, that the student was tested on the concepts, and whether the answer was correct or incorrect. It's important to note that each child gets tested on the concepts at multiple points in their automated examinations, both AMS and periodics, and each occasion is separately recorded. So, for instance, with the concept "Divide by a 1-digit number: 2-digit quotient with remainder," the child whose history file I was examining had been tested ten times, over an almost two-year period, ranging from 21 December 2009 to 20 September 2011.

For each concept then there is a summary number given, which shows the SABIS-adjusted score for that child. It looks like a fraction, although in fact it's not a genuine fraction. This number indicates four possible outcomes:

- No need to reteach (this is when the numerator is positive and the denominator is greater or equal to 20)
- Reteach and retest (the numerator is negative or equal to 0 and the denominator is greater or equal to 20)
- Retest only (the numerator is negative or equal to 0 and the denominator is below 20)
- More tests recommended (the numerator is positive and the denominator is below 20)

We don't need to understand how each of these outcomes and numbers is arrived at, although it's important to point out that the quasi-fraction actually weights the *intervals* between the tests, *as well as* whether the answer was correct or not. So, for instance, the history file that I was looking at showed that the student had been asked a question about a particular concept six times, and answered it correctly five of those times. His score was given as 13/25 – the algorithm is a trade secret, but it's to do with the intervals at which the tests are taken. Suffice it to grasp that for every single concept that is there in the SABIS curriculum, each child is tracked at this level of detail.

Importantly, this information goes to the AQCs and the subject heads of department, who then advise the teachers on what to take action on. The files are accessible to the teacher, but in general they have to teach according to the pacing charts they are given. Remedial teaching is decided upon by the AQCs and heads of department.

Similarly, I saw the same child's 154-page history file for English. For example, the topic "Narrative Elements" at Grade 7 is broken into ten concepts, each separately numbered as with the math concepts above:

- Identify the narrator
- Identify the speaker
- Identify and restate information about important characters
- Infer character traits from thoughts, feelings, words and acts
- Identify the feelings/emotions of a character
- Identify suitable adjectives to describe a character
- Identify the setting
- Identify subplots/conflicts and relationship to main plot
- Identify foreshadowing
- Recognize suspense within a passage

Again, each of these concepts is linked to particular questions in the AMS and periodic exams, and full details are given showing the student's understanding at particular intervals.

There are certainly curriculum materials available in the market, some of which do delve down to this level of detail in terms of the objectives to be taught. But none would then link these objectives automatically with questions in an automated question bank, with automatic alerts for remedial action. And remember, these tests are at least weekly per subject, so allow for constant monitoring of progress. The level of detail available at the individual level is quite astonishing. In the right hands, you could see how this would mean that no child need slip through the net; no child need be in the position of not understanding concepts essential to moving on to higher levels. In this way, SABIS, I believe, is unique and way ahead of the game.

Moving on from the *individual* files, there are the files for the *class as a whole*. I was given access to these for one complete grade (Grade 4 at the International School of Choueifat, Dubai – it's a very large school, with 324 students across ten sections of Grade 1 alone). Those for the "essential concepts" covered 44 pages alone. The tables showed "Failed concepts only per student," with the quasi-fraction as above to show where the child had not succeeded, and a running total of the number of correct answers. From these tables it's quite easy to see how each child is doing within the class and how the class as a whole is doing. Then there are a couple of summary pages, showing the concepts and the percentages of children who have understood each concept. Again, it's easy to see those concepts that are giving more or less difficulty and to think of how one could respond accordingly. It's all a very scientific way of approaching what children are learning.

The history files are also significant in terms of another aspect of course development. Supposing someone within the company proposes a new course for ninth-graders. The first move for SABIS is to ask: what is the prerequisite knowledge for taking the course? They can then "press a button," as Ralph puts it, and out will come a list of all students who can take the course without any problem, based on their prior understanding as recorded in their history files, together with further lists showing students who would need further attention before they could take it. "All of this would come out automatically," Ralph says proudly.

All this puts a new gloss on the notion of "data-rich" schools. These are not data obtained from termly or annual tests summarized too late for any remedial action. The information that SABIS has takes it to a whole different level. In all, they have 2,500 tables which are populated with data from their students. And on top of that, there are the processes and systems designed to ensure that the data get used to assist those students who are not able to perform. SABIS is also creating files for data on student behavior, attendance, even physical development – and again there will be a system of electronic alerts to warn of things that are going wrong.

Ralph Bistany muses, however, that they probably have more data than they can use at present. "Development is moving faster than the schools can move. We are not giving them enough time to absorb ... we know this. And again, we're thinking of ways to accelerate the situation. SABIS is working at maybe fifty percent or maybe even less of the power available to it." But, he hoped, it could move toward using all the power it was developing. "It's agony," he told me. "Mrs Saad always told me, 'Slow down a bit and let them absorb it.' Maybe I'm worried about my own time and I'm in a hurry."

The real power of this data, says Ralph, will be seen when you combine it with the power of the Integrated Learning and Testing model. "It can become even more powerful, and less adult dependent," he says. "Through Student Life," says Ralph, "we are already creating schools that can run themselves." We'll come to these developments in Chapter 11. But how in general is technology used throughout SABIS?

Technology tools

It's obvious that the "history files" depend upon the existence of the technology capable of handling such huge quantities of data. We saw in Part 1 how SABIS was a very early player in using technology for supporting the learning process, acquiring one of the first computers on sale in Lebanon in the late 1960s – inspired, as we've seen, by the need to analyze the large amount of data it was amassing because of the Yemeni students it had taken on, and the detail required for the granularity of student understanding they wanted. Using technology has been a crucial part of SABIS's educational and managerial practice ever since the days of the first computers.

I spoke to Serge Bakhos, group vice-president responsible for information technology (as well as having other responsibilities for book publishing), to gain insight into how technology was used throughout the organization. The Information Technology Department has 65 full-time employees, including 45 software developers. Serge is Ralph Bistany's son-in-law, having married Carl's sister. He's from Lebanon but studied robotics at master's level and mechanical engineering at undergraduate level in Cincinnati, which in the 1980s was a robotics hub. In 1985, Mr Ralph Bistany, who was by this time his father-in-law, drafted him into SABIS, to help set up their first private school in the USA, in Minneapolis. Mr Bistany had said, "You can continue your

PhD in Minneapolis and just check in on the school to make sure it is all going well." He did just that, enrolling for a PhD in Minneapolis, and spending just five hours a week in the school: "Those five hours soon became full-time hours"; after two months, he gave up his PhD to work full-time for SABIS. He stayed for five years, then went to work on some business projects in Abu Dhabi, all the time keeping in close contact with Carl Bistany. When Carl came to SABIS as president in 1996, Serge returned to the fold.

What are the key technological elements that fit into the logic of learning? The first that we've come across several times so far in the book is "AMS," the SABIS Academic Monitoring System. This is the key tool through which academic progress is tracked in each school – whether private or public–private. The system electronically monitors students' understanding of every concept taught on a weekly basis for each topic. Any learning gaps that are identified can be quickly dealt with.

As we saw, the AMS is a computer-generated exam, created from a databank of nearly one million questions prepared – and continuously updated – by the Lebanon-based curriculum teams and delivered to SABIS schools all over the world. The exams are customized according to required levels of difficulty, time, and topic categories. This is done automatically through the EGS (Exam Generation System) Wizard. An administrator in any SABIS school can specify to the head office in Adma:

- the subject and particular topics for the exam (as in the particular SABIS books – the book code and sections are entered);
- the level of difficulty (e.g. very difficult, difficult, average or easy);
- time to be taken – in minutes.

Within seconds, a unique test is created and available to use in a SABIS school.

In the vast majority of SABIS schools, the AMS tests are taken directly by the student on a computer, using the SABIS ITL – the Integrated Testing and Learning system, the kind of system we met through Hêro in Chapter 6. As we saw in the Kurdistan chapter, immediately a student finishes the exam, it is electronically marked, and students can straight away tackle again any questions on which they've not done well, being referred electronically to review material to help them. To this end, each student has a "My AMS," based on the "history files," which compiles the concepts or questions that students have not firmly grasped, and can then generate personally tailored exams to address those learning gaps.

Further developments are now linking the AMS with the student's "history files," so that if a child finishes the tests quickly in one subject, say biology, and gets all the questions correct, the program then automatically switches over to an area where they have difficulty, say Arabic grammar. This option allows them to spend time on areas of difficulty elsewhere in the curriculum, rather than wasting the time until the allotted end of the examination.

I thought it was very interesting that in order to use an expensive resource efficiently and effectively, no teacher is involved in invigilation of these exams; instead, SABIS employs full-time exam invigilators whose sole job is to ensure that all goes according to plan in the ITL halls. This is all part of SABIS's philosophy of disaggregating the roles that are typically bundled together under the rubric of "teacher" in normal schools and identifying those on which the professionally trained teacher actually needs to act and can add value by doing so.

Data from the AMS, plus a wealth of other data, are contained in the SSMS, the SABIS School Management System, the second component that Serge introduced me to. This is a fully integrated management tool, used for tracking everything related to the school application process (from initial inquiries to registration and enrollment), to monitor course enrollment, student attendance and discipline, and student progress.

Data are inputted into the system from the full range of administrators in the school, including the Academic Quality Controllers (AQCs), the Student Management Coordinators, supervisors, heads of department, and teachers. For monitoring student progress, the data are entered automatically from the AMS.

The SSMS features a "tracker" system, currently state-of-the-art for student performance tracking. A full range of reports is issued by the system, presenting and analyzing wide-ranging data for administrators and teachers to monitor student learning and progress. There are systems of alerts and reminders for teachers and administrators to identify those students who have learning gaps and who may have behavioral issues or attendance problems. Learning gaps are referred to the Student Life Organization, for peer tutoring and other remedial help, while other issues are dealt with by teachers and administrators.

The data from the individual schools' SMS are amalgamated into the SABIS Regional Monitoring System (RMS), the third component of SABIS technology. Quality control in SABIS emanates out from the school to the region. Relevant data from the Academic Monitoring System and the School Management System are available in this application to the SABIS regional administrators. They can compare and analyze data across schools in real time and quickly drill down to the level required in order to trace problems as they arise – for instance, with underperforming schools or classes – and suggest remedial action. SABIS schools are currently broken down into the four regions which use this system:

- USA
- Lebanon, Jordan, Syria and Saudi Arabia
- Europe (England, Germany, Romania), Egypt, Pakistan and Kurdistan
- The Gulf (UAE, Bahrain, Oman, Qatar)

The Regional Monitoring System is a further quality control instrument. In every region there is a center to which the results of the AMS and periodic exams are immediately relayed and full analysis is available within 48 hours. If there are common errors, the regional teams step in immediately and take remedial action for all schools in terms of quickly developing teaching and learning materials to help solve the common errors. If there are some schools not performing as well as others, then again the teams step in. This time, the teams can focus on locating what the specific issues are within a particular underperforming (or indeed "over"-performing) school and explore how to address these.

Finally, there is the SABIS "Web School," the social networking part of SABIS's web presence. It has three parts. First, SABIS Web Parent, a password-protected site, allows parents to view regularly updated information about their child's academic performance, behavior, attendance, and involvement in Student Life. Secondly, SABIS Web Student allows students to keep in touch with their school at any time, from anywhere. Students can check their school timetable, homework due dates, and view their academic progress. There's also a facility to allow students to carry out practice examinations. Third, SABIS® Web Teacher provides teachers with a means of communicating with individual students or groups of students to assign homework or send relevant messages or materials.

The "picture project" – assessment in kindergarten

SABIS is in a hurry to ensure that time is not wasted in its schools, so uses the full range of technology as above to check on children's progress. Many schools see the early years, kindergarten, however, as a time to be exempted from this pressure to measure what children are learning. SABIS thought along similar lines until recently. At kindergarten level, only simple teacher assessments were required to check how children were learning. But Ralph Bistany then became frustrated with this and wanted to know more objectively whether children were being prepared for the more rigorous years ahead. So his teams created a computer-generated assessment system for kindergarten too, the "picture project." It's based on the kinds of material that children at that age would already be familiar with from their everyday class books. Pictures are produced for children to see whether they can identify the object within them or make some other connection. So, for instance, when a child sees a picture of a car, does he know it is spelled "c-a-r"? Initially teachers were asked how many questions the children could do before tiring: "Everybody said ten to eleven questions are more than enough," Ralph says, chuckling. "But instead we find the children are enjoying it and they are doing forty-five and not wanting to stop. There's no substitute for experience to find out what children really are capable of."

The project was first piloted in the kindergarten of one of the International School of Choueifat schools in the Emirates. It caused a huge upheaval for administrators: "They've got a very big kindergarten of eighty children," Ralph explained. Usually, the teachers conducted the assessments themselves "and the children did pretty well." With the automated assessment, the children were getting very poor results. "This tells us that the information given to us by the teachers before was not correct and maybe we should do something about it." Ralph is positive about this finding: "We used to think that this is what the kids learned, all of them; now we know that a big fraction has not learned. But the advantage is now we know and can do something about it. However, it is part of human instinct not to want to know." Ralph is referring to the school's initial response, which was to stop the assessments because it feared that parents wouldn't like what they saw. Says Ralph, "This is equivalent to, if you go and check your blood and find you sugar is high, you simply stop checking."

This emphasis on testing young children mustn't make one believe that SABIS has a narrow view of what learning can be like for younger children. Ralph is clear, however, that for such children there's nothing wrong with stimulating their interest through more childish things than getting them to read texts. So, for instance, his teams are working on animation for younger children using cartoon characters to illustrate concepts. "There's no harm in making learning fun," he says.

The myth of class size

Often, when education reforms take place around the world, they are focused on making class sizes smaller. Could this be one way of making learning more effective in the SABIS logic of learning? In fact, precisely the opposite is the case.

The writer of the Harvard Business School case study on SABIS says that the company's system can "best be understood in the context of the founders' rejection of several commonly held beliefs about education, which they call 'myths.'"[4] He gives two examples of these myths relevant to the educational model.

One of these myths is that "the smaller the class, the better students learned, in part because small classes allowed instruction to be individualized."[5] SABIS firmly rejects this notion – indeed, it's one of the "core areas" that SABIS proudly – and boldly, given its potential controversy – displays in its literature, just as it does the issue of being a for-profit company (which we'll address in Chapter 12). So, for instance, in the 2011 *Closing Achievement Gap* report, in the section "What makes SABIS schools different," one of the five areas of difference noted is "Larger Class Sizes: SABIS Schools serve an average class size that is larger than typically found in public schools."

What educational reasons are there? "The idea that smaller class sizes allow 'individualized instruction' makes no sense at all," says Carl Bistany. "A simple exercise in arithmetic clearly shows this." Even with a very small class of only twenty students, and a 40-minute period, that would mean that the teacher has only two minutes per child. That's hardly enough to get going with. "Individualized instruction is a myth," he says.[6] Indeed, the research that is available seems largely to support the intuitions and experiences underlying SABIS's ideas on class size. The piece of evidence that advocates of smaller class size like to invoke is the STAR (Student–Teacher Achievement Ratio) project, an experiment conducted in the 1980s in Tennessee, USA. Usefully, this featured randomized assignment of children to different classes – making this potentially a very high-quality experiment. There were three types of classes to which students were randomly assigned: one was the normal size of between 22 and 25 students; the second was the same size but with a teacher assistant to aid the teacher; the third featured small classes of between thirteen and seventeen students, with just the teacher (no aide).

The study found no significant difference between the students in the normal-sized classes with or without the teaching assistant.

Children in the small classes, however, scored better by a 0.2 standard deviation than children in the normal-sized classes: "For a student who started at the 50th percentile – in the exact middle of the performance spectrum – this increase would be the equivalent of an improvement of less than 8 percentile points, which would bring the student up to a level between the 57th and 58th percentile."[7] This is "not trivial," even if it's not an "educational revolution."[8]

There are doubts about this evidence, however. For instance, students were not tested when they entered the program – there are no baseline assessments. But this means we can't be sure that students assigned to the three experimental groups really were of roughly the same average achievement. This is a pretty serious omission: "If the students assigned to smaller classes were higher-performing students to begin with, their higher test scores would be attributable to this pre-existing advantage and not to smaller classes."[9] Moreover, there's an oddity to the results in that they posted only this "one-time" benefit to test scores. Students remained in their assigned class groups for years afterwards, but the academic gap between those in different class sizes didn't increase anymore: "This is an unusual and unexpected finding because if smaller classes really do improve student performance, we would generally expect to see these benefits accrue over time."[10]

Further doubts arise when the results are viewed against the national trend in the USA, which has seen a consistent reduction in the ratio of students to teacher unaccompanied by an improvement of performance. From 1970 to 2001, the US national ratio of students to teacher fell from 22.3 to 15.9, but test scores and graduation rates were "flat over the same period."[11] A study by Caroline Hoxby of Harvard University looked at student achievement and variations in class size (from 10 to 30 students) that were occurring "naturally," i.e., not because of any experimental design, in 649 elementary schools in Connecticut. She found no link between smaller classes and higher achievement.[12]

International evidence also does little to support claims that smaller class sizes will lead to higher achievement. The international mathematics and science assessments – TIMSS – are regularly administered across a range of countries to compare student performance. A study by Ludger Wössmann and Martin West, also from Harvard, showed that in Singapore, South Korea, and Japan, three of the five highest-performing countries, average class size was larger than 30 – indeed, South Korea's was greater than 50. Comparing within-country performance, only two countries showed academic benefits for smaller class sizes – Greece and Iceland. Overall performance in these countries is low, and school resources and teacher salaries are also lower than average: it could be that in these two countries teachers' skills are considerably lower than in other countries and that this alone leads to the benefits of small class sizes. The authors of the study conclude: "the evidence on class-size effects ... suggests the interpretation that capable teachers are able to promote student learning equally regardless of class size (at least within the variation that occurs naturally between grades). In other words, they are capable enough to teach well in large classes."[13]

Perhaps rather than increasing class size – and this is true even if evidence like the STAR project could be shown to be robust – greater benefits might be obtained by doing what SABIS does: creating systems by which even average teachers can thrive and benefit the children they are teaching. This is a very important part of SABIS's critique of the "small is beautiful" movement: as long as you structure the lessons correctly, you can liberate teachers to teach concepts correctly, and it won't matter one bit if you have larger classes. With all the elements of the logic of learning, and the other elements that we'll meet in the next chapters, you can be in a position to have classes as large as you want.

What about discipline problems that might arise with larger classes? Again, SABIS has methods for dealing with these issues – discussed in the next chapter. Moreover, Ralph Bistany is clear where many behavioral problems come from. "Our experience is that very often poor behavior is triggered by learning difficulties that are not properly addressed." For instance, when SABIS opened the Chicago charter schools, "everybody was expecting us to have behavioral problems."

But they spent the first six weeks testing children to develop a profile for each and then regrouped them into classes appropriate to their "background knowledge vis-à-vis the course." In this way, completely unexpectedly to outside observers, "we had practically no disciplinary problems at all."

Learning "myths" and learning styles

Alongside the "myth" that smaller classes are better than larger, another educational "myth" mentioned in the Harvard case study of SABIS is that "learning by memorization" is bad.[14] Carl Bistany explains the SABIS point of view on the matter: "Rote learning would be bad if it really existed. Rote learning means memorizing without understanding, which is extremely rare, for it requires a very powerful memory and the amount memorized under these conditions can never be substantial. Through the justified attack on rote learning, memorization has been maligned, and this has led people to believe that learning does not require any memorization – a false belief for anyone who wants to acquire substantial knowledge in any field."[15]

Carl Bistany pointed out how this myth gets elaborated today – with information so readily available on the Internet the need for memorization in education is even more obsolete. "This is an insidious attack on mental abilities," he says. He pointed to the recent air crash, where US Airways Flight 1549 had taken off from New York's LaGuardia airport and suffered a bird hit; the captain had a small window of opportunity to make a decision about where to land. Quickly he mentally went through the possibilities, and finally went for the only one that seemed likely to bring success, bringing the plane down on to the Hudson river, in the process saving the lives of all 155 people on board. Could Captain Chesley Sullenberger have done that if he hadn't been able to memorize all the processes and procedures required in that Airbus? Carl thought this unlikely. It's an extreme example, but one which illustrates neatly the perils of throwing the baby out with the bathwater when it comes to embracing the impact of information technology on education.

The arguments against memorization were already there when

Ralph Bistany started teaching in Choueifat at the age of 22. He locates their source with Michel Eyquem de Montaigne, the sixteenth-century French Renaissance writer, widely regarded as having invented the genre of the personal essay. He quoted to me in French de Montaigne's pithy saying, "Since I would rather make of him an able man than a learned man, I would also urge that care be taken to choose a guide with a well-made rather than a well-filled head." In education now, this approach is taken to mean, says Ralph, "that you shouldn't memorize anything." For Ralph this makes no sense: "I'm sure Montaigne didn't mean it this way." For "there is no learning without memorizing"; indeed, "it's very difficult to memorize something you don't understand"; it's possible, he concedes, but extremely difficult. The role of the teacher can be to help children understand and to provide them with the tools to help them memorize too.

Ralph has explored over the decades different approaches to memorization, investigating how understanding and memorization can reinforce one another. It's been useful for Ralph because while being involved in education he's also himself been absorbing scholarly learning throughout. So, at the same time as he has been trying to instill learning in others, throughout he has been reflecting on his learning techniques.

For instance, early on in his time at Choueifat he developed the discipline of always trying to summarize any passage he was reading in his own words. This was based on the realization that "you can fool yourself that you have understood while you are reading, but you can't fool yourself when you have to write it all down." With this in mind, he decided to allow his early classes to bring a piece of paper into their exams, with the proviso that it must have a maximum of eight words on it. He told the students, "After revising the material for the examination, try to write it down. Every time you stumble, go back to the book, write one word to remind you of the concept you missed." Determining the words, recalls Ralph, actually reinforced their learning. After they'd spent time selecting those eight words, they didn't really need them on paper.

Another incident illustrating this interrelationship between understanding and memorization took place in the early days of SABIS's first private school in America, in Minnesota. The children were learning a poem by a famous American poet. It would take the class two weeks, the teacher told Ralph, to learn the poem by heart. Ralph was appalled – at the inefficiency, but also at the realization that this would be a sure way to kill the poem in the minds of the children, who would simply get bored learning it for two weeks. Ralph said, "You're joking?" No, the teacher was not joking. "Please," said Ralph, "this should take ten minutes." "No way," said the teacher. "These are only fourth-graders."

Ralph asked for copies of the poem to be sent to the class: "I'm going to teach them to learn this poem by heart in ten minutes." Then he explained to the children, "We are going to learn sixteen lines of poetry, and I took a bet with your teacher that you are going to learn these in ten minutes. We are going to turn the page to start the stopwatch, and we are going to read this poem through once. While reading it we are going to *count the ideas*, and come out with a number after our first reading. Are you ready?"

So they read through the poem, counting the distinct ideas that came up, and they arrived at seven ideas. Could they then remember all seven ideas? Yes, they could easily by creating a narrative linking them. This was the first step, memorizing the ideas underpinning the poem. Ralph then explained to them, "Now here is a secret. These ideas can be said in a limited number of ways. How did the poet say the first idea?" After answering this, they were asked to read how the poet put the first idea. The same approach was repeated for the other ideas. The whole process was repeated several times until, finally, they recited the poem exactly as it was written. That took around eleven and a half minutes. "But I lost my bet," muses Ralph, "as it took them longer than ten minutes." But certainly not two weeks.

The belief that memorization is important, and an aid to understanding, also underpins another part of the SABIS education model, homework. The SABIS take on homework is rather different from what is found in other schools – I was a little confused the first time I spoke to a student in the ITL hall, who told me she was doing "home-work," when she seemed to be doing a test in normal school time. For SABIS, "correcting homework done at home is meaningless because we never know whether you have done it or your aunt," says Ralph. He reflects back on his own schooldays: "Sometimes my friend wrote my homework, and I did his." So instead, SABIS gives children questions to which they not only have to work out the answers, they then have to answer the same questions under exam conditions the next day at school. They prepare their answers at home – and then it doesn't really matter whether or not they are helped by an aunt or a friend, as long as they know how to get to the answers. "So you know exactly what the questions are going to be, you don't have to guess, then you come in and recite them under exam conditions. It is a good form of learning," says Ralph.

Does all this mean that Ralph Bistany is against discovery learning and problem solving? Absolutely not. He thinks spending time solving real problems – as opposed to the kind of problem solving that is often demanded in schools – is really valuable. SABIS makes a distinction between problems and tasks. Most exercises and problems given at the end of chapters and in exams are actually tasks because the mate-rial on which they are based has been taught and is sufficient for the answer. Their role is to test the depth of knowledge and to reinforce it. Whereas a real problem arises when one has not encountered a similar situation before and the material learned is not enough to find the solution. The only issue is the efficient use of time. So for instance, Ralph points out, two weeks trying to discover particular proofs in geometry would be time superbly spent, "the benefit to you would be immense." However, "if I were to teach geometry by discovery, it would take two thousand years. Like everything else in life, you have to choose how to allocate the time. Just because something is beneficial, doesn't mean that you have to do it at whatever cost in terms of time." So he is entirely in favor of discovery learning as an important learn-ing style: "If we can get children to spend two weeks trying to find solutions to some problems, and even if they don't find the answers, this is beneficial, this is strong mental effort, this is very good. It's just that we can't do it all the time."

A further "myth" that Ralph Bistany objects to, which he also believes is having a similarly insidious impact on education, is the requirement that mathematics and sciences always be taught in a "hands-on" way.

This relates to Ralph's understanding of the nature of knowledge. He has no truck with the idea that there are different "forms" of knowledge: "I believe that if you can learn English grammar, geography, literature, then you can also learn mathematics and physics and vice versa." Many young people might not particularly like one subject or another – particularly true with regard to mathematics and sciences, "but that's just a very convenient excuse. But I don't see that math and science require special talent." What he does concede is that "*all subjects at a certain level*" will require a certain intellectual power and a willingness to make the effort. You are not going to be able to teach non-Euclidean geometry, quantum mechanics, relativity, to everybody. But that is because not everyone is willing to make the effort, *and* you need a certain power of abstraction."

The ability to abstract is something that unites the different subjects. And it's an ability that needs to be learned – and which can also be grievously undermined: in general, says Ralph, "This is why we tell our teachers, please avoid 'hands on' in mathematics because 'hands on' makes learning easier, but you aren't developing a part of the brain which is the power of abstraction." At most, in SABIS schools, hands on is used in mathematics as "scaffolding," for those who can't grasp the abstractions, to be removed as soon as the concepts have been understood.

Differentiated learning

In the SABIS system, the emphasis, for the communitarian reasons that we'll explore in the next chapter, is very much on children learning together as a class. This does not mean, however, that there is not room for children of different abilities or aptitudes to flourish. Some of the ways in which the SABIS system responds to different learning abilities are worth summarizing.

First, there are diagnostic tests. When children join a SABIS school, they take a set of diagnostic tests to explore how well they will perform at different grade levels. If students perform above or below their expected grade level, they do not have to be in their chronological grade. The logic of the SABIS design is to place children where they fit best, rather than simply according to their chronological age.

Secondly, the SABIS curriculum, as we have seen, is divided into "essential" and "non-essential" concepts. This means that it's designed with flexibility within it. The most able students will be able to learn *all* or most of the concepts, while the less able will simply be mastering the *essential* concepts. So the SABIS curriculum itself allows for extension of fast learners with the facility of built-in, more difficult material.

Thirdly, students who are fast learners become peer tutors (student teachers) and Shadow Teachers, and so learn by helping their counterparts. The premise here is that by having to explain material to another child, you deepen your own understanding. We'll explore this more in the next chapter.

Fourthly, conversely, slower learners are assisted by their peers in learning material they have difficulty mastering. In extreme cases, slower learners can be put in "intensives," where teachers and peers help them address the essential concepts.

Fifthly, in the ITL hall, children who finish tests quickly and get most answers correct can be given further, more advanced problems to solve, which really push forward their understanding of the subject. Similarly in the classroom. The key here is that it is pursuing learning at a *deeper* level, using concepts that all children will have learned, but pursuing their application and logic much further.

Sixthly, something that Ralph was "clamoring to introduce" for some time, and which has finally been introduced initially in SABIS schools in the UAE, is allowing students to opt out of a course entirely. So, for instance, if one or more students decide that they know eighth-grade mathematics sufficiently well, say, then they can opt out, provided that they pass a test given to them – which is actually harder than the end of eighth-grade math test – to check that their knowledge really is solid. If they pass, they then have four choices: they can adopt two or three of the weaker students and help them in their math. Or they can become a full-time Shadow Teacher in the class. In both cases, provision is made to allow the student's own grade to be raised higher, depending on how well the slower students do. "A bright student is usually better than a mediocre teacher at teaching his or her peers," says Mrs Saad.

Another option is that they can go to the library and work on development – such as producing materials, new tests, software, etc. Or finally, they can study a course on their own – completely on their own, which, as Mrs Saad says, "is a great preparation for life. We say we are preparing kids for lifelong learning; we had better instill it as early as possible in the children." Indeed, so successful has this option become that single studying is now part of the SABIS repertoire being offered to students – we'll discuss this further in Chapter 11.

Pointing to the range of ways in which fast students can move forward, Ralph told me: "I could kick myself for not having done this earlier because I remember in my class when I was a student, there were some very bright kids who were lost because they were too bright." So, he says, "the kids who love learning should not hate school and should not be bored."

Apart from the self-study opt-out, most of these methods for dif-ferentiated learning involve the faster students helping the slower ones – peer learning, adopting weaker students, Shadow Teaching, and so on. This fits into the SABIS philosophy that the class is a community and must take responsibility for all of its members, from the weak to the strong. This strong theme running throughout SABIS's model is the focus of our second education chapter, "The community of learners."

CHAPTER 10

The community of learners

THE SABIS SYSTEM has gone a long way to creating a learning environment which is logical in all its steps and efficient and effective in its progression. This is done in tandem with creating a community of learning, however, within the school and within each class.

Indeed, the importance of this community puts a dramatic brake on what it is possible to implement in their schools. Interestingly, this communitarian instinct appears to be shared by Ralph Bistany and Mrs Saad. I was surprised to see how strong and pervasive it is – as, on the face of it, it did seem to run slightly counter to the strong individualism that it is apparent in their thoughts on other subjects. In this chapter we'll outline three aspects of the community of learners. First, we'll explore Ralph Bistany's and Mrs Saad's reflections on the importance of the class, celebrating cooperation not competition. Secondly, we'll see how the community of learners in the school is expressed through the Student Life Organization. Finally, we'll focus on a dual aspect of this – the related peer learning and Shadow Teaching – to contextualize the SABIS method in terms of important historical precedents.

Cooperation not competition: the importance of the class

In the previous chapter, we noted in passing how the possibilities for "differentiated learning" were in general contained within the classroom itself – peer learning, Shadow Teaching and the like. In the next chapter, we'll see how technological possibilities are emerging which offer the prospect of teacherless classrooms, even schools. But when pushed on whether these technological possibilities could lead to the end of classes, to the possibility of purely individualized learning, both Mrs Saad and Ralph Bistany are reluctant to accept it. Yes, they want the faster students to be able to develop intellectually. But they believe that this can be done in many ways, including the lateral and social ways we discussed in the last chapter. There are huge benefits from being in a school, they believe, and being in a class, which are completely lost if you simply follow individualized learning.

I understood their position to be something like this: many people love their schooldays and feel loyal to their schools; this is because, after the family, it's our first connection with identifying with a body bigger than ourselves. So school is an important stepping stone to the larger adult world. We mess with this at our peril – it is part of the education system that has over generations proved its worth. You don't want a system of individualized "nerds" to develop, who have no sense of their community responsibilities and who know only how to satisfy their own intellectual impulses. Intellectual and cognitive development are, of course, hugely important. But education is about more than this; it's also about emotional and social development. The school and the class neatly encapsulate a way of developing all three at once.

Let's spell out two of the key reasons why it is so important to Mrs Saad and Ralph Bistany. The first is that it is a better preparation for adult life to be "rubbing along" with others of all kinds of ability, not just your own. Mrs Saad said: "We feel it's healthier for everybody. In real life you are not going to go out and mix with just the brightest anymore; you have to be able to communicate with people with a wide range of abilities if you are to succeed." Ralph Bistany reinforced the same message: "In classes we have this advantage: the bright and the average continue learning together. In real life, this is the way people work in teams; it's important they learn this in schools. Children should learn to work together; we like them to stay together."

But the second, and perhaps the most important reason, is to do with moral and social responsibility within the group. At SABIS, Ralph said, "we create a sense of general social responsibility and we are trying very hard to have our students *cooperate*. We are trying to create the spirit where in the class, if a student is failing, *every other student is concerned*." A SABIS class, he tells the students, "should be like the Marines; we don't leave anybody behind. The Marines sometimes lose four men in trying to save one man, but they don't give up on their comrades and we should have this attitude. If one student is failing, it's everybody's concern."

To this end, it is anathema in SABIS to rank students by ability – even though the data are available, no student must get to hear of their rank in class. (In fact, in larger schools, where a grade is broken up into different sections, the students' rankings are used to sort students so that each class is of mixed ability – the first-ranker goes into a different section to the second-ranker, and so on.) Neither Mrs Saad nor Ralph Bistany wants competition to distort the sense of community within a class. Collaboration is more important than competition, and that's why ranking of students is not allowed: "One of the results of rankings," says Ralph, "is that one kid has an interest in another kid's failure. Nobody in society should have an interest in somebody else's failure." He recognizes that there could be a problem with certain positional goods in society, but in general, "a good society would solve such problems." In general, "it shouldn't be you or me; it should be you *and* me." Society shouldn't be a zero-sum game, where if I win, you lose. Instead, "when people cooperate, wealth increases, and everybody has more."

People are misguided about competition when they say that it makes students work harder, says Ralph. SABIS has found this not to be true. "When we removed rankings from our reports, we had staff who said these kids are not going to work hard; but our kids are working harder and harder. They want to achieve and we tell them, there is one measure … anybody who is not achieving his or her full potential is not commendable, even if the student is first in the class." This approach has led to more cooperation among students and has improved the performance of the whole school.

A gifted student may come first without even trying. That student is not commended simply for coming first. Whereas if a student is doing his or her very best, they are accorded a lot of appreciation and respect, wherever the student ranks.

When they leave the cooperative school, won't students have to compete in a world of positional goods? How do they cope with that? Mrs Saad said: "They compete successfully. We are hoping that they will be more humane, if I may put it like that. But if they have to fight, they do fight."

In general, says Mrs Saad, "it's part of the character-building of the children. Sometimes we are accused of being totally and harshly academic. People forget that the other side is also of great concern to us ... building a concerned, responsible citizen."

The importance of the class has one important caveat, however, which links back to the earlier chapter on "The logic of learning." It depends upon how a "class" is defined – a point that so often gets overlooked, Ralph says, because most often a class is simply defined as children of the same age, thrown together without any further thought. This is completely the wrong way of going about it: "In education a class is defined necessarily by the course and if you have a course that's well defined, that starts at a point and ends at another point, and that has a set of concepts that are prerequisites, then any individual can be in this class taking this course if and only if he or she has the prerequisite knowledge." That's why the issue of the class children are in – the community of learners – is so intimately linked to the logical parts of the learning process, the essential concepts and so on that we met in the previous chapter.

Indeed, as we shall see in Chapter 12, SABIS is working to create a wholly new learning environment, "literally run by the kids themselves," in which this spirit of *cooperation* not competition will prevail. "The thirty percent or so who are brighter can learn from information technology and they can be assisting the rest of the learners," says Ralph. In other words, the value of peer learning and the social environment trumps ideas of competitive individualized learning, even when advanced technology is introduced.

For students by students

Going back again to Chris Whittle's radical school design: he outlines a program with the unappealing name of "Student Chores,"[1] which includes things such as student peer learning and teaching, students undertaking some functions in the school office, and supervising behavior. SABIS has been doing all of this already; its name, "Student Life," has a more positive ring, however – and it really is an exceedingly positive experience for all those students involved with it.

The Student Life Organization has developed into one of the key components of the SABIS program. You can't really understand the SABIS philosophy without understanding how Student Life works. In Part 1, I outlined the genesis of the program, as Ralph Bistany and Mr Germanos in particular explored ways of getting students involved with their schools. Figure 12 shows how Student Life is structured – and it is important to stress that this crucial element is found in all SABIS schools, whether private or public–private partnership or charter schools in America.

Within the Student Life Organization, there are eight "departments": Academics, Discipline, Management, Sports, Activities, Outreach, Lower School (itself divided into the same seven other departments), and Social Responsibility. The Academics Department brings into play Shadow Teachers and peer learning (student teachers); the Discipline and Management departments are part of ensuring an environment conducive to learning. Finally, the Sports, Activities, Outreach, and Social Responsibility departments are all part of the education of the whole child.

Although in each school there is a teacher taking on the role of "SLC," the Student Life Coordinator, who has a senior administrative role, the underlying motivation behind the SLO is that it is student-driven and student-led. As one SLC, the youthful Chris Matheson at

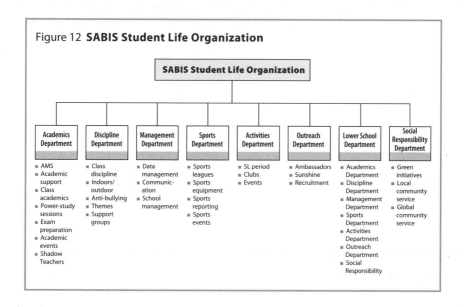

Figure 12 **SABIS Student Life Organization**

SABIS Student Life Organization

Academics Department	Discipline Department	Management Department	Sports Department	Activities Department	Outreach Department	Lower School Department	Social Responsibility Department
■ AMS ■ Academic support ■ Class academics ■ Power-study sessions ■ Exam preparation ■ Academic events ■ Shadow Teachers	■ Class discipline ■ Indoors/outdoor ■ Anti-bullying ■ Themes ■ Support groups	■ Data management ■ Communication ■ School management	■ Sports leagues ■ Sports equipment ■ Sports reporting ■ Sports events	■ SL period ■ Clubs ■ Events	■ Ambassadors ■ Sunshine ■ Recruitment	■ Academics Department ■ Discipline Department ■ Management Department ■ Sports Department ■ Activities Department ■ Outreach Department ■ Social Responsibility	■ Green initiatives ■ Local community service ■ Global community service

SABIS Flint, put it: "I am the coach on the sidelines, not more than that."

Such is the importance attached to Student Life that SABIS employs a Director of Student Life for all of SABIS's schools world-wide. The enthusiastic and energetic Roger Soweid currently has that role, engaging in training and implementation to further the SABIS vision. He was born in Lebanon, although he's been away for the past 36 years. He's now based in Phoenix, Arizona, and has dual national-ity, French-Canadian and Lebanese. He's been with SABIS for a decade now.

Roger took me through the core principles of Student Life: "Student Life is an organization within each of our schools that empowers our students to do everything they need to do for the other students. SLO is run by students for students. Our job is to empower students to take every single aspect of school life on their shoulders and run with it." The aim of Student Life is to allow children to "take matters into their own hands and empower them to really make a difference." SABIS wants its children to leave school strong academically, "but we also want them to go out into the world and be able to function and communicate and organize and lead."

In practice, students are appointed to senior roles in each department – there might be a head and a deputy head prefect for each department, sometimes more. These students are ultimately responsible for what goes on, but their role is to encourage as many other students to take part and take on smaller responsibilities and activities.

I saw Student Life operating for myself across different contexts and countries, and met with those students most closely involved with it in Lebanon, Iraq, the UAE, and the United States. It was certainly a key part of the standardized SABIS package across the world. (There was one important difference, however, which was unfortunate. In the USA, it is illegal to have students in a classroom without a teacher. In the rest of the world, SABIS students are totally in charge of all that goes on in the Student Life periods. In the USA, a teacher has to be in the class. In smaller schools this does have an impact on the number of clubs and activities; I would guess too that it could lessen students' feeling of involvement and responsibility for those activities.)

The Academics Department is an important vehicle through which weaker students are helped by stronger students. Roger put it like this: the student leaders would observe "these students are failing," and then discuss, plan and implement "what can we do to help these students succeed? What do we do to tutor them, each one separately based on their areas of weaknesses? What do we do to make sure they understand their homework? What do we do to help them pass their exams?" Students are empowered in this way to take charge of the success *of all the other students.*

We've seen how aspects of this, such as peer tutoring and Shadow Teaching, worked in Kurdistan, helping Hêro get up to speed with her English and helping her assist other students get up to speed in other subjects. In general, if you're not doing so well on a particular topic or subject, you'll be assigned to a study group, with a group leader, to work in the Student Life period (there's one period every day) on that topic. It won't be compulsory, but it will be strongly recommended. And likewise those who've done particularly well at a subject or topic can volunteer to help out those students who are not doing so well.

It's important to note that because of Shadow Teachers, the concept of "supply teachers," as we call them in England, or "substitute teachers," is unknown in SABIS schools. Supply or substitute teachers are supplied by agencies to cover for temporary teacher absences. Often children see the supply teacher as "fair game," a chance to let off steam and misbehave with impunity. In the SABIS model, if a teacher is absent, the Shadow Teacher in the class simply carries on teaching as normal. The children already know the Shadow Teacher, he or she is one of them. There is no upheaval, nothing different. It's again a very interesting efficiency measure that links the logic of learning with the community of learners.

How does the concept of Shadow Teaching work? A student in the International School of Choueifat, Dubai, told me: "We're given the pacing charts, so we look at what we've done and read up on that. We may see a review of what we have to do and learn from the books. They only choose Shadow Teachers that are good at a subject. So basically we have a good grasp of what we have to teach and get on with it."

Another told me: "I think Shadow Teachers work best when the teachers actually are not there. Because I'm a Shadow Teacher myself and our math teacher was absent for a few days, and for me as a person I thought it would be kind of challenging. But I was surprised because the class cooperated with me and there is some evidence that they really got on well with me." Because the math teacher was unexpectedly absent, the student had no time to prepare. Even so, it was a rewarding experience for him and for the class as a whole. To make it clear, one explained to me: "Whatever the Shadow Teachers are delivering to the students, it's an entirely new concept. They are not repeating what the teachers have already taught. So they do need to be prepared, and there is training done under the Academics Department of Student Life."

Another student told me that Shadow Teaching works well because "you're teaching your peers, everyone is on the same level, I mean you know your classmates, you know how they learn so you know how to teach it to them."

Why do the students think SABIS does the Shadow Teaching? "It's basically empowering the students to communicate and learn well," said one. "I think everyone can take something from that experience. Throughout Student Life, it gives us a chance to show what we are capable of, our management skills and how we can maintain discipline, organize everything. We can learn interpersonal skills, communication skills." Another added, "I think the best way to learn is to teach it to someone." That's certainly been my experience – I feel I really know something well only if I can teach it. Or write a book about it.

Moreover, the Student Life senior students also organize the system of "subject prefects" which features throughout the school during every lesson. In a normal classroom there will be about seven subject prefects, with the students arranged into groups of four, one subject prefect per group. The subject prefects are selected at the beginning of every term, usually assigned by the Academic Quality Controller and the teacher. They are subject-specific, so someone who is a prefect in English will not necessarily be a prefect in mathematics. Throughout each lesson, they will be part of the learning cycle by checking answers and helping those who need help.

Going back to the different departments, the Discipline Department is the key way in which students are tasked with ownership of creating a social environment conducive to learning. "Our students," said Roger, "are the ones who are helping other students behave in the right way. They are the ones who are patrolling the hallways, patrolling the playgrounds, making sure everybody is doing the right thing." There are discipline prefects in every classroom helping the teacher with classroom control. "If people are fighting, it is often our prefects who are there separating people, mentoring them, advising them, making sure they make up." And they also form "anti-bullying" squads, on the lookout for all types of bullying, mental, verbal, physical and now cyber bullying too. Again, "we empower our students to take care of discipline."

Roger gave me an example of how this works in practice, from the SABIS charter school in Flint, Michigan. Early on one visit, he told me, he saw "three big African-American guys" from Grades 10 to 12 "running in the hallway. There should be no running in the hallways; we don't allow that." But he saw their prefect badges, and so thought "something is happening; I need to go and check that everything is okay." From a distance he saw exactly what was going on. "Two students were about to start a fight – they were face to face, their noses nearly touching, shouting at each other." The three prefects dove in between those two students. Roger thought, "Oh no, now we're going to have a much bigger fight." But he was taken aback: "You should have seen it. They talked in the sweetest way to both of them and said, 'Hey, guys, what's going on? You seem to be tense. How can we help you?'" Two of the guys took one of the boys to the side and the other took the other student. "They talked to them and then got them back together to shake hands and to resolve the whole thing." It was quite impressive, all handled very professionally. And not for one moment involving any member of staff. How did the prefects know there was a fight about to start? Another prefect had got on the walkie-talkie and shouted, "I need back up; I need back up!" In schools like Flint, the senior prefects have these walkie-talkies, precisely to cope with emergencies like these.

The Management Department would very much appeal to Chris Whittle's revolutionary side: here students take responsibility for many of the school office functions. They manage data entry on to computers, they organize and manage "lost & found." School newsletters, bulletin boards, and yearbooks are all organized by students themselves. Students can also be in charge of school maintenance: "Something is broken; they are the ones who write the piece of paper and give it to the custodians. You have broken glass, and you need to fix it as soon as possible." Finally, of course, they manage the Student Life office itself.

Other departments are self-explanatory: the Activities and Sports departments, for instance. But the key here is that students take responsibility for organizing everything within these – such as field trips, clubs at school, the Student Life period itself, and the sports leagues and field days. The activities themselves extend the students' curriculum experience; being responsible for organizing the activities extends it even more.

I was particularly interested in the Outreach and Social Responsibility departments. Mrs Saad thought these very important: "The kids should become aware of those who are less fortunate than them." It's about social responsibility, toward the community, local and global. But it's also about getting children to engage with the complexities of modern life and the realities of multicultural society.

At the charter school in Springfield, Massachusetts, I was able to interact with the head prefect for Outreach. The student impressed me by saying that SABIS is the "give back" school – something that she in the Outreach Department is specifically involved with. They raise funds for local and global charities and raise awareness of important issues among the students: "The thing about SABIS is, outside of academics, it's a whole life experience. I take what I've learned here at SABIS and turn it into something I can give back to all the people that I've met." Her parents were refugees from Laos, who left as it was descending into chaos in the early 1970s. "When they came here they had nothing," she told me. Her dad finished high school when he was 25; he's a plumber now, while her mom works for an insurance firm. She grew up and is still living in a pretty rough part of Springfield: "Growing up seeing kids take advantage of everything, get caught up in all wrong causes. It has affected me; I want to do something to show the community around us that kids my age aren't only thinking about themselves but can give back to other people as well," she said.

She's been to Laos to visit her grandparents and other family members. "They live in a shack," she told me, "there's barely any food. They don't have running water; they don't have great electricity; they don't have a lot that I have." When she's in the mall with her friends and she hears them throwing tantrums about all they want, she responds: "Why can't you just appreciate the clothes you have, or the stuff you have at home, because there's others who don't have that. There are others who don't have education, who don't have food, who don't have a family." The experience of seeing where her family came from has inspired her. "When I'm finished with high school I want to go to college and study pharmacy so I can join, like, the Peace Corps and distribute medicine. There's a college in Boston, Mass., the College of Pharmacy and Health Sciences, and they have a really strong pharmacy program that I really want to join. So hopefully I'll get that shot."

There's a relatively new sub-department under Outreach, the Sunshine Department, or the "Sunshine Squad," as Ralph Bistany calls it. This had an interesting genesis: in 1985 or so, in the newly opened Minnesota private school, "a parent came with a daughter in fourth grade. She had red hands – her hands were actually colored for some reason. The father told the director, 'I know that the kids are going to make fun of her, and so on, *and there is very little you can do about it.*'" But at least they should be forewarned to stop any bullying taking place. Ralph wasn't in America at the time – the director called him to tell him of the problem. As she described it, Ralph thought, "*Why* is there 'very little we can do about it?'" He didn't want children in the school being miserable and lonely. If he could stop bullying, why couldn't he also address this more positive issue too? So he said to the director, "Choose two or three really strong girls from seventh grade and ask them to talk to the fourth-graders, fifth-graders and their group." They should tell the school that there was a girl coming with red hands, but this wasn't any big deal. And most importantly, the girls were to accompany this girl "for a while, making sure she had friends and knew where to go." The outcome was "the girl was happy and nobody was bothering her." This experience of helping children who are lonely and miserable is now formalized in one of the themes of Student Life.

It is especially important to SABIS that Student Life take hold in the public schools (charter schools in the USA) as well as the private schools. When introducing the philosophy into SABIS charter schools in America, Roger told me that when the students hear about the responsibilities that can be theirs under Student Life, "they look at me with wide eyes and say 'you're kidding me, you want me to make decisions, to be a leader, you want me to actually do something in the school rather than just be a spectator in the class?'" They've never seen anything like this in public schools. It's a tremendous way to boost their confidence and self-esteem, as well as their managerial and leadership potential.

In the charter schools, the system can take time to get going, maybe three or four years, especially if there is high staff turnover, as often is the case in a charter school when SABIS first takes over. But once underway, something interesting happens: "In Cincinnati this year," Roger told me, "the Student Life Coordinator had to undergo some surgery. I knew that she was leaving school September eighth and not returning until November." The school director called him and asked how he should go about replacing her. "I said, 'You don't replace her.'" If she has been doing her job properly, the students should be doing everything on their own. "No one could see any difference from when she was there to when she wasn't. Students did the tutoring by themselves, the activities by themselves, and the director was saying, 'Whoa, does she still have a job?'" But her job is vital still, said Roger, for the strategic and coaching roles.

As part of the Student Life Organization, there's also the summer leadership camp, which brings together students active in Student Life from SABIS's schools all over the world. Last year it was held in Bath, England; before that for a couple of years it was held in Egypt. It's all done at SABIS's expense. For all those who've been involved in it, it seems to be a hugely important, life-changing experience. One of the things mentioned to me time and time again by students from very poor neighborhoods across America, in New Orleans, or Flint or Springfield, or in the deprived communities in Kurdistan, was that they were taking part in an event rubbing shoulders with young people from all over the world. There you were all equals, no one cared whether you were from poor inner-city America or from some of the richest families in Europe.

For instance, Duane, a young African-American student from SABIS Springfield, is deputy leader for Sports. Tragically, I heard that he had recently lost his brother in a gang skirmish. He told me about the leadership summer camp: the whole experience was just "wonderful.

Learning about other cultures, for twelve days, learning about leadership and how our leadership affects those who follow behind us. Egypt was a terrific experience. One of the best opportunities of my life. Sometimes you wonder how lucky you are to be surrounded by these intelligent people from all over the world." From everyone who took part, I heard a similar response: "I'll stay in touch with everyone." And Maretta Thomsen, the erstwhile director of SABIS Springfield, told me of a young Latina woman, "from the north end in Springfield which is one of the poorest sections. She said to me, 'My future is that I'm going to get pregnant, or killed, or something like that.' She used to go home after school and close her bedroom door "and stay there. That's how frightened she was of what was outside in the world." Then she went on the summer leadership camp that year. "She came back and she said, 'My life has just changed.' She went on and graduated from high school in three years. The last time she came to visit me she was getting her doctorate in mathematics."

Student Life is a key part of the SABIS way, the world according to SABIS. But it is still evolving and developing. Ralph Bistany was at pains to point out to me the reality of this process of continual development – and also he was quite happy to ascribe credit where it is due. For instance, Ralph said: "I insisted that even at third-grade level we should have Student Life." He felt he was being radical, pushing the range down as far as it would go. "Anyway," he continued, "to my surprise one day we found out that a British lady teacher in our private school in Jordan had organized Student Life in kindergarten and it was working." This came at first as a shock to Ralph. But then he challenged his own thoughts: "I asked myself, 'Why on earth did I decide that it should stop at third grade?' Something was wrong in my thinking, I had no evidence that it would not work below third grade. I was stupid. And this woman made me realize that." He reflects on his fallibility; I reflect on the way that he is open to evidence to change his views.

Peer learning

Finally, we turn to the important concept of peer learning – or "student teaching" – in SABIS schools. This is a concept that could equally have been stressed in the earlier chapter, on the logic of learning. For one of the key motivations behind introducing it is the terrible waste of resources in most traditional classrooms. We already explored this in terms of Hêro's views in the Kurdistan chapter: just to reiterate these, if you were a Martian looking at a traditional classroom, what you'd see and assume is the reality is that there is one person who knows (the teacher at the front) and the rest who don't know anything (the thirty or so children). The reality of any classroom situation, however, is that several of the children will understand quickly – or will have grasped the concept even without teaching – and so there are many potential teachers in the classroom. But in traditional classrooms, the rest of this talent goes to waste. In SABIS schools it does not. Children are assigned peers to learn from – whether through the grouping in the classes, with "prefects," who are good in their subjects, assigned to help those who are slower, or through the Student Life Organization, where students who haven't done well at the AMS or periodic assessments are assigned to others to help them with their difficulties.

But I've included the idea in this chapter because it is also a key way in which SABIS keeps the communitarian spirit alive. As we've noted above, children in SABIS classrooms must feel like Marines in action – if one is suffering, then they all are suffering. Through peer learning the faster learners can exercise their moral responsibility to help those who have more difficulty.

I'm particularly fascinated by the way in which SABIS has evolved this method of peer tutoring because of what I've understood about the history of educational developments elsewhere. Problems that still haunt educational systems around the world today, including a short-age of expert teachers, high teacher turnover, and a general scarcity of resources, also faced educators in early nineteenth-century England and America; a viable solution was found through two methods of peer learning, the Madras Method and the Lancastrian Method. These methods, which transformed education for the poor across the world, prompted the creation of a different type of learning environment. To conclude this chapter, let's outline how these ideas developed in the world outside of SABIS.

The Reverend Dr Andrew Bell arrived in India in 1787 to take up his position as the principal of the Military Male Orphan Asylum, in Chennai. Faced with teachers who had "no knowledge of their duties, and no very great love for them," he had a moment of insight when he observed peer learning methods in the local village schools.[2] Testing this method in his own school, he found the older boys could successfully teach classes that "the master had pronounced impossible" to teach. Bell sacked all his teachers and the school "was entirely taught by the boys" under his supervision. On returning to England, he published a description of his "Madras Method," and began to introduce it in schools in England serving the poor, beginning in Aldgate, London. In 1811, the National Society for the Education of the Poor in Accordance with the Principles of the Established Church was set up to promulgate Bell's methods. By 1821, 300,000 children were being educated under Bell's principles. His ideas were taken up around Europe, and as far away as the West Indies and Bogotá, Colombia.

A parallel method of peer learning was created, apparently independently, by Joseph Lancaster, who had started a school to serve poor children in his parents' home when he was only eighteen. He was led to the "monitorial system" for straightforward economic reasons: "He could not afford to hire trained teachers and thus was compelled to rely on advanced students to educate the novices."[3] He published a description of his methods in 1803; by 1811 there were 95 Lancastrian schools. In 1808, a "Committee on the Rendering of Material Assistance to the Lancastrian Schools" was formed, and in 1814 the British and Foreign School Society was founded, to disseminate the methods at home and overseas.

Lancaster's methods became particularly popular in America: in 1806, the Free School Society of New York, set up to educate poor children, based its teaching methods on the Lancastrian monitorial system. In 1807, the New York legislature voted $4,000 aid to the Free School Society, since its Lancastrian method was considered a good way of reaching children. The method soon spread across other states in America: for instance, the Office of State Superintendent of Public Instruction for Lancastrian Schools was established in Maryland in 1826.[4] Lancaster himself came to the USA in 1818. De Witt Clinton, former governor of New York and president of the Free School Society, praised Lancaster for creating a system whereby "boys learned to read better and a better quality of discipline existed," compared to other methods of instruction. Governor Wolcott of Connecticut praised the Lancastrian system of instruction for being "efficient and economic."[5]

For both Madras and Lancastrian methods, the process was similar. One "master teacher" could teach between 200 and 1,000 pupils. The pupils were divided into groups of around ten, who were taught by monitors, who were themselves taught by the master teacher. Crucially, pupils were placed in a group of pupils of similar ability for that subject matter and were promoted between groups as soon as they mastered the material. Children were often given rewards/prizes for being promoted to the next level class. A contemporary witness of the Lancastrian model (in 1818) noted the school's importance in terms of the differentiated learning taking place, which sprang naturally from the peer learning model adopted: "That school was of more importance to me than all the others I ever attended for study, as it allowed the pupils to advance according to their industry and application to their studies, and were not held back by duller scholars, a fault I greatly fear often to be the case under our present school system, and which has a tendency to level down too much for the general good, if no improvement can ever be effected, by those having our schools in charge."[6]

Another contemporary report, in the *Westminster Review* (January 1824), also praised the differentiated learning possibilities inherent in the peer learning methods:

By this system the greatest possible assistance is given to the slow, and the greatest advantage to the quick. The slow are stimulated and impelled; the quick are never for a moment retarded. As soon as they get to the top of their class, remain there steadily, and thus show that they perfectly understand its business, they are promoted to a higher class. Here then is a free course for genius. The active and the indolent, the stumbling and the sure-footed, though they may be yoked together, are not forced to keep pace with each other; if stupidity be dragged along by the vigour of genius, it is a clear advantage gained: genius cannot be chained down by the weight of the stupidity.[7]

The *Westminster Review* also commented on some of the psychological benefits of the methods of peer learning:

it is evident that on this system children are better taught than on the old, because from the sympathy they take in each other, they learn everything communicable by one to the other more easily and perfectly. Whatever a child has been taught, he will communicate to his companions better than a master; because his manner of teaching, and the words he employs, will be suited to the capacity of his pupil; he knows where this difficulty lies, and how to remove it.

In other words, the "peer learning" wasn't just from monitors to pupils, it was also between pupils themselves, and this was encouraged as part of the system (as it is in SABIS schools, rather than being discouraged as it is in traditional schooling, where children are not usually allowed to help each other).

Peer learning methods went out of fashion in the new public schools that emerged in America, Britain and elsewhere. There was a revival of interest in peer learning methods in the late twentieth century, however: a study from Stanford University in 1984 compared four methods of raising educational standards in schools, viz., reducing class size, increasing the amount of time given to instruction in mathematics and reading, computer-assisted instruction, and peer tutoring. Peer tutoring was the most cost-effective, and the most effective in increasing achievement, regardless of cost.[8] Another meta-analysis[9] examined 153 studies to assess the relative merits of four distinct ways of teaching mathematics. Peer tutoring was found to be superior to computer-assisted instruction, programmed learning and individual learning packages. Looking at 65 studies comparing peer tutoring with traditional instruction, a further meta-analysis[10] found that in math, average pupils involved in a tutoring project were likely to score higher than about 73 percent of pupils receiving traditional instruction. In reading, the same figure was 58 percent.

Why does peer learning/tutoring improve achievement? One suggestion is that

> older pupils learn the work better than usual both because they have to teach, and therefore have a *reason* for learning, and because the very process of teaching causes learning. For example, the tutor has to find words to explain, has to emphasize and explain again, and has to mark the younger pupils' work. These activities all fix the work in the tutor's mind and produce better learning than normal.

Many younger students in particular express the feeling "that they can ask questions about the work more easily of a pupil-tutor than of a teacher."[11] A considerable body of academic work has been conducted since this time. This recent work suggests that well-planned peer learning "can yield significant gains in academic achievement."[12] Other researchers[13] also note that peer learning is a particularly cost-effective learning strategy.

In the light of this research evidence, again it is clear that SABIS has chosen methods that are likely to raise academic standards, as well as engage learners in their communities. Interestingly, historically we see how methods of peer learning emerged to serve the most poor and disadvantaged; in the next chapter we will see how SABIS is intending to use these methods, in tandem with technological advances, for precisely the same ends.

CHAPTER 11

The evolution of the learning environment

S ABIS HAS CREATED LEARNING ENVIRONMENTS in its schools which have a logic of progression within them within the constraint of respect for the community of learners. But the learning environment for SABIS can never be static, particularly with progress that is possible through information technology. It's not just new technologies which make this possible either – new ideas and realizations about the way learning happens also bring new possibilities, as with the example of students learning without teachers in SABIS schools. The application of information technology to learning also raises profound questions about the role of the teacher in learning; SABIS is pioneering ideas in the model for its teacherless school. This chapter outlines the progress SABIS is making on "learning without teaching" and "the teacherless school" before finally drawing the themes from the three educational chapters together, to "think the unthinkable" about educational developments.

Learning without being taught

For many years Ralph Bistany has been thinking about education and the role of the teacher:

For a long time I said to my colleagues that I don't understand why people need teachers if they can read. Whatever can be said can be written. If we can say something and it is understood, why should it not be understood if it is written? On the contrary, I would think it would be easier to understand written text than the spoken word. So why is it that people insist on having teachers if the books are written properly? And this still puzzles me to this day.

He's particularly baffled by the ways in which teaching is still done through lectures in many universities:

When people tell me I'd rather listen to a lecture than other forms of learning, I really can't figure it out. For a simple reason, if I'm listening to a lecture and my mind wanders for a short time, when I come back sometimes I've missed something important and the rest of the lecture stops making sense. If it is a presentation of an argument, if it's a story it's different, but if he's defending a case, making an argument of any kind, and I've lost something, it is difficult to recover.

When reading yourself, however, it is completely different: "If I am reading and I stray for a moment, then I can go back and restart from where I lost the thread. In my mind it should be easier for anybody to read rather than to listen. But people tell me otherwise. I'll probably die without understanding."

Indeed, the lecturer often has notes that he's reading to the class: why not let the students read them and ask questions on the notes, rather than have them listen to someone reading? "In today's world," Ralph Bistany says, "in general, lecturing should not exist anymore. It is a monstrosity." The only exception is if there is a lecturer with great charisma and presence – but there are only a handful of these: then "record him and let everybody listen to him and hit 'playback' if their minds wander."

This line of thinking was behind the motivation to develop SABIS's own book series. For "if the students read something and they still need an explanation, it means the book is not properly written." So SABIS started to develop books that *would* be properly written and which would enable students to read and understand by themselves.

But do they really know how the students are reading the books? Do they really know whether learning from their books is really successful? These kinds of questions have led to further development in SABIS's technology of learning, to the recent development of the ILT – Integrated Learning and Testing (not to be confused with the ITL, the Integrated Testing and Learning system, another core of the SABIS method; perhaps SABIS could devise more distinctive names to identify these two very important yet distinct concepts?).

The underlying principle here is that students can – indeed should – be learning by reading text; the important cycle of teach-practice-check (or, really, learn-practice-check) is integrated by having the young people answer questions based on what they've just read, and the system will not let them move forward until they've answered correctly. But it's still, if not teacher-centered (although the teacher still has an important role), then class-centered, for reasons explored in the previous chapter.

The basic hardware is simple. Each student has access to an individual laptop or computer, while the teacher has a larger console that enables him or her to see everything that is happening in the class. Everything is done wirelessly. The software has been under development for around eighteen months – although some part of that was simply brainstorming about the concept and gathering requirements for moving forward – by around seven full-time developers in the SABIS headquarters in Adma, Lebanon, with up to seventy others contributing as required. The content is adapted from the books that were already developed by SABIS. At the time of writing (January 2012), the system is currently being piloted in four locations in the UAE. Over the coming year, Ralph hopes that it will be rolled out to all SABIS schools.

The way I saw the system working in mathematics and science classes was as follows: the students log in, and the teacher, sitting at his or her console at the front of the class, clicks on an explanation or a paragraph, and this is then given to the students individually to read on their laptops. When they've finished reading, they click to show that they've done this and then questions based on this paragraph/explanation automatically appear. The teacher meanwhile sees a representation of his class on his console, showing those who have finished reading and their progress on the questions, which they've got right, which incorrect. Each individual pupil is shown with color coding by their names. For the "explanations," the codes are:

- Yellow – completed but activity not answered
- Green – completed and activity answered correctly
- Red – completed and activity answered incorrectly
- Gray – not completed

For the "activities," the color codes are as follows:

- Blue – not answered
- Green – answered correctly
- Red – answered incorrectly

Then there are graphs showing the progress of the class by each of these color codes.

Questions then automatically appear based on this explanation, and the students individually go through these; if they answer correctly, they go on to the next, usually more difficult one, until they have completed a set of questions based on the explanation. The way the system is configured at the moment, they can't carry on unless the teacher gives them permission – so that in some ways the class is moving at the same pace. I say configured "at the moment" because Ralph and the developers acknowledged that this may change, depending upon how students and teachers respond during the pilots. The teacher at his or her console meanwhile can see which students are having difficulty and who has finished. He or she can bring up the screen of particular individual students to see how they are working, or he or she can take in – through a series of colorful graphs – how the whole class is doing.

In what is taken for granted as normal in the SABIS classroom, the teacher then electronically alerts those who have mastered the questions to help the slower ones, the usual method of peer learning; "the students are organized to self-correct," as Ralph Bistany put it. The students are as usual grouped in fours, and the prefect in that subject helps those who are having difficulty. If more than 50 percent of the class have got the key questions wrong, however, then the teacher stops and formally teaches the explanation, as in a traditional class.

Once all the children have got the questions right, then the teacher clicks again on his or her console, and a new paragraph or explanation is brought up on to the children's screens, and again they follow through this process. For experiments in science, there are video demonstrations for the students to watch, again at the click of the teacher's laptop.

Importantly, there is a wealth of data being collected through this process, just as there is through the AMSs and periodics, all stored in the history files, as already discussed. I was shown the printouts for one of the classes I'd watched, a 45-minute session on square roots with 29 students. Here the printout came to a staggering 299 pages of information, with a two-page summary. Here, for each student is recorded the exact time in seconds that they took to read the explanation, the exact time they devoted to each question, and how many incorrect answers were submitted until they came up with the correct one, and so on. For instance, one student took 47 seconds on the first explanation, one second to "Navigate to Item" and then sixteen seconds to deliver the correct answer to the first question. The student then took two seconds to navigate to the next item, and 40 seconds to solve the next question, first submitting an incorrect answer, then submitting the correct answer.

Now clearly, this type of information is not typically intended for teachers, or indeed anyone else, to read. It's electronically analyzed, primarily for two purposes. The first is the usual one associated with all SABIS assessments, to help ensure all the children get all of the "essential" concepts. A system of automatic alerts is set up, so that the

Academic Quality Controller (AQC) and the head of department can be advised on classes or children who have particular problems or issues, and then these can advise the teacher on how best to deal with this. The same kind of proprietary algorithm that was there for the history files appears to be used for this too.

The second purpose, however, is to help course developers across SABIS, and this brings us back to the questions at the beginning of this section. How do we know how children are actually reading the SABIS texts? Now, instead of estimating how long students take on various tasks, the developers can access full scientific information on how long different tasks took, and what the variation and averages were. This kind of information will be invaluable as they move on to develop further course materials. They can take the pacing charts that have been developed over the years and see how accurate they are or where they need to be changed. The curriculum can now develop much more scientifically.

For instance, every time a teacher has to intervene, the developers can establish what the reasons are. It may be a fault of the administration – they had not realized properly that there was an essential concept required before children could move on to the next stage, in which case this is "system failure," but something that the administration can rectify. But it could also be that the text is not clear enough, that some or all children are misunderstanding the writing. In which case, the teams can scrutinize the text and try to make it clearer, so that all can understand it.

The data obtained are immensely important to Ralph: "This paragraph, how many seconds does a child need at this age to absorb it and understand it? I don't know and nobody knows ... and now we are going to be able to find out." The whole experiment, Ralph says, "it's dear to me. I have an instrument now that I have dreamed about for all my life. Now we can begin to think properly about how to learn efficiently."

He tells me that his sense is that if learning is done efficiently, without all the waste that is there in any school day – even, implicitly, in SABIS – then over the twelve-year schooling period, children will need to learn for only "three hours a day," in which they can cover all the curriculum and learn several languages: "Twelve years is more than enough with three periods teaching every day to cover the French Baccalaureate and the Advanced Placement and the A-levels and what have you easily. Many periods are really giving very little return to the students in terms of absorbed knowledge. And at the end of the day if you ask the kids, 'Let's list what we've learned today that we didn't know yesterday,' you'd be shocked at how little this often is." And then, with the time liberated through this efficiency, "I would want to make life at school more fun, to have more soccer and more music, as well as more learning for those who want to." All this, he believes, will be possible now that they have this technology in place, and the data that flow from it.

Now, some of the questions I saw the children answer were multiple choice. Not all were, however. While there will always be a place for multiple-choice questions, SABIS believes, multiple choice does have its drawbacks – not least that children can sometimes guess correctly, especially after a couple of attempts. So SABIS is investing considerable resources in computer-correctable working – it's a huge project for them. The team is looking to be able to correct most subject areas apart from English composition. Tools are being developed that allow students to write in complete answers in their subject, whether mathematics or science or grammar, and for these answers to be corrected electronically. One of the areas the teams are working on is the possible different answers that need to be allowed for. They've made a decision, for instance, in science, that spelling mistakes are considered to be incorrect answers – they could have gone for the opposite but decided that accuracy in these areas is important. So "alectron" will not be accepted for "electron." But then there are often large numbers of correct answers that could be submitted, which the computer correction programs must be able to spot. To see this on a very simple level, consider a mathematics question that has the answer "1,000." A student could write this as I've written it here, or as "1 000" or as "one thousand," or perhaps as 10^3 or 1×10^3, and so on, depending on the context. Computer-correctable assessments must be able to accept all the ways of correctly writing the answer.

The processes put in place to ensure that all possibilities are taken into account again show the meticulous way in which SABIS operates. First, the teachers and curriculum writers have been asked to give for every question what they believe are all the acceptable correct answers, as I've tried to do above. Secondly, fitting in very much with the way SABIS values student opinions, for any answer deemed incorrect by the program, a student can simply click the appropriate icon, and his or her answer is automatically referred to the Academics Department in the Student Life Organization – that is, to the student's peers. Two Student Life prefects will then go through this disputed answer. If they reject it, they have to explain to the student why it is incorrect, and how to obtain the correct answer. If, however, they believe the answer is correct, or potentially correct, they send the answer to the head of the appropriate academic department. If he or she accepts it, then the student's grade is automatically changed, and the new answer added to the computer-correctable program.

Thirdly, if the student doesn't accept the two fellow students' views, he can appeal directly to the head of department. If the head of department agrees with him, then the process continues as before – except the two students who rejected the answer are given a point against them. If they accumulate three points in this way, then these particular students will no longer be asked to adjudicate whether answers are correct or not; they have disqualified themselves. If the head of department thinks the original student is wrong, however, then *the student* is given a point against him. If he accumulates three points in this way, then he is no longer able to take objections directly to the head of department, although he can still object to the Student Life academic team as before.

So the system is developing to ensure that the computer-correctable tests have as comprehensive a range of answers as possible, and also that students are intimately involved in this process of creating the database of answers.

The system as it was being trialed when I was observing it (in

October 2011) still had the teacher very much in control of the pace – there was still a function for class learning, rather than the fully individualized system that perhaps one might have expected given the technological possibilities. This comes down to their philosophy of the community of the classroom, which we've already explored. Ralph agrees that the technology does create the option of everyone moving at their own pace – and indeed, they are trialing this in language acquisition, where the disparity in abilities is simply too great. I was given the example of a South Korean student arriving in class with excellent English and mathematics, but absolutely zero Arabic and French. Where do you place that child if there is no streaming or setting by subjects, given that the Lebanese children they're studying with have been speaking French and Arabic from the beginning of their schooling? So in this case, they are already using and further developing software to enable completely independent learning. The student will stay in the same physical class, but will learn at his or her own pace.

So in foreign languages, there will be a break with Ralph's ideal of the class learning together. But is this the thin end of the wedge? Could this lead to the breakdown of the class altogether? Are they willing to trial this in other areas, even the sacred math and English too? Ralph says, "I don't want to. I'm not keen," for all the reasons we've explored already. But I wonder whether the pilots will bring about different ways of working with this advanced technology.

There have been obvious teething difficulties in their initial pilots – teachers who just simply couldn't let the children read, but immediately started talking through the explanation, as in a normal classroom. Ralph observed: "The children are supposed to be reading; the teachers are not supposed to be saying anything. But they forget! I am amazed at the power of routine!"

Perhaps there are deeper reasons why people don't want to learn from text – even adults, Ralph notes, want to register for a course and go and listen to someone talk, even though reading the text could be a much more efficient way of learning. "And that beats me," says Ralph. But nonetheless, "I believe it is important to learn from text and ultimately it is *easier* to learn from text. I believe it is so, but of course if it's something you never did before, you think it's difficult and you don't even try! I want to break that cycle and I want our kids to choose to learn from text." And that's a major reason why he's persevering with this new method. Note that this idea of focusing on students reading the text is an interesting difference between this and the approach of Khan Academy, which we'll touch on in the next chapter – which brings another approach to students learning on their own, at their own pace, without teachers. There, it is very much still as if the teacher is teaching the concept; children follow as if they were following a teacher on the blackboard. With the SABIS method, however, children have to read. That's a higher-order function, says Ralph, who is adamant that he wants children to be able to do this, rather than always have to be spoon-fed by a teacher taking them through each step.

The students I spoke to seemed to enjoy it. At the SABIS Military High School in Al Ain – a public–private partnership in the Emirates – they were deeply enthusiastic about it. Here eleventh- and twelfth-graders are in the pilot program. One explained to me that "it's very good for advanced students because before when we got stuck on one activity, the teacher kept on explaining and explaining, but other students who are understanding, they can't solve anything else. So now each student, when he finishes he can press 'complete' and then move on to other exercises ... so advanced students solve like seven activities and other students three activities." "It's a very mature way of learning," said another. "You can't hide behind the rest of the class's understanding; if you don't know, you can't carry on."

And at the International School of Choueifat in Dubai, students were equally enthusiastic. "It's way faster and quicker than class," said one. "You don't have to wait for the teacher to explain to everyone." Another said, "It's a sensible way to teach, more productive and more efficient." And another, "When a teacher explains something, we always rely on him, we never study ourselves, and most of the time we always get confused and we end up blaming the teacher, when it's just our fault for not reading the text."

It's not only through information technology that these developments are possible either. We noted in the chapter "The logic of learning" how some students are able to opt to study courses on their own as part of the SABIS repertoire being offered in schools. So ideas on how children could learn without teachers preceded what is now being pursued through the power of technology by some time: Ralph talked of how he was working particularly closely with Mr Germanos in the Emirates in the 1980s. "We spent most of the time together, we went out to different restaurants together, we played sports together, and we spent a lot of time together talking and rearranging world politics." And, of course, as they sat and talked, "We'd always slip back into school matters." One of the ideas that came up between them was the idea of creating a pilot in one of their schools where children would learn part of the course entirely without a teacher: "For every class we left part of the course without a teacher, telling the kids, 'You take care of it.'" At the end of the course, as usual, they would take the same exams as others who had the teacher for that section of the course: "We never noticed any difference," Ralph says, laughing. "This grew into a bigger and bigger thing."

It really was quite dramatic to visit several of the SABIS schools in the Emirates, for instance, and hear many of the senior students in quite a blasé fashion say that they're learning subjects completely on their own. It's particularly relevant when you also read in, say, the British educational press about young people who can't study subject X because there are no teachers for that subject available, and how unfair this is. SABIS kids have got into the habit of self-reliance strongly enough that they can simply get on with it.

I spoke to some of the students who were engaged with this "self-study" program. It was quite surprising to see that these were normal students, not at all fazed by the fact that they were studying whole courses on their own. Initially, one student described the pilot process that they had been involved with:

It began when I was in Grade Six or Five; they introduced this new concept of "self-study." We were studying fractions and decimals at the time. They gave us the pacing chart and the core material, and a free study class twice a week. So we would get the books and study fractions and decimals by ourselves. And we would have a weekly AMS as usual on these areas we had studied ourselves. It was very difficult at first – I remember that initially I got eight out of twenty, that sort of thing, but slowly I started to grasp the concepts. Now I guess it's made it much easier for me to study on my own, so I am able to tackle more easily things that I don't understand, just through reading and reflecting.

Another said, "When we go to university, they won't teach you material like in school, so you have to do a lot of self-study. So they sort of get us ready for that."

From this initial pilot, the process has been brought in for whole courses now. The students have to obtain 85 percent in the subject or a related subject in Grade 9, including getting all the essential concepts correct, before they are allowed to go on to self-study. The students I spoke to in Grade 11 at the International School of Choueifat, Dubai, were taking AP (College Board Advanced Placement) courses in business studies, psychology, environmental science, biology, computer science, English literature, and history. The results show that the self-study students do as well or better as taught students in other schools.

The students had started in Grade 9 and have weekly tests in their self-study subjects in the ITL hall, just as in any subject they are learning. They study in their own free time, at home or after school: "You have to manage your time, that is the whole point."

Returning to the technology-based ILT: using the rich data coming from the trials, as the curriculum developers iron out any difficulty with the texts, to ensure universal understanding and make sure that they are crystal clear about what prior concepts are needed to move on, won't all this make the teacher in fact obsolete? Ralph thinks it might do: "As the system develops, there will be no need for the teacher at all. Now, the teacher is there ... it's like because this car broke down, you need the mechanic to fix it. Once the car becomes really very dependable and cannot break down, you don't need a mechanic with you."

SABIS is not shy of this logic. They are exploring it fully in their "experiment" of the teacherless school.

The teacherless environment

There's a logic behind the Integrated Learning and Testing pilots which could lead inexorably to the idea of educating children in teacherless regions. Initially, SABIS is linking this to a philanthropic project – but if it's successful, it could be rolled out commercially to be an integral part of the SABIS system. Although this wasn't said to me by anyone in SABIS, I can see possible reasoning behind the need for a philanthropic pilot: as Ralph Bistany pointed out to me several times, he is inhibited in what he can bring into SABIS schools by market demand, particularly by what parents demand from schooling – and Mrs Saad is sometimes the bearer of the news of what parents will and will not tolerate. In their philanthropic work, however, SABIS had been pushed into experimenting with, if not teacherless schools, then teacherless grades, and this work was so successful that it showed an obvious venue in which they could experiment with the technology-led teacherless approach.

The humanitarian desire to serve the poor brought up the business problem of the scarcity of a required resource, namely higher-level teachers. In effect it's really just the extreme of a problem that SABIS has been meeting for some time, the shortage of the right kind of teachers. For instance, Carl Bistany said: "Today if you got me twenty physics teachers that could teach at Grade Twelve, I would take them all," such is their scarcity. It's a predominant issue in the international media too, which points to impending or indeed actual crises in public education in America, Britain and around the world owing to the shortage of competent teachers.

For governments this scarcity is a source of much hand-wringing and political point-scoring. For SABIS the scarcity, instead, led to a more subtle challenge. The SABIS philosophy led to Shadow Teachers, who take part in teaching to strengthen their expertise and substitute for teachers when absent. It also led to student teachers – peer learning – who can help students who are having difficulty. Places with *no* qualified teachers led to the question: "Can we find a way to give access to learning ... *without* teachers?" Mrs Saad said: "The lack of availability of teachers in poor areas should be no reason why kids are deprived of learning. We're trying to prove that you can take education to even remote areas."

Thus the idea of the teacherless class was born, even though this was a time when the technological resources were less advanced. But now the present resources, especially of ILT, seem to make it even more viable than before.

Mrs Saad sees this development as crucially important: "We are continuing research in every field to make education cheaper and accessible to deprived areas. If you can develop the tools for children to learn effectively on their own, if you can make the text easy enough for the kids to understand and with questions to make sure that it has been understood, if you can automate all of this, then the cost of education can come down and high-quality education can be accessible to all children."

But surely, however good the software is, children – especially deprived children– need a *social* framework for their learning? This is where the SABIS system again comes to the fore with processes that have already been developed and which we've already outlined in the previous chapter. Here it is the peer tutoring methods and the school management and discipline parts of Student Life Organization that come into their own. In a normal SABIS school learners are *already* increasingly responsible for their learning, for that of their peers, and for maintaining an environment suitable for learning. It's not a huge step to think that these kinds of processes can be further extended into an entirely teacherless setting.

But it doesn't have to go as far as having no adult supervision, in case that was making anyone uneasy. In poor regions there are many young people in their early twenties, especially girls, "who have not had a chance to continue their education," said Ralph. These young women can be brought in to supervise parts of the school, in conjunction with the Student Life Organization. This brings another neat twist to the potentially beneficial outcomes of this work. The supervisors themselves can also be learning, as they co-supervise the children: "Ultimately we will encourage them to take an external exam and register at a remote university." The beauty of it all is that "the kids are learning and some of those young people who have not had an education will get a second chance."

If this demonstration is successful, it could dramatically transform all of what SABIS does in the future – and with it, the whole education industry: "Just imagine," Ralph said, "if we manage to create a school using technology where the cost per student is extremely small and yet the educational outcomes are high – the kids are totally bilingual, they are well read, excellent at math and science. What would be your reaction?" For Ralph the reaction of those who want to bring quality education into difficult areas would be very clear. They would clamor: "We want this everywhere." It would be a classic example of a potentially "small margin, large volume" business, exportable to many parts of the world.

It goes against much of what is taken for granted in the education literature today. Mrs Saad points out, "Most of the studies that appear" – she and I had been talking about the recent report from McKinsey[1] – "end up with the finding that the only thing that really makes a difference in the classroom is the quality of teacher; therefore, we have to make sure we have the best teacher in the classroom. We are going against the trend there; we are trying to create a teacher-independent classroom. Because if you want to apply it at a scale, it's extremely difficult to build that based on exceptional teachers. You cannot change the level of education worldwide if what you are doing is centered only on the ability of exceptional professionals."

In SABIS's programs with the teacherless class, three imperatives that seem central to the company, the educational, business and humanitarian, converge. Coming together in this way, they create the potential for huge transformation of the way we think about education.

The outcome could well determine how SABIS approaches educational development in the future. Certainly it provides a possible framework on which the company can build in achieving its goal of serving five million children by 2020 – through remote learning or teacherless "schools" in underserved areas. But SABIS clearly sees this kind of pilot as having potentially generalizable results. Through innovation of this kind, SABIS is fashioning new models of educational delivery that could have much wider impact than on just the particular communities they are serving.

Thinking the unthinkable in education

SABIS has an education model that brings a distinctive logic and efficiency to the learning process. It embeds students in a community of learners, always conscious of their responsibility to each other. But SABIS is restless too; restless to ensure that the model it brings to its students has taken into account the world of technological possibilities, while still equipping them with the values that make society possible.

I like the fact that SABIS is "thinking the unthinkable" in this way. To me, this is the beauty of having global companies like SABIS involved in education now – for as they grow in strength and reach they can help liberate education from what I've argued elsewhere[2] is the straitjacket in which it has found itself for the last one hundred or more years.

Through its preparedness to innovate and grow, SABIS is showing the way toward an alternative educational paradigm to the one in which we've been immersed for so long. The educational paradigm of the twentieth century was one of government monopoly. SABIS, and educational companies like it, are part of the vanguard which can challenge the power of this government domination. People within SABIS seem to recognize the profound importance of the role they can play, which can lead to a new educational renaissance.

I see this happening on two levels.

On one level, perhaps it's relatively uncontroversial: government monopoly in education breaks the crucial link of accountability between parents/students and their schools. That's not good; it leads to lower standards and complacency. Charter schools and other schools of choice aim to reinvigorate that accountability link. Some of the evidence reviewed in Part 2 here suggests that higher standards do result from these kinds of school choice reforms. SABIS's place in the forefront of this school choice movement, in the USA, and in countries new to these ideas, such as the Emirates and Kurdistan, is clearly beneficial in raising educational standards. And SABIS's concerted attacks on the educational establishment – challenging shibboleths like the smaller the class size the better, or memorization is bad, or frequent testing is anti-educational – show the benefits of having strong counterbalances against the power of governments.

But as we move forward, as SABIS continues in its relentless quest to develop the learning environment, there's a more insidious government monopoly in education that I believe educational companies like SABIS, as they grow in strength and global impact, can begin to challenge.

Governments all over the world dictate the "What?", "Where?" and "How?" of education. What is to be taught, where is it taught and how is it taught, and to whom? In doing so, they tend to obscure and neglect the even more important "Why?" Why should we learn this, rather than that?

But governments have been shown not to be good at second-guessing which industries will succeed, when and where. This was the fundamental lesson learned through the denationalizations of the mid to late twentieth century. Governments across the world getting out of the way of industries liberated the spirit of entrepreneurship in areas such as telecommunications, transport and energy, which had for so long been restricted under state monopoly.

In education, however, governments still second-guess the kind of education required by young people for preparation for adult life and where and how it is delivered. But the mechanisms governments have at their disposal are cumbersome and bureaucratic; in any case, they can't be attuned to issues such as the ways in which humans flourish, central to any ideas of what education is for. And once procedures are put in place, they're exceedingly hard to modify and change. And they're shored up by all sorts of politically vested-interest groups that resist change that will be beneficial to the people. In other words, this second, most insidious form of government monopoly is the control of the *framework* of educational provision.

One way of challenging government monopoly is through the emergence of a vibrant global education industry. Strong and innovative education companies can bring new concepts to the marketplace of ideas, allowing these to be tested – some to destruction, some through refinements and an interactive process of testing and retesting to application and thence to scale. Yes, these ideas can work *within* the framework of government regulation on schools, curriculum, assessment and the kinds of destination for students, and can effectively raise standards within these areas. That's as far as companies like SABIS have moved to date. It's clearly beneficial, and if they did no more than this, then it would be a powerful contribution to improving educational opportunities.

But they can, if they wish, do more than this – and the programs SABIS will conduct in poor environments show how it may be willing to engage on this second level too. An emergent education industry can begin to challenge government monopoly *of the framework itself* – where education takes place, and areas such as the curriculum, the assessment system and student destinations, all to be tested and refined to suit the conditions we find ourselves in today, rather than being subject to acquiescence to the political realities of yesterday. An emergent education industry, with companies like SABIS at the forefront, can begin to provide a counterbalance to what governments say should be the ends of education, as well as challenging what they say should be the means.

Writing this extended case study of SABIS has reinforced in me this belief, and given me new cause for optimism about the future of education. This optimism seems to be echoed by Chris Whittle in the book with which we opened this narrative. Here, he looks ahead to the next 25 years of education: in "other sectors of our life and economy, twenty-five years is a *transforming* period of time, a period in which the magical and unimaginable can occur."[3] There's no reason why educa-tion should be any different, he says, provided that we can break away from the reality of education as "The Last Great Cottage Industry."[4]

In education – he's referring largely to public education in America, but the message is applicable across the world – the crucial problem is that there's no opportunity for *scale*. Compared to other industries, education is organized in a "highly splintered, highly local" way,[5] and this is the fundamental reason for the low quality of America's schools. Take the five largest of America's school districts; they are tiny com-pared to the five top American companies. New York City, the largest of America's school districts, has revenues of $12.1 billion; this is dwarfed by America's largest company, the family business Wal-Mart Stores, with revenues of $288 billion, some 24 times larger. Broward County, the fifth-largest school district with revenues of $2.0 billion, is 75 times smaller than America's fifth-largest company, General Elec-tric, at $152 billion.

But it's not that the revenues aren't potentially there in education: the USA spends "over $400 billion per year to educate our children from kindergarten through high school."[6] The odd thing about the gov-ernment monopoly in education is that it is so splintered – it is a monop-oly but at an extraordinarily prescribed localized level. No one decides it should be this way – or at least no one decides this on an ongoing basis. Reinforcing my point above about the great difficulty in changing the way government organizes education, Whittle notes that the way education is organized now in America is not "some well-considered judgement. Perhaps it was, one hundred years ago, but today's politi-cal leaders did not explicitly make this decision. They inherited it. The way our schools are controlled and provided came about over a century ago."[7] And no one has been able to change it since.

So Whittle argues that it's this lack of scale which leads to the many problems we see in public education, including the low standards and disaffection of millions of the most deprived and ill-served students. Why would scale make any difference? "The power of scale – and the only reason we should care about its impact on education – rests in the way it gives birth to certain types of creativity, in its capacity to make large-scale research and development possible."[8] Research and development – R&D – is the motor of "the most exciting transformations in our world. R&D has enabled us to have transportation systems and medical systems and power systems that routinely deliver success rates of 99 percent. R&D leads us down two great roads to quality – better design and better systems – ingredients American schools are sorely lacking precisely because of their fragmented organization."[9] R&D in education could make it relevant to the needs and aspirations of the young people being served.

If we can bring scale into the education sector so that emerging companies can invest more in R&D to create new designs, then we can begin to see the transformation of education. Clearly SABIS is part of that movement – and we reflected in the Introduction on Whittle's discussion of why companies like SABIS are important. In particular, large global companies – as SABIS is becoming – can invest in the R&D required for educational innovation; but they can also stand up to the government monopoly of the educational framework, beginning to challenge government ways of doing things. Take some very simple examples. The school calendar, for instance. This nine-month year "was developed in agrarian times, so children could work in the fields during the summer."[10] You may have noticed that most children don't work on farms anymore. But try to change that system within the political system, and you'll come up against all sorts of vested interests trying to defend the status quo – even if it's completely indefensible in terms of our modern world. In particular, it's anti-educational, as research shows that the long break leads to children forgetting and losing interest, an especially pronounced tendency for children of the poor.

Or take the school day – which typically finishes mid-afternoon – "developed in an era when Mom was home with milk and cookies at 2:30," but which is now "so wildly inconvenient for working parents" and leads to another potentially anti-educational phenomenon of "latchkey" kids and their associated disaffection.[11] Again try to change that within political systems at your peril.

It hasn't happened yet. But education companies working globally can begin to effect changes in the fundamentals of the educational framework too, trying to explore what really is educationally required and effective, and instituting appropriate changes. But this can happen in more profound ways too.

Chris Whittle writes about the problems of student motivation – a crucially important area, and one where I feel a lot of sympathy for his views. He writes: "Motivation is not part of our standard curriculum. Very simply, our schools do an absolutely miserable job of showing students *why* education is important."[12] He continues:

> The problem here is palpable and easy to see – hard to miss, in fact. Visit a school that serves students from kindergarten through twelfth grade. It is a study in contrasts. Visit the younger grades first. At that level, schools don't have to worry about the motivational issue. School is new, an adventure for children. As educators, we're still surfing on the natural desire of these kids to explore, to find out. But then go directly to a middle school or high school class and you can literally *see* a drop in the level of energy and engagement. The children are leaning back, not forward. There is a tactile listlessness to classes. You can feel it. Participation is limited, awkward. It is easy to say this is just adolescence, yet adolescence is not always so – a fact made very clear by a trip to the lunchroom in the same school. There, energy abounds.[13]

I identify with this description completely – in my field notes of trips to schools around the world I often reflect on precisely the same phenomenon. Why do schools seem fine for young children, but so unpleasant for older ones? One of the areas where we've got to explore why motivation may be so hard to foster is in the *content* of the curriculum itself:

> as much as we should find and stoke motivation, it is equally important that we not kill it. When something we are teaching is just mindless,

we should stop doing it. Or if we must teach children something so that they can pass some equally mindless exam, then it's best that we admit it. Better that students know we know.

Whittle gives an example:

I run a reasonably complex $400+ million company, and I cannot recall needing most of the higher-math material that I learned. I know that statement is heresy, but ask yourself: if 99 percent of children are not going to use it, why is it, again, that we're teaching it? (If the answer is that it helps them to learn in a more general sense or identifies those with particular aptitudes, let's let them know that.)[14]

I think this comment is profoundly important. My guess is that those like Ralph Bistany and Mrs Saad in SABIS will disagree with the actual example he gives. But this is irrelevant: the important point is that within the monopoly of the government framework in education we have to take, whether we like it or not, the curriculum topics prescribed; what Whittle is saying, and I agree, is that as strong global education players emerge, we don't have to just accept what is given by governments. We can start to think through these issues again, back to first principles, and have alternatives explored within the marketplace of ideas. And as and when we decide what we want in the curriculum, we can make sure that students know why, and are motivated to work with us.

Thinking of curriculum, you have to think of assessment – and it's interesting in this context to note that SABIS participated in creating the new International Baccalaureate in the mid-1960s, as an alternative form of assessment to those offered in international schools largely under the British government system of GCSEs and A-levels. Perhaps as SABIS grows in strength it could again think about improvements to assessment systems, perhaps to reflect what it deems most important in the curriculum, and either develop its own alternative baccalaureate, or be a market leader that adopts alternatives to government assessments developed by other global education players.

These are the kinds of thoughts I have when I see strong, global educational players like SABIS emerging. They are in a position to really challenge the myths and fads in education wherever they emerge. SABIS has been doing this for years, within the frameworks set by governments. As the education industry grows in strength, it can also start challenging the framework too. With its Integrated Learning and Testing methodology, with its thoughts on teacherless classes, SABIS is challenging the notion, an essential core of the framework, that you need classes run by teachers for learning to take place. This seems to be a huge step toward liberating education from the constraints that government monopoly has brought.

The award-winning author Matt Ridley, writer of the provocative but deeply positive *The Rational Optimist*, recently wrote about education thus:

> One of my philosophical passions is bottom-up order. Human beings have a hard time understanding that some of the finest complexity in the world comes about through spontaneous emergence, not top-down diktat. This is true of ecosystems and economies, of genomes and cultures, of embryos and encyclopedias.
>
> Education, though, feels like one of those things that has to be top-down: There has to be a teacher and a taught. But plenty of people educate themselves. Is it possible for everybody to be an autodidact, now that knowledge is so accessible online?[15]

Perhaps more clearly than anyone else is currently doing today, outside of small-scale experiments, SABIS is challenging both the "top-down" notion of teacher to pupil and the equally important "top-down" notion of government control of education. We can't predict how things will develop in the education market in which SABIS is a crucial player. But I believe we can feel confident that with organizations like SABIS engaged in the process of trying to find what works best, where, when and for whom, there is huge cause for "rational optimism" about the enterprise of education.

CHAPTER 12

The education industry

W E'VE EXPLORED THE THREE THEMES underlying SABIS's education model – the logic of learning, the community of learners, and the evolution of the learning environment. We've also seen how SABIS is operating across the globe, from Kurdistan to "Katrina" and a multitude of places in between. In this final chapter, it's time to turn to the underlying business model that makes all this possible. Ralph Bistany and the SABIS team have continually reinforced that SABIS is a *for-profit* education business, part of the *global* education *industry*. The following are the questions that arise from this, particularly in connection with the words I've italicized above:

1. Should education be for profit?
2. If so, what sort of business is it? What form can standardization take? Are there useful analogies to be made with other industries?
3. Finally, what kind of business is SABIS? What are some of its peculiar features?

We'll explore each of these in turn.

For-profit education

The chapters on the American experience showed again and again how obstacles were put in the way of a company like SABIS. Why? Why isn't it allowed to make a difference in America, and in other countries? Behind most of the objections from organizations like the teacher unions and school districts, behind many of the objections from academics in universities, is a simple issue: SABIS is for-profit.

For-profit education is hugely controversial. In my own country, the deputy prime minister, Nick Clegg, recently gave a speech in which he made clear that the profit motive was not going to be allowed in any public–private partnerships the coalition government was introducing in England: "To anyone," he began, "who is worried that we are inching towards inserting the profit motive into our school system ... let me reassure you ... Yes to greater diversity; yes to more choice for parents; but no to running schools for profit ..."[1] He was highly applauded for this statement by his party and by the teacher unions.

In America, except in Arizona, only non-profit organizations can hold charters for schools. The eminent American philosopher Martha C. Nussbaum, currently Ernst Freund Distinguished Service Professor of Law and Ethics at the University of Chicago, recently gave a series of lectures entitled "Education for profit, education for freedom." To her it is clear that these two ideas are fundamentally opposed.

SABIS is, surprisingly, given the controversy this could engender, completely open about being a for-profit company. Its recent report, for instance, *Closing the Achievement Gap: The SABIS® Story!*, aimed at an American audience, has a section entitled "What makes SABIS® schools different." One of the five areas is "For Profit": "As a for-profit educational service provider, SABIS® has a built-in incentive to succeed. There is built-in accountability for results that encourages SABIS® to continuously seek to improve" (p. 11). Profit here is connected with accountability and incentives.

What are the major objections to for-profit education? In the SABIS case study published by Harvard Business School, the objection to for-profit education is characterized thus: "... quality education could only be achieved if it were not-for-profit, because, ostensibly, the profit motive would cause educators to cut corners and sacrifice quality for profit."[2] The profit motive will lead greedy businessmen and women to lower the quality of provision.

Applied to other businesses it might seem a strange criticism. Do we believe that in other competitive markets, such as food or airlines, the profit motive leads to Wal-Mart selling us substandard meat and vegetables (sacrificing quality for profit) or British Airways dropping us in France rather than taking us all the way to Ghana (cutting corners for profit)? In general, we assume that competition between suppliers in an open market leads to higher-quality provision at a lower cost – because the supplier knows we can take our business elsewhere, and so tries to keep our custom using quality and price as attractors.

Is there any reason why an education business should be different? We've already seen how SABIS is working in difficult places – such as Kurdistan and inner-city America – to raise standards and promote educational opportunity. Certainly nothing in those descriptions suggests that they are sacrificing quality for profit or abandoning their principles; quite the opposite in fact.

Prompted by conversations with Ralph and Carl Bistany and Mrs Saad, and through my own thoughts about these issues, I've actually begun to think that the question of whether education should be "for-profit" is a bit of a red herring. The issue is rather educational freedom. If we are seeking freedom of education, in the same way that we seek freedom of association or freedom of speech, then the parallels and contrasts between the different situations are important to explore. Concerning freedom of association, for instance, it's not an issue to anyone that some people and organizations may be able to make a profit from this freedom – it's not an issue provided the freedom is upheld and not obstructed. So, for instance, no one seriously objects – in fact, I doubt anyone thinks of these matters at all – if bus companies and bicycle manufacturers and those who make a living from restaurants and pubs, to name a few, make a profit from the abilities of people to exercise their freedom of association. Similarly, it's not a matter of huge controversy that there are companies able to make profits out of freedom of speech – television broadcasters, newspaper, magazine and book publishers, for instance. The freedoms we cherish simply make such considerations irrelevant.

Why couldn't education be considered in the same way – pointing to a freedom we cherish, and consigning any quibbles about whether profit should or should not be allowed to the sidelines? I think it may be because people everywhere have given up on having freedom of education, so much so that they take it for granted that governments can intervene in a multiplicity of ways – including questioning the profit motive. For arguments *against* freedom of education are those *for* state intervention in education. I've written in detail about these elsewhere, and this is not the place to rehearse them at length.[3] But very briefly, the strongest argument, and the argument put most commonly, refers to "social justice" or some synonym, such as "equity." This is that without government intervention in education, the neediest children will not be able to access quality educational opportunities.

Historically this was not true at all. This was the profound insight of Professor E. G. West, whose seminal book *Education and the State* brought these issues to light again in the twentieth century.[4] In nineteenth-century England, for instance, according to the official report of the Newcastle Commission of 1861, only 4.5 percent of school-aged children were not in schooling, at a time when state intervention in education was only minimal. Forster's educational act of 1870 was explicitly designed to top up the extensive private provision in education, explicitly not to create an alternative state system. But E. G. West and others have also shown similar evidence from Scotland, New York, Massachusetts, and New South Wales. Historically, we didn't need the state to get education going for the masses. We didn't need state intervention in order to promote social justice.[5]

It's not true in terms of contemporary evidence either. Across the developing world, the poor are accessing low-cost private schools in huge numbers in the slums and shanty towns and villages of Africa and Asia. In Lagos State, for instance, at least 75 percent of schoolchildren in poor areas are in low-cost private schools, which outperform the government schools for a fraction of the cost. The same is true across Indian slums and shanty towns. It is a huge and inspiring success story.[6] So again, it's not the state which is helping give poor children in developing countries today the education they desire – it is through the vehicles of educational freedom, private schools, that they are so doing.

So my suggestion here – argued at length elsewhere – is that the argument for social justice does not stand up as a justification for the state overriding educational freedom. (Can educational freedom *guarantee* that the poorest will be served? No, but neither can the state guarantee it. But educational freedom, combined with philanthropy, can better ensure that all are served.) Neither do other arguments for state intervention hold water.

So if the arguments against educational freedom don't hold up, then the issue of whether or not education should be for-profit should also be sidelined, as it is when we discuss any of our other fundamental freedoms, such as freedom of speech and freedom of association.

This is a high-level discussion, depending on arguments defended elsewhere. Can we not say anything more about the particular facets that profit or non-profit bring to education?

Interestingly, when people are asked to spell out their objections to profit in education, they often talk about the profit *motive* in education – this is exactly what Nick Clegg did in the excerpts of his important speech above, for instance. This way of putting it highlights precisely why those objecting are mistaken. The reason for this goes back all the way to Adam Smith. His famous and pithy expression of how the public interest can arise from individuals pursuing their own interest was set out in *The Wealth of Nations* in 1776: "It is not from the benevolence of the butcher, the brewer, or the baker that we expect our dinner, but from their regard to their own interest. We address ourselves, not to their humanity but to their self-love, and never talk to them of our own necessities but of their advantages."[7]

In other words, it's crucially important to distinguish intentions (the profit *motive*) and results: *what we should care about is whether the goods get delivered, not the motivation behind those who deliver them.* The butcher, the brewer and the baker are all concerned with their self-interest – their profits. In general, says Adam Smith, there's no point in pleading with them about your own needs and problems, addressing "their humanity." Instead, if you stump up what they require – cash on delivery, which satisfies their "self-love" and their "advantages" – they'll make sure you get all you desire. Crucially, as Adam Smith and others have also pointed out, when competition between different butchers or brewers or bakers is brought into the picture, then the individual providers are kept on their toes, ensuring quality is high and price is kept low.

Ralph Bistany and Mrs Saad are adamant that for-profit education has the potential to transform education. There are three major reasons why the profit motive is better in other areas of our lives. It is better for quality and innovation. It attracts talent. It brings down cost. The same could be true for education. Moreover, there are some interesting thoughts to be had when we consider how philanthropists are drawn to education too.

Ralph Bistany is very clear on this: "How does anybody who is seeking profit, make a profit? Only when they make a better product for less money than the competitors. The better the product is and the less it costs to the consumer, that's the door to profit!" So it's all about quality and price, as far as Ralph is concerned, and no one should be worried about that being applied to education. "If not-for-profit had been better, then communism would have conquered the world." He points to the motor industry – one of his favorite sources of analogy. Do you remember the Trabant? It was the most common car in East Germany; as Wikipedia notes, in its admirably balanced appraisal: "The main selling points were that it had room for four adults and luggage in a compact, light and durable shell and that it was fast (when introduced) and durable." It was not all good, however: "With its mediocre performance, inefficient two-stroke engine, noxious fumes and production shortages, the Trabant is often cited as an example of the disadvantages of centralized planning."[8] That's how Ralph Bistany remembers the car:

Those who built the Trabant in East Germany, they didn't seek to make profits. In West Germany, those who built Mercedes, Audi, Volkswagen – they were all after profits. But does anyone suggest that the Trabant is a better car than a Mercedes? Because the search for profits means that the West Germans had to invest in quality improvements and because they were in competition they had to make these improvements while still lowering the price. I don't understand why anyone suggests anything is any different in education.

In other areas of our lives (again Ralph points to the motor industry, and I would point even more to the mobile telephone and information technology industries), the pursuit of profit by manufacturers and service providers leads to such dramatic improvements in quality *and* such dramatic reductions in price that what was available only to a tiny minority becomes available to the majority: the luxury car he first owned in 1948 was an Oldsmobile 88. An ordinary car now – say a Honda Civic – "is superior in every way to the dream car that was available then to only a very few people. Now everybody can have a Honda. Why did that happen?" If the car industry had been like education, "then it would have stayed the same. If the car industry had been a not-for-profit thing, only Mr Gates and Steve Jobs and maybe the president of the USA would have a car now."

What is it about the profit motive coupled with competition that leads to these outcomes? And why shouldn't education be any different? The mantra – or perhaps "nightmare" would be a better word – of anyone in business is "Exit, exit, exit" – your customers can exit at any time, if you don't satisfy them in terms of high quality and low prices. So that's why you need to invest in research and development (R&D) for innovations that will help you raise quality and/or reduce prices. Much of the discussion in the previous three chapters about the education model can now be viewed from this dimension – and it is fascinating to see how often in the education industry educational motivations are aligned with business imperatives too. For instance, it makes no sense educationally to waste talent in the classroom, so ideas on peer learning and Shadow Teaching educationally make sense – to help develop the talents of those who are faster in their work, while at the same time giving support to those who need help. But clearly this also satisfied the business imperative of providing a higher-quality service to customers, so that "no child is left behind," this time at the same cost. Or think of the ILT – the computer-based learning in which SABIS is investing heavily. The educational motivation for this is clear – it can help focus exactly on how children learn and where their difficulties are, to make the process of learning more efficient and effective, educationally speaking. Now at the moment it's all a cost to the SABIS business, profits are being diverted that way. If it succeeds in making learning accessible without the need for highly paid teachers, however, then this R&D will lead to both high quality and much lower costs, so will satisfy the business imperative too.

Notice another important dimension that comes in here, and which Ralph Bistany and Mrs Saad are very clearly aware of. In most areas of our lives, if successful innovations lead to higher quality and/or to lower prices, they'll be copied, or at least adapted and refined, by the competitors in the industry. Competition ensures the rapid spread of ideas. The same could and should be true in education: for instance, if SABIS is successful with the ILT, competitors in the education industry will surely want to copy, or adapt or refine, what they have delivered – because it will lead to higher profits. If it works, the innovation won't remain long with SABIS alone.

So the outcomes of profit in industries other than education – and Ralph Bistany and Mrs Saad argue that the same should be true for education – are increased investment, especially in R&D leading to increased innovation, the rapid spread of ideas and the lowering of prices. But it's also important to reflect on the alternatives to profit in education. If there is no profit, and no prices, how are decisions on allocation of scarce resources to education made? They're made by governments, by politicians and civil servants. Now, when politicians like the British deputy prime minister round on the profit motive at the heart of business, they make it sound as if their motives are pure, disinterested.

Before Adam Smith, that's how people thought of merchants too, disinterestedly pursuing the public good through commerce; Adam Smith's insight was to show that self-interest was at the heart of business. Similarly, we don't have to think of politicians or civil servants in this selfless way anymore – hugely important work in public choice theory[9] has led to the insights that, no less than businessmen, politicians and civil servants are also and equally guided by self-interest. Not the profit motive; for politicians it's the *vote* motive – they need to get elected and to maximize their votes and standing among their different constituencies. Indeed, that's probably why Nick Clegg was making that particular speech about profit and education at the time, in order to show his party, the Liberal Democrats, that they were distinct from their coalition partners, the Conservatives, so votes for them were not wasted. Similarly, civil servants are concerned with maximizing the size of their bureau, and their budget allocations – the *power* motive, perhaps it can be dubbed.

So if you're not allowing the price mechanism and the profit motive to allocate scarce educational resources, then the alternative is to hand over to politicians and their civil servants. They too are guided by self-interest. And it's their self-interest over the decades which has led to education turning out more like the Trabant than the Mercedes. The argument of Ralph Bistany and Mrs Saad is that, rather than think we need to insulate education from the profit motive, it's far better to argue that it needs protection from the vote and power motives of the politicians and bureaucrats.[10]

Clearly, Ralph Bistany and Mrs Saad are keenly aware of interesting developments in non-profit education. At one meeting, Ralph showed me a recent article about Khan Academy and its youthful founder, Salman Khan. He was very happy to learn about others who were also seeking innovative solutions: "Apparently he was asked to help his brothers and sisters, or nephews and nieces, with their school work, and hit on the idea of these twelve-minute bite-sized chunks of videos, that they could watch and rewind at their own pace, to make sure they had really grasped the concepts." It has parallels to what SABIS is trying to achieve with the ILT and the teacherless class – although Ralph is adamant that he wants to see whether the higher-order skill of being able to read an explanation can be the way that students develop, rather than what he sees as the lower-order skill of having a concept explained to the student. Homework too – Ralph noted how SABIS has also seen traditional homework as being wasteful, and likes the fact that Khan Academy, like SABIS, is thinking differently about it – in Khan's case, homework involves children watching his videos, then coming back with queries to the teacher in class, in effect reversing the role of classwork and homework. Clearly, Ralph was interested in what Khan Academy was doing and believed that it was an important way of getting people to think "outside of the box" in terms of educational delivery.

Except on one level, and this is where his disappointment arises: "People are excited about him, as we are. Even if what he does is of value, the fact that he is *non-profit* is sending out the wrong message: an exciting new education opportunity is reinforcing the sense that education has to be non-profit." For Ralph and Mrs Saad in this case it is reinforcing the key difficulty: "Any area based on non-profit is going to attract only a few talents, and there will be no competition." There are clearly some people in the world who are not motivated by finan-cial gain. Good people, such as Mother Teresa, and presumably Salman Khan. But if education is seen as primarily something for non-profit motivation *only*, then "It would just be Mr Khan and only a few ... very few. When it is for-profit, everybody who thinks he can do it will jump in and will want to compete." Mrs Saad put it like this: "Education has been stagnant for so long, you need fresh blood, fresh thinking, fresh minds to be injected into it, and only business can bring that."

Ralph Bistany gave another illustration to convey some of the advan-tages of the profit motive – in this case how being for-profit can make much better use of philanthropic resources. Again, without wishing to disparage what they were doing, he points out how a non-profit competi-tor in the charter school arena such as KIPP is totally dependent on phil-anthropic funding to survive. But if you're a philanthropist who wants to make a difference in the charter school arena, where are your resources better spent? Suppose you have $20 million to give away, which would build a reasonable charter school, say. As a philanthropist, you can give that money to a non-profit organization like KIPP and you'll see the one school created. And that's the end of your money – indeed, you also have the misgiving that, unless the non-profit institution can continue to attract other philanthropic donations, it could go under altogether.

Now consider the same philanthropist with the same $20 million. If he builds a charter school for a for-profit company like SABIS to operate, he can lease it to them, or loan them the funds; after a maximum of ten years, the funding can be repaid with interest, and so the same $20 million can be recycled if the philanthropist wants to build another school – without him coughing up any more money, he now has two schools rather than one. And you don't have to worry either about the company needing other philanthropists to step in – because it's a for-profit business it doesn't need any scarce and hard-to-get donations to survive. All it needs is to be able to conduct its business freely and without interference.

Ever since he's been involved, Ralph has insisted upon the fact that SABIS is a for-profit business, even when it could have been financially advantageous otherwise. Ralph told me proudly about the school they opened in Bath, England: "We think we are the first school that was *officially* for profit." Discussing the legal processes when coming to England, their lawyers said that they should register, as schools normally do in England, as a non-profit charity; it was easy enough to channel surpluses out of such charities, they were told, and they needn't pay taxes. It wasn't even tempting. To the consternation of their lawyers, Ralph and Mrs Saad said they wanted it to be known that they were a for-profit education company, even if it meant losing money. The same thing happened when they registered their school in Minnesota as "for-profit." Again their lawyers thought this most eccentric.

I got the sense that Carl Bistany and Mrs Saad may have been slightly sensitive to the way Ralph Bistany talked about for-profit education to me – that I might misinterpret what he was saying, or at least

that I might fail to capture the full picture of where SABIS stood in rela-
tion to profit. Perhaps they were afraid that Ralph Bistany liked to play
to the gallery on this important issue. Mrs Saad certainly seemed to
suggest this: "I think his message is so typical of him, he wants to challenge because people are against schools as businesses." They needn't
have worried that I would misinterpret – the humanity of the man and
the principled vision of the company were manifest in much of what he
was saying and in what the company was doing.

Perhaps he did like to grandstand: when I asked him what motivated SABIS to go into Kurdistan, he said, "Profit." Period. But then,
as he described his visits, he was clearly deeply moved by the plight of
the Kurdish people and clearly inspired by how wonderful it was to be
helping bring education to the country he'd fallen in love with.

When I asked him what had motivated them back in the 1950s
to take on the Yemeni students, again it was "Profit." "I'm brutal in
this," he said. "I felt that I needed to do a lot of things and that I needed
money to do it." But as he elaborated, he couldn't hide the immense joy
he shared with Mrs Saad in educating these young people and in the
intellectual excitement of developing the required educational tools:
"I love the Yemenis, you know. Those kids when they came, they were
amazing. But they learned within a very short time; you wouldn't have
known they had no schooling before."

In neither case was there any contradiction for him between the
twin motivations of profit *and* a humanitarian vision and raising educational quality.

I could see what Ralph was trying to do – and had some sympathy for this. He wanted to convey that there should be no embarrass-
ment about being a for-profit company. You don't have to qualify it, add
caveats, because the more you do that, to appease those who object to
for-profit education, the more you make it seem as though *you* believe
there *really is* some cause for concern." Ralph really believes, and wants
everyone to know, that there is no inconsistency between seeking profit
and having humanitarian impulses or a vision of quality education. I
guess that's why he's so adamant.

But there are other positives about the profit motive in education. Ralph pointed to initiatives whereby the company will carry out substantial R&D in order to better serve an area of huge need and social deprivation. But, of course, they can afford to spend funds on this R&D only because they have already made sufficient profits from other work. Without profit, there is no way they could have conducted this work, nor continue it until it reaches sustainability. Because of the profits it has generated from its work, SABIS can create the SABIS Foundation, and afford to channel 14 percent of all its shares into this non-profit institution, and so dividends from the company are earmarked to go into research to improve education and develop tools that make it accessible in deprived areas. But Ralph didn't want me to focus too much on the importance of the foundation vis-à-vis the company itself. Again resorting to one of his favored motoring analogies, he said: "Making the Model T Ford helped the world a lot more than the creation of the Ford Foundation."

So SABIS is a for-profit education business and not ashamed of being labelled as such. But this does not mean that it thereby eschews high principles, nor lowers quality, nor that it cannot be motivated also by humanitarian concerns. Indeed, the more one sees of the company, the more it appears that these principles do come before consideration of profit; but that without profit, these principles could not hope to be met. That's the dialectic. And that's the relationship that a study of what SABIS is doing helps illuminate; it's the relationship that critics of for-profit education fail to understand.

Ralph was nonplussed when I offered him this observation. I'll give him the last word.

"Let me ask you a question," he said. "Why is it that people who seek profit should have no principles?" There was nothing notable to him about this. People have principles, and for everyone there are principles that will override the desire for profit. For him and SABIS, the educational principles would inevitably be foremost, whatever this meant for profits. "There are things I don't accept. But many people who seek profit also have a lot of principles. There's nothing remarkable about that."

Standardization in a global brand

So if education can legitimately be thought of as a justified for-profit business, what kind of industry can it be? Can we really talk about a global *brand* in education, as the title of my book suggests? Perhaps a key determinant of the extent to which a company can be a global brand would be the level of *standardization* it shows. What form can standardization take in the education industry? Are there useful analogies to be made with other industries?

We've noted already how Ralph Bistany enjoys making parallels between the motor manufacturing industry and education. In the Harvard Business School case study of SABIS, Carl Bistany gives similar parallels:

> If you go to a Lexus manufacturing plant, you don't hear anyone telling you "This line of Lexus is not as good as last year's because the plant engineer left and we haven't found a replacement yet." But in schools we hear all the time, "Mrs Brown left, what a pity, the class is not doing as well." The engineer in a Lexus plant cannot break the process. We need to make sure that no one along the educational conveyor belt can damage the process either.

Carl continues the analogy with manufacturing when he challenges the idea that education cannot be for-profit:

> Our "product" is the enhanced minds and characters of our students; we have about 13 years [K–12] to maximize our enhancements so that our children will be prepared for college and beyond. The college is the immediate customer we are selling our enhanced product to. The 13 years are a conveyor belt, and we need to continually look at every stage of production to ensure a high quality product.[11]

He expanded again on these ideas when I spoke to him:

> What is important is *the system*. Because when you have the system,

then a bright teacher can enhance the productivity of the system or the output of that system. But an average teacher should not break the system. And in a way, the parallel I like always to draw is this: you never hear that a model 2010 Jaguar is not as good because the head engineer left the company or the production manager died or retired. The production quality is there no matter who the individual is. Now if the head is a superb production manager, maybe instead of producing fifty Jaguars a day, they can produce fifty-five Jaguars a day – but still the quality is the same. So that is what drives our thinking, that what should be behind any teacher, average or excellent, should be the system.

How do these analogies with manufacturing hold up for the education industry? These examples are powerful tools to make us think about education differently and the possibility of standardization within it. There are significant differences, however, which seem to undermine some of the analogy's power.

One is that the products from an automobile factory *can* be identical, because they can be fashioned from identical components using identical procedures, irrespective of whether or not "Mrs Brown" is around to help. In schooling it can't be like that, for the important reason that the "product" is not a thing, but a person, the child or student who goes through the processes of education. And apart from anything else, he or she will have a relationship with Mrs Brown or her successor, and relationships can matter to the process and outcome – in a way that it doesn't matter in the automobile case which particular person is engaged in the assembly line, *as long as they are correctly following the processes.*

Does this insertion of the reality of people and the relationships they make mean that we can't have any satisfying analogies like these between education and other industries? Carl Bistany made some comments about another business which set me thinking of other possible parallels. It was in the context of a discussion about how, as a businessman, he is concerned with optimizing resources: "Teachers may spend, say, the first fifteen minutes of every day explaining certain disciplinary procedures. Multiply that by a hundred in a large school. We can ask ourselves is this making use of their valuable and expensive time? How much of a return on that time are we getting?" It's because he is thinking, Carl said, "from an *industrial* point of view," he must think about teachers' time as being "an expensive resource. I will need to optimize my return."

He pointed to how the safety procedure announcements are automated in the *airline industry*: instead of having individual cabin crew having to read through the procedures on every flight, these are automated into the safety video, shown at the press of a button to the passengers. Importantly this means that the cabin crew is released from this repetitive chore for other tasks, and the possibility of error or individual nuance of expression is removed: every passenger will, at least, have been put in front of an identical safety briefing, not matter which crew is on the flight that day. He suggested that you could also easily automate things like school announcements in the same way, to release the burden on teachers and to ensure that there are no inconsistencies between classes.

This set me thinking about the parallels between the airline industry and the business of education. On reflection, I guess that traveling with an airline is perhaps the closest experience that most adults get to being like children in school again; in part for this reason, the similarities between the two areas of business appear strong.

First, there is the time spent with staff *at the point of delivery* (cabin staff in the airline, teachers in the school). In the car manufacturing example, there was little chance of human relationships getting in the way of product standardization, provided that correct procedures were strictly followed. But even in *service* rather than manufacturing industries, in general the chance of human relationships getting in the way of standardization, and hence of a uniform experience for the consumer, is usually low. When I go to buy a burger from McDonald's or a coffee from Starbucks, there isn't usually sufficient time for the relationship with the person serving me to get in the way or enhance the enjoyment of my food or beverage. Or at least, it is relatively easy to train staff so that their interactions in this relatively short space of time are tolerably the same for every customer. When you fly with an airline, however, because the cabin crew are involved in "servicing" you over a prolonged period, *there is time for human relationships and therefore foibles to emerge* and to impact on the standards and standardization of service received.

This is a crucial similarity with schooling. The three airlines I travel with frequently are British Airways, KLM/Air France, and Emirates; in each I am or have been a gold/platinum member. I can categorically state that on each of those airlines the quality of the experience is *extremely* variable, dependent to a large extent on the cabin crew and the team leader. Sometimes staff members are wonderful, full of controlled energy and kindness. Sometimes you really hit it off with an individual, just because that's the way any relationship develops: a member of the cabin crew likes you because you are similar in some way, and so helps you more than he or she helps others. Sometimes you don't hit it off, and are helped less than at other times. Sometimes you get what you might call a "cabin crew pet" (in analogy with "teacher's pet" in a classroom), and that can be irritating if it's not you. Because of the nature of flying – with journeys often taking hours across continents and time zones – sometimes members of staff get tired, disgruntled, jet-lagged, and, with the best will in the world, behave differently to how their training suggests they should. Sometimes – often, even – passengers get the same.

All this means that, although of course there is considerable training of staff, the variety of experience can be extreme. I've stepped off a flight feeling how wonderful the world is, because members of staff were so positive and caring. Other times I've stepped off a flight from the same airline thinking I'll never, ever, ever fly with them again. Just because of the way members of staff have behaved. However good a company's training of cabin crew, it means that it is impossible to standardize fully the interactions between staff and customers, because of the time that is spent in each other's company and the possibilities that arise there.

That said, there may be differences *between airlines* – so you can probably rank airlines for better or worse service. A couple of friends who've spent time on East Asian airlines tell me they are more consistent. But my experience suggests these friends – all men of a certain age – are actually making an observation about the consistency of gender and age of the cabin crew rather than the consistency of the service. I flew Alitalia recently – it was the only airline flying because Icelandic volcanic ash had closed the airports of northern Europe. The headset in my seat was not working, so I couldn't watch the video or listen to the radio. I mentioned this to a member of the cabin crew at the beginning of the flight: "Many headsets are not working" was his full response, delivered with a meditative shrug. Who could argue with that?

Finally, these differences are there because of the fact of human relationships. Much of the experience, however, *is* nonetheless standard. For each airline, there is a clear standard of food, entertainment, seat comfort (or lack thereof), legroom, toilet cleanliness, etc., etc. And it's also clear that the interactions with the staff rarely if ever descend beneath a certain minimum standard. In a sense, it's these standards which define the brand. And it's these factors which ensure that, however differently the staff may behave, the customer still has a relatively uniform experience – the food served is still the same food whether or not the person serving it smiles sweetly or greets you with a forced smile; and of course you still get to your destination, whether speeded by smiles or not.

All this strikes me as being very similar to schooling. In schooling, it's the age and hormones of the children and young people which create the unpredictability, rather than tiredness, jet lag and alcohol as in the airline industry; but the effect is the same. In other words, no matter how good your training and support, you cannot expect teachers to behave in identical ways with students, nor can you expect that the experience of each student will be the same whatever teacher they have. The extent of time that teacher and student are together militates against that, because there is time for human relationships and foibles to emerge, just as in an airline situation. So in a sense, it *can* matter in schooling if Mrs Brown is not there this year; she may have made the whole process more enjoyable or productive than Mr Smith, who takes her place.

But here perhaps Carl Bistany's choice of words in his car manufacturing example is more careful than a perfunctory reading might suggest – he writes: "We need to make sure that no one along the educational conveyor belt *can damage the process* either." In other words, just as in the airline case, although we can't guarantee an identical experience for students, we can make sure that the processes and procedures are not damaged. So the aspects of the brand that have to be consistent include all the parallels to the food, cleanliness, entertainment, and so on that I mentioned for airlines. In the case of schooling, these would include elements like the curriculum, the resources, the approach to teaching and learning, and so on.

Moreover, you can certainly compare across brands, as you can do for airlines. In this way you can say that the consistency of standards across SABIS schools is superior to that of other brands and chains in the market – indeed, others do not even require there to be consistency of approach.

With this standard in mind, then it seems we can think about the consistency of the SABIS network of schools. Using the standard of the car manufacturer, perhaps the level of consistency required was harder to see – clearly the way I saw a teacher behave in New Orleans was different from the way a teacher behaved in Springfield, and both were different from the teachers I saw in Kurdistan. If you think more of the general consistency of approach, however – the consistency of the curriculum, the teaching and learning methods, the materials used, the way students are involved through the Student Life Organization, and so on – then you can point to the consistency of the standards of the SABIS brand. It behaves like, and features the standardization of, not the Lexus factory maybe, but certainly a big international airline.

Consideration earlier of how being confined with members of staff for prolonged periods means that staff behavior may not be consistent also raises the issue of the different type of experience that will be introduced because of your fellow passengers – your peer group – exactly parallel to the way your experience can be affected in schools. We don't normally travel alone, unless we are absurdly wealthy and can afford the lonely luxury of a private jet. The social nature of the traveling experience brings in parameters which are often largely outside of the control of the airline provider. Selfishness comes in – the individuals who insist on bringing too much cabin baggage, blocking the overhead bins so that you can't load your own. Then there's the over-fat person, whose body invades your seat space. The person with a screaming baby. The person who keeps talking, or who snores loudly, or who eats with his mouth open or who laughs raucously at the television shows. All these impinge upon your experience as a passenger. All this is similar in schooling too, where you are thrust together with people you don't necessarily want to be with, and you have to rub along somehow. That's why the "community of learners" that we explored in Chapter 10 is so important for a company like SABIS. Rules and regulations, norms of behavior and ways of harnessing the goodwill of people can all help in schooling, as they do in airlines too.

There appear to be two crucial differences in this analogy between airlines and schooling – where the analogy breaks down and which might make education unique among businesses. First, there is the *voluntary* aspect of education. In terms of flying, once you board the aircraft, almost irrespective of how you behave or engage with the experience, you will leave airport X and arrive at designated airport Y. There are exceptions – for instance, weather can mean you're transferred to another airport; the same can happen if you or a fellow passenger misbehaves in a serious way, or if you or a fellow passenger is really ill, etc. But in general, once on board, you arrive at your destination.

This is not true for schooling. You have to *want to engage* in the process of education in order to benefit from it. The great educational philosopher Professor R. S. Peters made this a fundamental of his theory of education: education is a voluntary process.[12] You cannot be forced to learn. You *can* be forced to engage with *the process*, but this doesn't necessarily mean you will learn and benefit from the opportunities. You can take a horse to water, but you can't make it drink. I'm not sure there are other businesses outside of education or training that have this peculiar quality. It may be thought that health has it to a certain extent: You can refuse to take your tablets or take bed rest. You can continue indulging in unhealthy alcohol or tobacco products even if they go against your health needs. But even in health, *if* you follow the instructions of your doctor, *then* you will benefit. In education there are some extreme cases where you can do everything you are instructed to do, but still come out without the benefit.

This can be for a variety of reasons, including lack of preparation, emotional upheaval, tiredness, distraction of hormones, etc. Given this uniqueness, one would expect any education business to attempt to make sure that this "variety of reasons" doesn't impinge on the learning process too much. One interesting possibility would be to have rote learning very early on. My guess is that it's almost impossible *not* to learn something when rote learning is conducted effectively. I recall doing some teacher training in India where my colleagues and I performed a skit showing the school's over-reliance on rote learning, as I saw it at the time: but I still remember everything we learned, even down to the specifics of the intonation. I still know my multiplication tables too, chanted when I was six or seven. Having this chanting from an early age may be one method that can be used in order to suck people into the learning process, to ensure that the *voluntary nature* of education doesn't get in the way of learning.

You'd also need a mixture of carrots and sticks in order to make sure that the putative learner becomes a real learner. Sticks would be the various punishments that could be meted out, to keep you on task as much as possible. But carrots would emerge too, and ways of making you feel responsible for your own learning. Within SABIS, perhaps the Student Life Organization is precisely one of these carrots, which has emerged through the evolution of the learning environment – so SLO may be an absolutely critical part of the business model as well as playing an important role in the educational model. It's required in order to make sure that the unique aspect of the business of education – the voluntary aspect of learning – doesn't stop young people learning. You might also create myths and stories about the importance of what you are doing and the absolute dangers of not conforming to what is required. You'd want to engage loyalty to the school and to the teachers. You'd make sure that children are adequately prepared and not left to flounder. You'd make sure they were working at their appropriate level. You'd have counselling and emotional support so that emotional stuff doesn't get in the way. You'd try to make sure that teenage hormones don't obtrude through rules and rewards (the end-of-term prom if you behave and get your grades; detention if not). What is interesting to me is that all these ideas – all part of the SABIS culture – could well have emerged because of the business imperative as much as for their educational value. As noted earlier, when exploring SABIS, it's often hard to separate the two sides, the enterprise of education and the educational enterprise itself.

But there's another important difference between the education industry and the airline industry which may cause the analogy to break down. When I discussed this model with Ralph Bistany, he came up with another way in which the business of education is different from other businesses: "Education has one particular characteristic that I don't see in other industries. The product can improve itself, if you prime it to do so." The SABIS model has seen this specifically with Shadow Teachers, self-tutoring: "If you get them going, children can continue without you. That's a big difference."

To put the difference in terms of the analogy with the airline industry: you can't start flying with British Airways, get dropped in Sydney but carry on to Auckland anyway (unless, of course, you take another airline or mode of transport). The parallel in education would be that you can go far with an educational provider and continue very much on your own once you're on your way.

We've explored some ways in which SABIS is pushing the envelope toward the end of more and more of the responsibility for learning being put on to the student. As developments progress here, we may have more insight into this crucial difference between education and other industries.

SABIS company miscellany

We can consider the delivery of educational opportunities as a business and not be convinced by arguments against for-profit education companies. SABIS's business model shows that it has created a global brand in somewhat comparable ways to another type of global business, viz. the airline industry. Our final question is: what kind of business is SABIS?

In my experience, when many people think of private school chains, they tend to think that a major part of the business consists of the property portfolio for the schools. This is to misunderstand the true nature of an educational business like SABIS. The previous three chapters, where we looked at the education model, and the earlier chapters, where we looked at licensing, will have suggested that there is a considerable intellectual property in the brand. This is the core of the SABIS business.

While some capital is tied up in property, this is kept as low as the business can manage: "Ideally," says Ralph Bistany, "as far as I'm concerned, we want to be a private school manager because to own means tying up our capital, and capital is limited, whereas to manage, well, really that's unlimited." Carl Bistany concurs: "Primarily we are a school operator, not a property owner. If I had a choice, we'd like to just be involved in operating the school, not having an equity stake in the school at all."

With SABIS's private schools, the degree to which the company participates in owning the school property ranges from 0 to 100 percent. Typically, SABIS will enter into a partnership with one or more local promoters, who are important for the business because they have local knowledge and political connections. The partners typically want SABIS to have some equity stake in the building, claiming that this makes SABIS more committed – although Carl Bistany says that this is completely to mistake where their commitment comes from. Typically, SABIS will take a minority stake. So, for instance, they have a 49 percent equity stake in their first private school in Egypt, 25 percent in their first school in Abu Dhabi, while in each of Jordan and Bahrain,

SABIS's stake is 10 percent. The private schools in Minnesota, USA, Bath, England, and Lebanon are 100 percent owned by SABIS.

Usually, SABIS will then sign a management contract with the company that owns the school property, typically a fifteen-year, renewable agreement. For those fifteen years, the partners basically entrust SABIS to run the school. There is a clause in these contracts allowing for them to be cancelled, but in the case of the private schools it is very different from the American experience with charter schools. No board has cancelled a contract during the whole period in which SABIS has operated schools.

Who has ownership of the property can be an issue with the charter schools – SABIS's PPPs in America. SABIS has built and 100 percent owned several of its charter schools, including in Springfield (an investment of around $20 million, now bought by the board), Arizona, and Cincinnati. This presents a big risk for SABIS capital – if, as we've seen too frequently occurs, SABIS and the board fall out, then the board can move the charter school somewhere else, and SABIS is left with a building that they would find difficult to use for any other purpose in the kinds of neighborhoods in which they have charter schools. (This has happened to them more than once. In one case, they were forced to sell at a loss of $6 million because the charter school board moved their school elsewhere.)

The four business models (plus one university in Kurdistan) that we've met throughout this book are worth summarizing, showing the geographic spread and the number of schools at the time of writing (January 2012):

- Private schools – 27 (in the USA, the UK, Germany, Egypt, Pakistan, UAE, Qatar, Oman, Bahrain, Lebanon, Jordan, Syria, Saudi Arabia, Kurdistan)
- Public–private partnership (PPP) schools (outside the USA) – 18 (in UAE and Kurdistan)
- Charter schools (US PPP) – 8 (all USA)
- Licensed – 5 (4 public schools in the USA, 1 private in Romania)

So SABIS is operating in fifteen countries, in schools catering to 60,000 students.

The *brand* is the same wherever it is found in the three school types (private, PPP, and charter schools), but in fact there has not been consistent naming of their schools until a decision was recently taken to do this. The original mother school, as we have seen, is called "The International School of Choueifat," and this has been the major brand name used by the company as it expanded: one other of their schools in Lebanon, and all their schools in Jordan, Syria, Kurdistan, UAE, Oman, Bahrain, Pakistan, and Egypt, are called by this name. This has led to the name of the small village on the slopes of Mount Lebanon being widely known throughout the world – there is now a *Choueifat Street* in Cairo and a *Choueifat Quarter* elsewhere.

As they expanded into Germany and the USA, the company used different localized names (so the US school is "The International School of Minnesota"). The company now appears to be moving to a new name for some of its private schools, however: SABIS International School was the name given to the third and most recent school the company opened in Lebanon. And although their school in England was originally called "The International School of Choueifat," at its reopening this year it will be named, in accordance with the newly preferred brand, "SABIS International School."

Twin peaks

Finally, SABIS is a family business – or rather a two-family business. The name, coined by Mrs Saad in 1990, takes the "Sa" from the Saad family and combines it with the "Bis" from Bistany. It has a reassuring educational ring to the people involved; "It sounds like *saber* [the Spanish verb "to know"]," says Ralph Bistany. Indeed, in Chilean Spanish *tú sabís* means "You know."

Mrs Saad notes the importance of the family business to her: "It is extremely important to me because I feel that in times of great conflict, when things are going wrong and we have seen them, we've been through times of difficulty, the blood tie and the pride of being part of this can play a major role."

When one thinks of family businesses, one might be forgiven for thinking only of small-scale "mom-and-pop" enterprises. In fact several well-known and large companies are family businesses:

Italy: Salvatore Ferragamo, Benetto and Fiat Group
France: L'Oréal, Carrefour Group, LVMH, Michelin
South Korea: Samsung, Hyundai Motor, LG Group
Germany: BMW, Siemens
Japan: Kikkoman, Ito-Yokado
USA: Ford Motors Company, Wal-Mart Stores

The American examples I found particularly surprising. The Ford family still has 40 percent of the voting stock in their eponymous motor company – incorporated in 1903 and the second-largest automobile manufacturer in America, by sales. Sam Walton founded Wal-Mart in 1962; his descendants still own 38 percent of the shares.

SABIS already spans four generations, while the fifth generation (Ralph Bistany's grandsons and Carl's sons) seems ready to come on board:

- *First generation*: the Reverend Tanios Saad (and Miss Louisa Procter)
- *Second generation*: Charles Saad, son of the Reverend Tanios Saad
- *Third generation*: Mrs Leila Saad (the grand-niece of the Reverend Tanios Saad: she could also be considered second-generation, as Charles's wife and daughter-in-law of the Reverend Saad) and Ralph Bistany
- *Fourth generation*: Carl Bistany (Ralph's son), Serge Bakhos (Ralph's son-in-law), Victor Saad, George Saad (great-grandsons of the Reverend Tanios Saad), Ghassan Kansou, Mahdi Kansou (grand-nephews of Mrs Saad)
- *Fifth generation*: Carl's sons (Ralph's grandsons)

These generations, however, are slightly artificial – the "fourth" generation actually spans what seems like a generation in itself – Carl is 56, Serge is 50, Victor is 41, George is 37, Madhi is 34, and Ghassan is 30. Victor, George, Madhi, and Ghassan are all grand-nephews of Mrs Saad, whose grandfather was the brother of the Reverend Tanios Saad. Victor and George are related directly to the founder, being great-grandsons of the Reverend Saad. Madhi and Ghassan are related to the founder as great-grand-nephews.

The fact that members of the fourth generation are firmly in positions of responsibility – Carl is president and Victor is vice-president, for instance – means that SABIS has survived what is reportedly the most tricky stage in family businesses: around 95 percent of family businesses "do not survive the third generation of ownership" because of "a lack of preparation of the subsequent generations to handle the demands of a growing business and a much larger family."[13] In part, they've survived because of some of the mechanisms they've developed – indeed, these were praised by the International Finance Corporation as being exemplary.[14] What the IFC commended SABIS on doing was bringing in a framework while the key players of the third generation – Mrs Saad and Ralph Bistany – are still able to take part and *before* any areas of conflict have already arisen.

There were two likely problem areas. First, ever since Ralph Bistany joined in 1954, one of the advantages of the businesses as far as he and Mrs Saad were concerned was the ease of decision-making. Mrs Saad put it like this: "What Ralph and I wanted, happened. We took, rather Ralph took, opportunities as he saw them." Ralph concurred: "We've been doing this for fifty-five years; we make a telephone call and we make a decision big or very big or small, and that's end of it; it takes five minutes. I'm not used to board meetings."

But around 1987, Mrs Saad started thinking seriously about what sort of company structure they needed to move things forward – she was aware that to ensure the continuity of the International School of Choueifat, careful succession planning was necessary. The first attempt was to create a foundation in Liechtenstein (in Liechtenstein, this does not have the connotation of being a non-profit institution), in 1988. Then, with the assistance of their lawyers, Mrs Saad and Ralph Bistany explored a structure that could work to ensure continuity and bring the two families together – under the newly coined name SABIS, in recognition of the contribution of both families. Mrs Saad and Ralph informally approached a number of members of the families. Carl was the first to join in 1996, followed by Victor a year later. By the year 2000, all the "fourth generation" had already joined SABIS.

Board governance was crucial, to replace the informal arrangements that had prevailed before. The International Finance Corporation[15] recommends that family businesses separate out the different circles of stakeholders: the family, shareholders, management, the board – which are usually, as was the case with SABIS, merged into one. So the new generations started to disaggregate these functions. They created executive management teams of which Mrs Saad and Mr Bistany were not members. These teams also included senior executives who are not family members, while the board was also supplemented in this way. Mrs Saad and Mr Bistany are on the board but are not now part of the management team. And even when the people overlapped under these different headings, they tried to get people to separate their interests: "Now put on your board hat."

One of the new structures put in place was the family employment policy. This begins from the premise that employment at the company is neither a birthright nor an obligation to any family member. If SABIS hires family members, it will only be on a merit hiring basis, based both on their abilities and the availability of a position within the company. The policy also stipulates that the company will not create a position just to suit the needs of a family member. (It may be worth noting that the families are genuinely discriminating about who they allow into the business. Other family members have wanted to join but were not allowed to.)

The second major issue that faced SABIS was this: much of what SABIS has been doing has been because of the sometimes brilliant insights of one man, Ralph Bistany. It's his understanding of education which has dominated the company. It's his exposing of educational myths and shibboleths which has led to the distinct educational emphases. And, as we've seen, it's been his and Mrs Saad's experiences over the decades which have led to the evolution of the educational model. Of course, Ralph Bistany and Mrs Saad won't be there all the time. But the education business is one that needs constant appraisal of new educational trends, sifting the fads from the good ideas, sorting which are worth adopting and which they should shun. Who is going to do that in the future? Obviously a different mechanism was needed.

The "different mechanism" was the Academic Task Force (ATF). This is a group of senior management people from within SABIS. Part of their work is to try to do what Ralph was doing: looking at innovations in education and trying to decide which are fads and which are ideas worth adopting. Exploring which fit into their philosophy of learning and core values and which don't. "We're certainly not going to adopt something just because a hundred people are talking about it," Carl said. But they're certainly open to new ideas and also to critically examining those they already have.

Mr Ralph Bistany isn't a member of the Academic Task Force, obviously, but all the other family members of the fourth generation are. Carl sees the group as the "caretakers of what we have, the curriculum," charged with "enhancing it all the time."

So SABIS is now building structures but trying not to lose its prior nimbleness and flexibility: "Sometimes we still take decisions for ten million dollars over tea and carrot cake," Carl said. "We are very nimble; we are very fast in taking decisions, and we'd like to keep this." One way of maintaining this, at least for now, has been not to bring in private equity investors. Certainly that would inhibit the making of quick decisions, if they had to entertain new board members who were not used to the culture: "All equity investors who came and talked to us were always concerned about their exit strategy after five years. But my short term is twenty-five years; the long term is the next one hundred years," said Carl.

These systems can keep the company focused; but can they replace the charisma and passion that Ralph Bistany and Mrs Saad have brought?

"People have different characters and different levels of intensity and passion," Carl commented. "But the commitment to our core purpose brings with it the passion of why we are doing this." The fourth generation is infected by the passion of the older generation – that is obvious from any interactions with them. Carl commented, "I've continued that passion but am trying to institutionalize the passion." The organization at this stage, he told me, "cannot just depend on one person or a good director. We have to continue delivering no matter who is there."

This realization hit him very forcibly when he first went to the board meetings for the SABIS charter school in Springfield, Massachusetts. We've already seen how enamored with Ralph Bistany the board members in Springfield became. They weren't shy about letting Carl know this: "Their first question to me was, 'We've known your father for the past seven or eight years and he's very committed to our school and to what we are doing in Springfield. We know him and we know his values ... how do we know if *you're* committed?" It dawned on Carl that this was his challenge: it never should depend upon who visits. "If I visit or George Saad visits or anyone from SABIS, they should know that these people represent the values of a company, not an individual." Every person within the company must be like the "ambassador of a country: when you send the ambassador, it's not the values of that person that matter, but the values of the country he or she represents. The same must be true for SABIS."

Interestingly, when I met with Dr Peter Negroni, formerly school superintendent for Springfield, and again one of the characters we've already met in the American chapters, this issue of passion came up. Dr Negroni was also very impressed by Ralph Bistany's passion. But Dr Negroni volunteered how impressed he has been by Carl since. Of Carl, he said, "He carries his father's heart together with acute business acumen. But he's got his father's heart there, his passion ... No question about it. The whole family, they are just wonderful people."

Thus prompted, I put the question to him: can SABIS survive without Mr Ralph Bistany and Mrs Saad? Dr Negroni had no hesitation: "Absolutely, because it's a family business and that's what makes them different. The belief system is embedded in those people's hearts and souls."

Conclusion

F ROM ITS ORIGINS in a humble village school for girls in Choueifat in 1886, the company now called SABIS operates in fifteen countries and has grown to serve, in its 125th year of operation, 60,000 students.

Many of the company's schools are strong and vibrant independent schools, providing an outstanding education to children across continents: in America, Europe, the Middle East, North Africa and Asia. Across the world, SABIS is the upholder of a highly respected education system, providing a beacon of excellence from which other organizations can learn and whose standards others can aspire to meet.

The company also has schools in public–private partnership with governments – with the aim of combining the innovation and excellence of the private sector with schooling free at the point of delivery. These schools are serving children in some of the world's most difficult places – such as in Kurdistan, northern Iraq, where a once oppressed people are finding SABIS ready to help them build schools and colleges for their emergence into nationhood. The same will be true across Iraq in general, and in other difficult places where SABIS can help make a difference through education. The company is also trying to create public–private partnerships in a wide range of settings, from the United Arab Emirates to the United States. For deprived inner-city children in America, from some of the most crime-ridden cities to the poorest parts of Louisiana, including hurricane-devastated New Orleans, SABIS is building charter schools to raise educational standards among these deprived groups. Often in these places politics seems to get in the way of growth and development. The tenacity and compassion of those involved in the company sticking with their attempts to expand in America and elsewhere inspire respect and admiration.

In both types of schools, private and those in public–private partnership, the SABIS system ensures that no teacher can get in the way of excellence – indeed, the system allows for, in Steven Wilson's memorable phrase, "Excellence without heroics." Created over decades of incremental, evolutionary innovation, there's a complete and organic system of educational content and delivery that is rich in data, strong on basics, and leads to mastery in a standardized way for all students, rich or poor, wherever they are in the world.

SABIS is a for-profit company, but its engagement over the years confounds critics who say that this means the company will cut corners or abandon principles in pursuit of profit. On the contrary, the company seems steeped in values, including compassion and integrity. These values seem to be rooted in the ideals of the company's founders. The family business is inspired by, and upholds for the future, the values of its earlier generations. In its dealings around the world, it is clear that the company often puts its principles before profit; crucially, however, *without its profits*, it wouldn't be able to extend its reach and capacity for humanitarian and educational ends.

But it's not static. It's not static in its understanding of education. The company is spurred by a need for innovation. Education needs to respond to the future of unknown possibilities, while remaining grounded in the virtues that have stood the test of time. Mrs Saad put it like this:

> If we ever think that we have got it all right, it would be the beginning of the end for us. We are constantly investigating ways of improvement because anything that stagnates begins to die. We will never stop; everything can always be improved. Look at the athletes, how they keep breaking records, a record now is not one in five years' time. I don't want anybody in our organization to think that we have made it once and for all.

And it's not static in terms of geographic reach either. The founders saw the need for education in an area devoid of opportunities and built a school accordingly. Around the world in the international sphere, the family members still see a world of needs and possibilities. Carl Bistany put it like this: "Being able to affect different areas in the world is important because deep down our SABIS founders really felt that making the world a better world through education would be better for humanity as a whole." By helping lift poor people out of poverty, you're helping to create a better environment for them. "And a better environment for them will mean a better environment for everybody." This humanitarian vision of changing the world through education also inspires the leaders to grow the company, reaching out beyond its current borders, to serve increasingly wider audiences, wider groups of people with needs.

When one chronicles the progress of SABIS, one is chronicling the influence of an idea – an idea that those less fortunate and less privileged, initially girls in a remote village on the slopes of Mount Lebanon, deserve a decent education. Through their shared passions, the idea became rooted in the hearts of men and women with compassion, intellect, and the business acumen to turn it into reality.

In particular the idea took root in the hearts and minds of the core team of Mrs Saad and Ralph Bistany. In the Introduction, I began this book with my journey to Kurdistan, to see how SABIS was making a difference in difficult places. Let me finish with my journey to interview Ralph Bistany and Mrs Saad, giving them the final word.

Footprints on the sands of time

I first interviewed Ralph Bistany over two days in Lebanon. It was an extraordinary experience, feeling that one was in the presence of someone of quite exceptional intellect, erudition, taste, and sensitivities. A humorous man, and generous too – always willing to ascribe ideas to others when appropriate. When he smiled, he reminded me of Anthony Hopkins, with wonderfully sparkling eyes in his warm, open face. And although wise and sincere, he had a boyish innocence about him; especially when Mrs Saad was playfully scolding him.

The first time I met him was when, with Amy Wesley and Carl Bistany, I'd flown from Erbil, Kurdistan, leaving at 3:30 a.m., flying to Amman in Jordan, and then changing aircraft to take the early morning flight, flying over the Golan Heights to traverse the austere mountains of Lebanon, before turning down over the coast, over the ancient city of Byblos, to land in Beirut. After a very quick shower and change of clothes, we drove the few miles to Mrs Saad's apartment, where we were to meet for our first day of discussions.

Mrs Saad organized the seating arrangements so that I could sit next to Mr Ralph Bistany. Amy and Carl had been away for a few days, so catching up was in order. In any case, the normal way into an important meeting of this kind is to have some small talk – indeed, the more important the meeting the more valued the small talk, to put one at ease. Mrs Saad, Amy and Carl duly partook of this, and I turned to "Mr B" to take part myself. But he just looked at me, conspiratorially, his expression saying something like: we don't need that, do we? We have work to do, an interview to go through, shall we get started? And so he cut through the small talk, asked me for my first question, and off we went.

I'd been nervous that I would feel too tired to interview him properly – for an interview so important for the book, it wasn't exactly the best way to be arriving, having hardly slept the night before and having flown across several borders. Amy had caught me yawning several times; Carl Bistany had scolded that I'd better not be too tired for this encounter. But I needn't have worried. Mr Ralph Bistany was so alert, so strong, and so interesting; all thoughts of my tiredness and nervousness were quickly banished. It was riveting talking to him; I waited with excitement and eagerness to hear what he would say next. Later I would understand exactly what people in America meant when they told me how he could mesmerize a room of skeptical people as he told them of his educational understanding. I felt in the presence of a truly great man.

We were in the middle of a discussion about the role of teachers and the possibility of a teacherless school when Mrs Saad announced that lunch was ready. Mr Bistany sounded disappointed at first. But then he said decisively, "We will carry on while eating," and with that he took my tape recorder and propped it next to him on the dining table. Over lunch he continued talking about the nature of education and the role of teachers and the definition of a classroom and how technology could liberate learning; everyone was eating in silence, listening to him, there were no side conversations, except over how delightful the pickled garlic was and please to pass the tomatoes, and did we want lemon with our hummus?

"You can carry on after lunch," Mrs Saad said to me, "as long as he's not tired." Indeed, at all times I was told I must be sensitive to Mr B's need to rest. He could carry on after lunch only for perhaps an hour, then he would need to rest. But it wasn't him, the 79-year-old man who'd recently had heart surgery, who needed to rest at all. A couple of times, those present hinted to him that he might want to rest, me included, but he would just carry on: "When I get tired everyone will know," he said. Eventually, late in the afternoon, it became clear that *I* was becoming muddled about a couple of things, and Mrs Saad, in her motherly, scolding way, said, "Ralph? I think by now, you must realize that everybody is tired." Ralph said that they should call his doctor and congratulate him because "I'm *not* tired."

Anyway, in the end we got ready to go on our way. I traveled in the same car as him, as my hotel in Adma was near his apartment. He continued talking about education. Then suddenly, mid-sentence, he said: "I'm tired now," and closed his eyes and slept.

The next day I met with Mr Bistany for breakfast, in his beautiful apartment on the top floor of the Bistany block of apartments: Mr Bistany is on the top floor, Carl Bistany and his family have the floor beneath, and his sister and brother-in-law Serge are on the first floor. It's an apartment block situated on a hill overlooking a bay in the Mediterranean, looking across to the city of Beirut proper. And it's just three minutes away from the SABIS headquarters next to the Adma school.

For breakfast we had a healthy but extensive spread of tomatoes and cucumbers, parsley, hummus and eggs – much of which had come from their own fertile gardens below. Ralph was pleased to tell me that "Bistany" is Arabic for "gardener." We talked the whole day in his study. And in between conversations, he guided me around his bookshelves – full of advanced texts on theoretical physics and mathematics, topology and quantum mechanics and calculus, then shelves of novels in three languages, a history of law in Spanish, then further shelves of economics, history and philosophy. He was particularly proud to show me an early edition of *Théorie des Ensembles* (Set Theory), by Nicolas Bourbaki, which of course he reads in the original French. There was no person called "Bourbaki" – the name is actually a collective pseudonym for a group of twentieth-century mathematicians concerned to expound mathematics with the maximum of rigor.

Ralph told me that he tried to keep abreast of developments in mathematical physics, including quantum theory, although he eschewed reading popular science, wanting to understand the real mathematics behind the developments. He was currently looking at tensor calculus; if he came across areas he didn't understand, "I go back and look at the prerequisites; I go back as far as I have to until I understand." He's doing this simply because he loves to learn – but he's also excited about the possibilities of SABIS opening a university (the first one has been opened in Kurdistan – "I would love to have a university here in Beirut," he says) and although he's too old to teach, he wants to keep abreast of things that the students might be learning. He studies every day, he told me. In the morning, he has three sessions, "of twenty-three minutes each. I want to do twenty minutes, but I know that I get phone calls and other interruptions." So he adds three minutes of stoppage time, as it were. "I use a stopwatch. I want the hour to be concentrated, that's the minimum. Whatever I am doing and wherever I am, I have to have this time."

Ralph does not drink, nor does he smoke. But he has a weakness – chocolate. At several points in the day he offered me various varieties of chocolates, Swiss chocolates, Belgian chocolates, chocolates that had just been brought to him from afar by various well-wishers. While I drank tea, he drank hot chocolate. At one point I had chocolate overload, so he got me some biscuits: these are "ginger biscuits," he advises me, pronouncing them "biscwits." He gets cold easily, he told me ("The only place I couldn't open schools," he said, "is Alaska"). In the middle of the afternoon, he went off to add another layer, then came back in his outdoor coat to resume our discussions. For me, the early winter Lebanese weather was pleasantly balmy.

I interviewed him at length, about the history of the company and his theories of education; some of our discussions have found their way into this book and I hope I've been able to convey something of the magnificent breadth and depth of his thoughts and experience. But discussions with Ralph can't be contained in this way – because the history of the company is intimately connected with the politics and history and economics of the nineteenth and twentieth centuries; his theories of learning and education are intimately connected with his ideas on logic and ethics, on the universe, and on love, religion and the meaning of life. We touched on all these areas; I wish I could have included more of these discussions here. What was extraordinary throughout was his humility in the face of knowledge, his lack of arrogance. He knew what he didn't know, and what he couldn't know, and felt awe at the epistemological shakiness of it all; and where he did know something, he was willing to concede that there could be alternative explanations. It was all quite surprising and refreshing.

He was very keen to teach me something – a method that he had developed of mentally extracting the cube roots of fifteen-digit numbers. He's teaching fifteen- and sixteen-year-old children in the Adma school this method, and he says they're really enjoying it. An Indian woman has apparently published a book with a parallel method, and apparently a Mr K. K. Thomas, an Indian engineer, had won a place in the *Limca Book of Records*, the Indian equivalent of the *Guinness Book of Records*, for his abilities to also calculate the cube root of a fifteen-digit number within a minute. "I find these timings excessive," said Ralph, "our kids can do it much faster."

He had asked his office to prepare a list of random fifteen-digit numbers together with their cube roots on the other side of the paper, which he folded over to obscure from view. To demonstrate the method he asked me to choose one of the numbers and he started to take me through the method. He was painstakingly thorough, and very patient with me – a mathematics teacher once for sure, but now slightly rusty. But then he began hesitating and became less confident. "The number there should be six zero seven ... I have made a mistake ... where do I get ... what did I do?" For a 79-year-old man to get in a slight muddle while demonstrating something to a younger interloper while being recorded seemed completely understandable and no cause for alarm. But he was alarmed. He kept on examining and reexamining what he'd done, looked at the table of figures, kept running different scenarios around in his mind, sighing and saying things like "Ah, I'm sorry. What did I do?" Then eventually, he stopped and smiled. "This table is wrong," he said categorically. "This table is definitely wrong ... Get me the calculator." And we got the calculator and found that, yes, it was not the man of nearly eighty years who had made a mistake, but the younger people in his office.

We tried again with another pair of numbers, and this time the numbers they gave us were correct. We spent an hour or so on the method. I understood what was going on, but I'm not sure I could replicate it now. He reassured me: "It looks tougher than it really is, but once you understand ... I mean, I make it a point for the kids to understand. I'm rushing you, otherwise we would spend all the afternoon on this."

Learning these mathematical methods with Ralph, and realizing how much he still loves to learn and to share his learning with others, made me realize something very beautiful about the company that I'd been researching. It's been run by someone whose passion is education, who wants to keep learning for himself, and is always keen to teach. And his genius tempered throughout by Mrs Saad's practical arts, combined with the humanitarianism of both, is what has influenced and continues to influence all the others in the fourth generation. In their turn Mrs Saad and Ralph Bistany were influenced by the strong values of Charles Saad and his father, the Reverend Tanios Saad, who founded the humble village school in Choueifat.

Mrs Saad joined us for tea; I asked her what she would like from the next 125 years of SABIS. She started with a rather standard business-school-type definition: "We'd like SABIS to be a world trademark of excellence in education," she said. Ralph concurred: "I'm overambitious. I would like that by then there are thousands of education companies including SABIS. We would be one of the giant companies of the world, bigger than General Motors. But there will be many other competing education companies. And because of this, education will stop being a problem for the poor. SABIS would have the honor of being one of the pioneers for solving the education problem."

Later, when I was on my own with Mrs Saad, she was more reflective: "When I was at school, many, many years ago, I studied Longfellow. Do you know his 'Psalm of Life'?"

I had to admit that I didn't know it particularly well, unfortunately. So she recited the poem by Henry Wadsworth Longfellow (1807–82):

Tell me not, in mournful numbers,
Life is but an empty dream! –
For the soul is dead that slumbers,
And things are not what they seem.

As she finished, she said, "I remember everything I studied when I was fifteen," adding, with a warm chuckle but a tinge of both remorse and self-admonishment: "But sometimes I can't remember things I studied two weeks ago."

Mrs Saad had ended with this stanza:

Lives of great men all remind us
We can make our lives sublime,
And, departing, leave behind us
Footprints on the sands of time.

This is what she wanted for SABIS's legacy in the next 125 years: "I'd like to feel that SABIS has played a role in making the world a tiny bit better, for some people, somewhere. I would like to think that SABIS will leave its footprints on the sands of time," she said.

Notes

Introduction

1. Throughout this book I will be using "public schools" to mean government schools, the international usage, rather than to mean "elite private schools," which is the idiosyncratic British and Indian (and possibly other parts of the Commonwealth) usage.
2. Chris Whittle, *Crash Course: A Radical Plan for Improving Public Education*, Penguin, New York, 2005, p. 97.
3. Ibid., p. 267.
4. Ibid., p. 180.
5. From here onwards, the registered trademark symbol ® is implied in every use of the term SABIS.
6. Steven F. Wilson, *Learning on the Job: When Business Takes on Public Schools*, Harvard University Press, Cambridge, Mass. and London 2006, p. 52.

Chapter 1: Climbing Mount Lebanon

1. Quotations from "Reverend T. Saad's first visit to England, 1897". Reprinted from *The Rock*, 1 October 1897.
2. *A Visit to Schwifat*, by Ellwood Brockbank. Extract from the School Report for 1897.
3. *History of Schwifat's School*. Extract from *The Rock*, 1 October 1897.
4. Mahmoud Khalil Saab, *Stories and Scenes from Mount Lebanon*, Saqi Books, London, 2004, p. 213.
5. Ibid., p. 213.
6. There's more than one way of calculating what this is worth in today's money. Using a measure of average earnings gives a value of £42,200 per annum in 2010 money (see http://www.measuringworth.com/

ukcompare/), which seems like quite a lot. Of course, her funds may have had to cover other expenses in England too.

7. Saab, 2004, p. 213.
8. This story is adapted from ibid., p. 213, and interviews with Mrs Saad.
9. *History of Schwifat's School*. Extract from *The Rock*, 1 October 1897.
10. *A Visit to Schwifat*, by Ellwood Brockbank. Extract from the School Report for 1897.
11. Matthew 26, 10, about the poor woman who had anointed the feet of Jesus with an expensive perfume that the disciples complained could have been "sold at a high price, and the money given to the poor."
12. Obituary letter signed by the Reverend Tanios Saad, dated Schwifat, 12 March 1907.
13. References in this paragraph to Saab, 2004, p. 212.
14. References in this paragraph to ibid., p. 213.
15. References in this paragraph to ibid., p. 212.
16. References in this paragraph to ibid., p. 214.
17. *A Visit to Schwifat*, by Ellwood Brockbank. Extract from the School Report for 1897.
18. Saab, 2004, p. 214.
19. All quotes here from *Mr Saad's Visit to England this Year, 1913*. Extract from the School Report for 1913.
20. Saab, 2004, p. 214.
21. Ibid., p. 215.
22. Ibid., p. 212.

Chapter 2: The good life

1. Henceforth, the registered trademark symbol ® is implied in every subsequent use of the term "Point System."
2. Henceforth, the registered trademark symbol ® is implied in every subsequent use of the term "Student Life Organization."

Chapter 4: An American roller coaster

1. The data used here were obtained from the Massachusetts Department of Education and the Michigan Department of Education. In Massachusetts, the tests used to give the comparative data are the Massachusetts Comprehensive Assessment System (MCAS), which

is administered every spring for Grades 3–10 in English Language Arts (ELA), mathematics, and science and technology/engineering. In Michigan, the comparison tests are the Michigan Educational Assessment Program (MEAP), administered every fall for Grades 3–9, in reading/ELA, mathematics, science and social studies.

2. Names of all American students have been changed to protect their identity.

Chapter 5: American antidote

1. Jay Mathews, *Work Hard, Be Nice: How Two Inspired Teachers Created the Most Promising Schools in America*, Algonquin Books, Chapel Hill, NC, 2009.

Chapter 6: A school fit for Hêro

1. Henceforth, the registered trademark symbol ® is implied in every subsequent use of the terms "Integrated Testing and Learning" or "ITL."

2. Henceforth, the registered trademark symbol ® is implied in every subsequent use of the term "SABIS Academic Monitoring System" or "AMS."

3. Henceforth, the registered trademark symbol ® is implied in every subsequent use of the term "Shadow Teacher."

Chapter 8: Licensed to ascend

1. *New York Daily News*, 3 January 2009, http://articles.nydailynews.com/ 2009–01–03/local/17915172_1_three-robberies-murders-violent.

2. Wilson, 2006, p. vii.

3. Ibid., p. ix.

4. Mathews, 2009.

5. Steven F. Wilson, "Success at scale in charter schooling," American Enterprise Institute for Public Policy Research, *Education Outlook*, 3, March 2009.

6. Ibid., p. 1.

7. Ibid., p. 1.

8. Ibid., p. 1.

9. Ibid., p. 2.

10. Ibid., p. 4.

11. *Growing Pains: Scaling up the Nation's Best Charter Schools*, Education Sector Reports, November 2009, p. 10.
12. Ibid., p. 11.
13. Wilson, 2009, p. 5.
14. Ibid., p. 5.
15. *Growing Pains*, p. 13.
16. Ibid., p. 13.
17. "US expands 'axis of evil'," BBC News, 6 May 2002, http://news.bbc.co.uk/1/hi/1971852.stm.

Chapter 9: The logic of learning

1. Whittle, 2005, p. 97.
2. Ibid., p. 105.
3. Ibid., p. 115.
4. Daniel Isenberg, *SABIS – a Global Education Venture from Lebanon*, Harvard Business School Case Study N9–809–167, 30 June 2009, p. 6.
5. Ibid., p. 6.
6. Quoted in ibid., p. 6.
7. Jay P. Greene, *Education Myths: What Special-Interest Groups Want You to Believe about Our Schools – and Why It Isn't So*, Rowman & Littlefield, Oxford, 2005, p. 52.
8. Ibid., p. 52.
9. Ibid., p. 53.
10. Ibid., p. 53.
11. Ibid., p. 54.
12. Caroline M. Hoxby, "The effects of class size on student achievement: new evidence from population variation," *Quarterly Journal of Economics*, 115(4), 2000, pp. 1239–85.
13. Ludger Wössmann and Martin West, *Class-Size Effects in School Systems around the World: Evidence from Between-Grade Variation in TIMSS*, Harvard University, Program on Education Policy and Governance, Working Paper no. PEPG/02–02, 2002, pp. 31–2.
14. Isenberg, 2009, p. 7.
15. Ibid., p. 7.

Chapter 10: The community of learners

1. Whittle, 2005, p. 115.
2. See James Tooley, *The Beautiful Tree: A Personal Journey into How the World's Poorest People Are Educating Themselves*, Penguin, New Delhi, 2009, ch. 11.
3. Judith Cohen Zacek, "The Lancastrian School Movement in Russia," *Slavonic and East European Review*, 45(105), 1967, pp. 343–67; p. 344.
4. Marlow Ediger, *The Lancastrian Monitorial System of Instruction*, Report, Northeast Missouri State University, 1987, p. 5.
5. Ibid., p. 5.
6. B. O. Williams, "My recollections of the early schools of Detroit that I attended from the year 1816 to 1819," in *Pioneer Collections: Report of the Pioneer Society of the State of Michigan*, 5, Lansing, 1884, pp. 549–50.
7. "The psychology of monitorial instruction," *Westminster Review*, 1, January 1824, pp. 53–5, www.constitution.org/lanc/psychmon.htm.
8. H. H. Levin, G. V. Glass and G. R. Meister, *Cost-effectiveness of Four Educational Interventions*, Project Report no. 84-A11, Institute for Research on Educational Finance and Governance, Stanford University, 1984.
9. S. S. Hartley, *Meta-analysis of the Effects of Individually Paced Instruction in Mathematics*, Doctoral dissertation, University of Colorado, 1977.
10. P. A. Cohen, J. A. Kulik and C. L. Kulik, "Educational outcomes of tutoring: a meta-analysis of findings," *American Educational Research Journal*, 19(2), 1982, pp. 237–48.
11. C. T. Fitzgibbon, "Peer tutoring projects: social education improves achievement," *Journal of the National Organisation for Initiatives in Social Education*, 4(2), 1985, pp. 5–10 (reprinted as Curriculum, Evaluation and Management Centre Publication no. 45, to which page numbers refer); p. 2.
12. Keith J. Topping, "Trends in peer learning," *Educational Psychology*, 25(6), 2005, pp. 631–45; p. 631.
13. H. M. Levine, G. V. Glass and G. R. Meister, "A cost-effectiveness analysis of computer-assisted instruction," *Evaluation Review*, 11, 1987, pp. 50–72.

Chapter 11: The evolution of the learning environment

1. McKinsey & Co., *How the World's Most Improved School Systems Keep Getting Better*, Report, 29 November 2010.
2. See James Tooley, *Reclaiming Education*, Continuum, London and New York, 2000; and James Tooley, *E. G. West: Economic Liberalism and the Role of Government in Education*, Continuum Library of Educational Thought, Continuum, London and New York, 2008.
3. Whittle, 2005, p. 159.
4. Ibid., p. 25.
5. Ibid., p. 29.
6. Ibid., p. 28.
7. Ibid., p. 28.
8. Ibid., pp. 29–30.
9. Ibid., p. 30.
10. Ibid., p. 32.
11. Ibid., p. 32.
12. Ibid., p. 110.
13. Ibid., p. 111.
14. Ibid., pp. 112–13.
15. Matt Ridley, "Turning kids from India's slums into autodidacts," *Wall Street Journal*, 4 December 2010.

Chapter 12: The education industry

1. "Nick Clegg rules out running free schools for profit", BBC News Education & Family, 5 September 2011, www.bbc.co.uk/news/education-14781392
2. Isenberg, 2009, p. 6.
3. See Tooley, 2000 and 2008.
4. E. G. West, *Education and the State*, Institute of Economic Affairs, London, 1965.
5. See Tooley, 2008.
6. See Tooley, 2009.
7. Adam Smith, *An Inquiry into the Nature and Causes of the Wealth of Nations*, ed. R. H. Campbell and A. S. Skinner, 2 vols, Glasgow Education of the Works and Correspondence of Adam Smith, Oxford University Press, 1976, Book 1, Chapter II, p. 19.

8. Trabant, from Wikipedia, the free encyclopedia, en.wikipedia.org/wiki/Trabant

9. See, for instance, J. M. Buchanan and G. Tullock, *The Calculus of Consent: Logical Foundations of Constitutional Democracy*, University of Michigan Press, Ann Arbor, 1962; A. Downs, *An Economic Theory of Democracy*, Harper, New York, 1957; G. Tullock, *The Vote Motive*, IEA (Institute of Economic Affairs), London, 1976; G. Tullock, A. Seldon and G. L. Brady, *Government: Whose Obedient Servant? A Primer in Public Choice*, IEA, London, 2000; G. Tullock, G. Brady and A. Seldon, *Government Failure*, Cato Institute, Washington, DC, 2002.

10. I've also argued this at length in Tooley, 2008.

11. Isenberg, 2009, pp. 6–7.

12. See, for instance, R. S. Peters, *Ethics and Education*, George Allen and Unwin, London, 1966.

13. IFC, *IFC Family Business Governance Handbook*, Washington, DC, 2008, p. 11.

14. Ibid., p. 11.

15. Ibid., p. 11.

Acknowledgments

I AM DEEPLY GRATEFUL to all within SABIS, and those outside who are part of the SABIS story, who gave generously of their time and ideas to help me write this book. Many of my interviewees are mentioned in the book, and I am thankful to each one. Unfortunately, in order to keep the book to a manageable size, I had to omit mention of several people. Their ideas and stories gave me essential scaffolding for the book and I am appreciative to each one of them for giving me of their time. All interviews were digitally recorded; I am grateful to Christopher-John Counihan and Lisa Simnett for their conscientious and careful transcriptions.

On my journey, Amy Wesley was an indispensable help throughout. She expertly organized most of my trips, and accompanied me on journeys to America, Lebanon, and Iraq. She also gave much editorial guidance for the book – including translating the text into American English. Jose Afonso also accompanied me on some American visits, as did Udo Schulz. I've known Udo as a friend for many years and he's always been a source of great wisdom and insight on the global education industry. Indeed, he was behind the invitation to the SABIS conference where the idea for this book was first mooted. At Profile Books, I must thank Paul Forty, Lisa Owens and Daniel Crewe for being courteous guides through the publication process.

Finally, I must mention the members of the SABIS twin families. In particular I'm grateful to George Saad, who guided me in Louisiana, Victor Saad who accompanied me in the United Arab Emirates, and Carl Bistany, who generously gave of his time and kept the project on track. Carl was always there to support me through the sometimes intense writing and editing process, and I was privileged to spend time with him in Lebanon and Iraq. Mrs Leila Saad and Ralph Bistany allowed me unprecedented access to the organization they created, and were exceedingly hospitable and generous. I've dedicated the book to them in expression of my gratitude.

Index